Cost Accounting and Financial Management

Cost Accounting and Financial Management

Dr. Anoop Pant

RANDOM

RANDOM PUBLICATIONS

NEW DELHI (INDIA)

Cost Accounting and Financial Management

ISBN 978-93-5111-395-9

Published in 2014 in India by

RANDOM PUBLICATIONS

4376-A/4B, Gali Murari Lal, Ansari Road
New Delhi-110 002
Phone : +91-11-43580356, +91-11-23289044
e-mail: randomexports@gmail.com, sales@randompublications.com, info@randompublications.com

Reprinted 2022

Type Setting by : Keystoneprintads, Delhi-110051
Digitally Printed at: Replika Press Pvt. Ltd.

Preface

In India, prior to independence, there were a few Cost Accountants, and they were qualified mainly from I.C.M.A. (now CIMA) London. During the Second World War, the need for developing the profession in the country was felt, and the leadership of forming an Indian Institute was taken by some members of Defence Services employed at Kolkata. However, with the enactment of the Cost and Works Accountants of India Act, 1959, the Institute of Cost and Works Accountants of India (Now called as Institute of Cost Accountants of India) was established at Kolkata. The profession assumed further importance in 1968 when the Government of India introduced Cost Audit under section 233B of the Companies Act, 1956. Many times we use Cost Accounting, Costing, and Cost Accountancy interchangeably. But there are differences among these terms. As a professional, though we use interchangeably we must know the meaning of each term precisely.

Cost Accounting may be defined as "Accounting for costs classification and analysis of expenditure as will enable the total cost of any particular unit of production to be ascertained with reasonable degree of accuracy and at the same time to disclose exactly how such total cost is constituted". Thus Cost Accounting is classifying, recording an appropriate allocation of expenditure for the determination of the costs of products or services, and for the presentation of suitably arranged data for the purpose of control and guidance of management.

Financial Management is managerial activity which is concerned with the planning and controlling of the firm's financial resources. Financial Management as the name suggests is management of finance. It deals with planning and mobilization of funds required by the firm. There is only one thing which matters for everyone right from the owners to the promoters and that is money. Managing of finance is nothing but managing of money. Every activity of an organization is reflected in its financial statements. Financial Management deals with activities which have financial implications. The very objective of Financial Management is to maximize the wealth of the shareholders by maximizing the value of the firm. This prime objective of Financial Management is reflected in the EPS (Earning per Share) and the market price of its shares. The functions of Financial Management involves acquiring funds for meeting short term and long term requirements of the firm, deployment of funds, control over the use of funds and to trade-off between risk and return.

I thank all members of my team who have helped in the preparation of the book. My special thanks go to "Random Publications" who have published the book.

– Dr. Anoop Pant

Contents

1

Introduction

ACCOUNTING OF MANAGEMENT

DEFINITION

Process of preparing management accounts that provide accurate and timely key financial and statistical information required by managers to make day-to-day and short-term decisions. Unlike financial accounting (which produces annual reports mainly for external stakeholders such as creditors, investors, and lenders) management accounting generates monthly or weekly reports for the firm's internal audiences such as department managers and the chief executive officer.

These reports typically show the amount of available cash, sales revenue generated, amount of orders in hand, state of accounts payable and accounts receivable, outstanding debts, raw material and in-process inventory, and may also include trend charts, variance analysis, and other statistics. Also called managerial accounting.

MANAGERIALACCOUNTING

Managerial accounting is concerned with providing information to managers-that is, people inside an organization who direct and control its operation. In contrast,financial accounting is concerned with providing information to stockholders, creditors, and others who are outside an organization. Managerial accounting provides the essential data with which the organizations are actually run. Managerial accoun-ting is also termed as management accountingor cost accounting. Financial accounting provides the scorecard by which a company's overall past performance is judged by outsiders. Managerial accountants prepare a variety of reports. Some reports focus on how well managers or business units have performed-comparing actual results to plans and to benchmarks.

Some reports provide timely, frequent updates on key indicators such as orders received, order backlog, capacity utilization, and sales. Other analytical reports are prepared as needed to investigate specific problems such as a decline in the profitability of a product line. And yet other reports analyse a developing business situation or opportunity. In contrast, financial accounting is oriented toward producing a limited set of specific prescribed annual and quarterly financial statements in accordance with Generally Accepted Accounting Principles Financial accounting vs. Managerial accounting: Managerial accounting differs from financial accounting in a number of ways that are briefly discussed below. Click here for a detailed study of the difference between financial and managerial accounting.

Financial Accounting	Managerial Accounting
Reports to those outside theorganization owners, lenders, tax authorities and regulators.	Reports to those inside theorganization for planning, directing and motivating, controlling and performance evaluation.
Emphasis is on summaries of financial consequences of past activities.	Emphasis is on decisions affecting the future.
Objectivity and verifiability of data are emphasized.	Relevance of items relating to decision making is emphasized.
Precision of information is required.	Timeliness of information is required.
Only summarized data for the entireorganization is prepared.	Detailed segment reports about departments, products, customers, and employees are prepared.
Must follow Generally Accepted Accounting Principles (GAAP).	Need not follow Generally Accepted Accounting Principles (GAAP).
Mandatory for external reports.	Not mandatory.

Managerial accounting is managers oriented therefore its study must be preceded by some understanding of what managers do, the information managers need, and the general business environment. Accordingly we shall briefly examine these subjects.

Need for Managerial Accounting

Every organization-large and small-has managers. Someone must be responsible for making plans, organizing resources, directing personnel, and controlling operations. Every where mangers carry out three major activities-planning, directing and motivating, and controlling.Continue reading.

History

Managerial accounting has its roots in the industrial revolution of the 19th century. During this early period, most firms were tightly controlled by a few owner-managers who borrowed based on personal relationships and their personal assets. Since there were no external shareholders and little unsecured debt, there was little need for elaborate financial reports.Continue reading.

Code of Conduct for Management Accountants

Practitioners of management accounting and financial management have an obligation to the public, their profession, the organization they serve, and themselves, to maintain the highest standards of ethical conduct.

In recognition of this obligation, the Institute of management Accountants has promulgated the following standards of ethical conduct for practitioners of management accounting and financial management. Adherence to these standards internationally is integral to achieving objective ofmanagement accounting. Continue reading.

Certified Management Accountant (CMA)

A management accountant who possesses the necessary qualification and who possesses a rigorous professional exam earns the right to be known as a certified Management Accou-ntant (CMA). In addition to the prestige that accompanies a professional designation, CMAs are often given greater responsibilities and higher compensation than those who do not have such a designation. Information about becoming a CMA and CMA programme can be accessed on the Institute of Management Accountants

To become a Certified Management Accountant, the following four steps must be completed:

- File an application for admission and register for the CMA examination
- Pass all four parts of the CMA examination within a three year period
- Satisfy the experience requirement of two continuous years of professional experience in management and/or financial accounting prior to or within seven years of passing the CMA examination.
- Comply with the standards of ethical conduct for practitioners ofmanagement accounting and financial management.

WHAT IS MANAGEMENT ACCOUNTING

Management accounting is the internal business building role of accounting and finance professionals who work inside organizations. These professionals are involved in designing and evaluating business processes, budgeting and forecasting, implementing and monitoring internal controls, and analyzing, synthesizing, and aggregating information—to help drive economic value.

The role of management accounting differs from that of public accounting, since management accountants work at the "beginning" of the value chain, supporting decision making, planning and control, while audit and tax functions involve checking the work after the fact. Management accountants are valued business partners, directly supporting an organization's strategic goals. With a renewed emphasis on good internal controls and sound financial reporting, the role of the management accountant is more important than ever. It obviously takes more people to "do" the work than it does to "check" the work. In fact, of the five million finance function professionals in the U.S., more than 90% work inside organizations as management accountants and finance professionals.

Some common job titles for management accountants in organizations of all sizes and structure include:

- Staff Accountant
- Cost Accountant
- Senior Accountant
- Corporate or Division Planner
- Financial Analyst
- Budget Analyst
- Internal Auditor
- Finance Manager
- Controller
- Vice President, Finance
- Treasurer
- Chief Financial Officer (CFO)
- Chief Executive Officer (CEO)

ROLE OF COST IN DECISION MAKING

DECISION MAKING

Decision making is central to the management of an enterprise. The manager of a profit making business has to decide on the manner of implementation of the objectives of the business, at least one of which may well relate to allocating resources so as to maximize profit. All organizations, whether in the private or the public sector, take decisions, which have financial implications.

Decisions will be about resources, which may be people, products, services, or long term and short term investment.

Decisions will also be about activities, including whether and how to undertake them. Where the owners are different persons from the manager (for example, shareholders of a company as separate persons from the directors), the managers may face a decision where there is a potential conflict between their own interests and those of the owners. In such a situation cost considerations may be evaluated in the wider context of the responsibility of the managers to act in the best interests of the owners. The name of my project is " The role of various cost concepts in decision–making process " In this assignment I am trying to define the cost first then show how they are playing role in different situation.

The costs that I discuss about are as follows:

- Manufacturing costs
- Non-manufacturing costs
- Fixed costs
- Variable cost
- Absorption costing
- Variable costing
- Opportunity costs
- Sunk costs
- Product costs
- Period costs
- Differential costs
- Standard costs
- Direct cost & Indirect cost
- Mixed cost.

ELEMENTS OF A DECISION

A quantitative decision problem involves six parts:

- An objective that can be quantified Sometimes referred to as 'choice criterion' or 'objective function', e.g. maximisation of profit or minimisation of total costs.
- Constraints Many decision problems have one or more constraints, e.g. limited raw materials, labour, etc. It is therefore common to find an objective that will maximise profits subject to defined constraints.
- A range of alternative courses of action under consi-deration. For example, in order to minimise costs of a manufacturing operation, the available alternatives may be.
  - To continue manufacturing as at present
  - To change the manufacturing method
  - To sub-contract the work to a third party.
- Forecasting of the incremental costs and benefits of each alternative course of action.
- Application of the decision criteria or objective function, e.g. the calculation of expected profit or contribution, and the ranking of alternatives.
- Choice of preferred alternatives.

RELEVANT COSTS FOR DECISION MAKING

The costs which should be used for decision making are often referred to as "relevant costs". CIMA defines relevant costs as 'costs appropriate to aiding the making of specific management decisions'.

To affect a decision a cost must be:

- *Future*: Past costs are irrelevant, as we cannot affect them by current decisions and they are common to all alternatives that we may choose.

- *Incremental*: 'Meaning, expenditure which will be incurred or avoided as a result of making a decision. Any costs which would be incurred whether or not the decision is made are not said to be incremental to the decision.
- *Cash flow*: Expenses such as depreciation are not cash flows and are therefore not relevant. Similarly, the book value of existing equipment is irrelevant, but the disposal value is relevant.

Other terms:

- *Common costs*: Costs which will be identical for all alternatives are irrelevant, e.g. rent or rates on a factory would be incurred whatever products are produced.
- *Sunk costs*: Another name for past costs, which are always irrelevant, e.g. dedicated fixed assets, develo-pment costs already incurred.
- *Committed costs*: A future cash outflow that will be incurred anyway, whatever decision is taken now, e.g. contracts already entered into which cannot be altered.

Opportunity cost

Relevant costs may also be expressed as opportunity costs. An opportunity cost is the benefit foregone by choosing one opportunity instead of the next best alternative.

Example

A company is considering publishing a limited edition book bound in a special leather. It has in stock the leather bought some years ago for $1,000. To buy an equivalent quantity now would cost $2,000. The company has no plans to use the leather for other purposes, although it has consi-dered the possibilities:

- Of using it to cover desk furnishings, in replacement for other material which could cost $900
- Of selling it if a buyer could be found (the proceeds are unlikely to exceed $800).

In calculating the likely profit from the proposed book before deciding to go ahead with the project, the leather would *not* be costed at $1,000. The cost was incurred in the past for some reason which is no longer relevant.

The leather exists and could be used on the book without incurring any specific cost in doing so. In using the leather on the book, however, the company will lose the opportunities of either disposing of it for $800 or of using it to save an outlay of $900 on desk furnishings. The better of these alternatives, from the point of view of benefiting from the leather, is the latter. "Lost opportunity" cost of $900 will therefore be included in the cost of the book for decision making purposes.

The relevant costs for decision purposes will be the sum of:

– 'Avoidable outlay costs', i.e. those costs which will be incurred only if the book project is approved, and will be avoided if it is not
– The opportunity cost of the leather (not represented by any outlay cost in connection to the project).

This total is a true representation of 'economic cost'.

Exercise

Zimglass Industries Ltd. has been approached by a customer who would like a special job to be done for him, & is willing to pay $60,000 for it. The job would require the following materials.

Material	Total units required	Units already in stock	Book value of units in stock $/unit	Realisable value $/unit	Replacement cost $/unit
A	1000	0	-	-	16.00
B	1000	600	12.00	12.50	15.00
C	1000	700	13.00	12.50	14.00
D	200	200	14.00	16.00	19.00

- Material B is used regularly by Zimglass Industries Ltd, and if units of B are required for this job, they would need to be replaced to meet other production demands.
- Materials C and D are in stock due to previous over-buying, and they have restricted use. No other use could be found for material C, but the units of material D could be used in another job as a substitute for 300 units of material E, which currently costs $15 per unit (of which the company has no units in stock at the moment).

Calculate the relevant costs of material for deciding whether or not to accept the contract. You must carefully and clearly explain the reasons for your treatment of each material.

Assumptions in Relevant Costing

Some of the assumptions made in relevant costing are as follows:

- Cost behaviour patterns are known, e.g. if a depart-ment closes down, the attributable fixed cost savings would be known.
- The amount of fixed costs, unit variable costs, sales price and sales demand are known with certainty.
- The objective of decision making in the short run is to maximise 'satisfaction', which is often known as 'short-term profit'.
- The information on which a decision is based is complete and reliable.

Cost-Volume-Profit (CVP) Analysis

CVP analysis involves the analysis of how total costs, total revenues and total profits are related to sales volume, and is therefore concerned with predicting the effects of changes in costs and sales volume on profit. It is also known as 'breakeven analysis'. *The technique used carefully may be helpful in the following situations*:

- *Budget planning*: The volume of sales required to make a profit (breakeven point) and the 'safety margin' for profits in the budget can be measured.
- Pricing and sales volume decisions.
- Sales mix decisions, to determine in what proportions each product should be sold.
- Decisions that will affect the cost structure and production capacity of the company.

Basic Principles of CVP Analysis

CVP analysis is based on the assumption of a linear total cost function (constant unit variable cost and constant fixed costs) and so is an application of marginal costing principles.

The principles of marginal costing can be summarised as follows:

- Period fixed costs are a constant amount, therefore if one extra unit of product is made and sold, total costs will only rise by the variable cost (the *marginal cost*) of production and sales for that unit.
- Also, total costs will fall by the variable cost per unit for each reduction by one unit in the level of activity.
- The additional profit earned by making and selling one extra unit is the extra revenue from its sales minus its variable costs, i.e. the contribution per unit.
- As the volume of activity increases, there will be an increase in total profits (or a reduction in losses) equal to the total revenue minus the total extra variable costs. This is the extra contribution from the extra output and sales.
- The total profit in a period is the total revenue minus the total variable cost of goods sold, minus the fixed costs of the period.

Revenue	**X**
Variable cost of sales	(X)
Contribution	X
Fixed costs	(X)
Profit	X

Sabre Products Ltd. makes and sells a single product. The variable cost is \$3/unit and the variable cost of selling is \$1/unit. Fixed costs total \$6,000 and the unit sales price is \$6. Sabre Products Ltd. budgets to make and sell 3,600 units in the next year. Draw a breakeven chart, and a P/V graph, each showing the expected amount of output and sales required to break-even, and the safety margin in the budget.

Solution: A breakeven chart records the amount of fixed costs, variable costs, total costs and total revenue at all volumes of sales, and at a given sales price as shown:

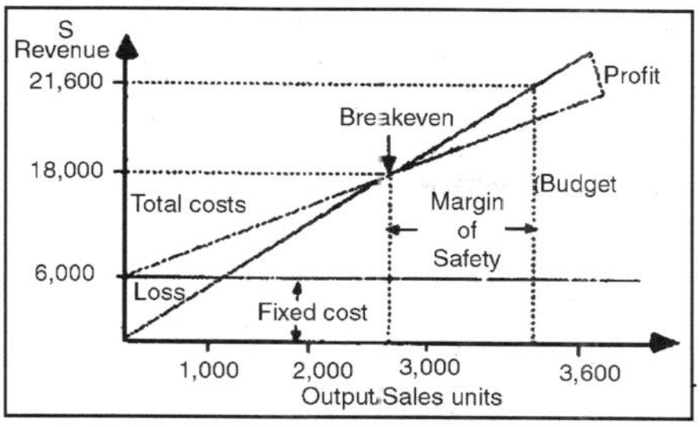

The 'breakeven point' is where revenues and total costs are exactly the same, so there is no profit or loss. It may be expressed in terms of units of sale or in terms of sales revenue. Reading from the graph, the breakeven point is 3,000 units of sale and $18,000 in sales revenue. The 'margin of safety' is the amount which actual output/sales may fall short of the budget without a loss being made, often expressed as a percentage of the budgeted sales volume. It is a rough measure of the risk that Sabre Products might make a loss if it fails to achieve its budget. In our example, the margin of safety is calculated as follows.

	Units
Budgeted sales	3,600
Breakeven point	3,000
Margin of safety (MOS)	600

As a percentage of budgeted sales; the

$$\text{Mos} = \frac{600}{3,600}$$
$$= 16.67\%$$

A high margin of safety shows a good expectation of profits, even if the budget is not achieved.

Profit/Volume (P/V) Graph

The P/V graph is similar to the breakeven chart, and records the profit or loss at each level of sales, at a given sales price.

It is a straight line graph, drawn by recording the following:

- The loss at zero sales, which is the full amount of fixed costs.
- The profit/(loss) at the budgeted sales level.

The two points are then joined up. In our example above, the PA/graph would look like this.

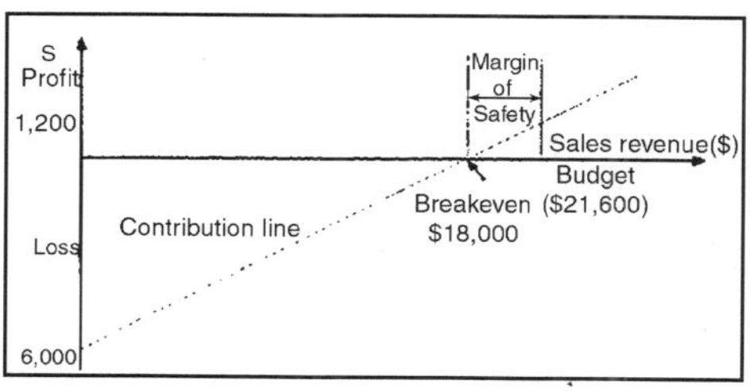

The breakeven point may be read from the graph as $18,000 in sales revenue, and the margin of safety is $3,600 in sales revenue or 16.67% budgeted sales revenue.

Arithmetic of CVP Analysis

- To calculate the breakeven point the following formula applies.
  S = *V*+ *F* at the breakeven point,
  where:
  S = sales revenue
  V = variable costs
  F = fixed costs (so that V + F = total costs).
  Therefore:
  (*S* - *V*) = F
  At the breakeven point, total contribution (S - V) equals the amount of fixed costs (F).
- To calculate the amount of sales needed to achieve a target profit the following formula applies:
  S = *V* + *F* + *P*
  Therefore,
  (S - V) = (*F* + *P*)

To earn a target profit, the total contribution (S - V) must be sufficient to cover fixed costs plus the amount of profit required (F + P).

Exercise: Arithmetic of CVP analysis. Ndlovu Ltd. manu-factures a single product, which has a variable cost of sale of $8/unit and a sales price of $12/ unit. Budgeted fixed costs are $24,000.

Calculate the volume of sales that would be required to achieve the following:

- Breakeven
- Earn a profit of at least $6,000.

The contribution/sales ratio (C/S ratio). The C/S ratio shows how much contribution is earned per $1 of sales revenue earned. Since costs and sales revenues are linear functions, the C/S ratio is constant at all levels of output and sales.

It is used sometimes as a measure of performance or profitability, and in CVP analysis to calculate the sales required to breakeven or earn a target profit or the expected total contribution at a given volume of sales and with a given C/S ratio.

As an alternative method of calculation, the breakeven point in sales revenue is calculated as follows:

$$\frac{\text{Required Contribution}}{\text{C/S ratio}} = \frac{\text{Fixed Costs}}{\text{C/S ratio}}$$

Similarly, the sales volume needed to achieve a target profit is calculated as follows:

$$\frac{\text{Required Contribution}}{\text{C/S ratio}} = \frac{\text{Fixed Costs} + \text{Profit}}{\text{C/S ratio}}$$

In exercise 5.2, the C/S ratio is,

$$\frac{\$4}{\$12} \text{ or } 33\frac{1}{3}\%$$

- The breakeven point is therefore

$$\frac{\text{Required Contribution}}{\text{C/S ratio}} = \frac{\$24,000}{33\tfrac{1}{3}\%}$$

Required sales to breakeven
= $72,000 or divided by $12
= 6,000 units

- To achieve a target profit of $6,000 the required sales are calculated as;

$$\frac{\text{Required Contribution}}{\text{C/S ratio}} = \frac{\$30,000}{33\tfrac{1}{3}\%} = \$90,000$$

or divided by 12
= 7,500 units

MAKE OR BUY DECISIONS

A company is often faced with the decision as to whether it should manufacture a component or buy it outside. Suppose for example, that *Masanzu Ltd.* make four components, W, X, Y and Z, with expected costs for the coming year as follows:

	W	X	Y	Z
Production (units)	1,000	2,000	4,000	3,000
Unit marginal costs	$	$	$	$
Direct materials	4	5	2	4
Direct labour	8	9	4	6
Variable production overheads	2	3	1	2
	14	17	7	12

Direct fixed costs/annum and committed fixed costs are as follows:

Incurred as a direct consequence of making W	1,000
Incurred as a direct consequence of making X	5,000
Incurred as a direct consequence of making Y	6,000
Incurred as a direct consequence of making Z	8,000
Other committed fixed costs	30,000
	50,000

A subcontractor has offered to supply units W, X, Y and Z for $12, $21, $10 and $14 respectively. Decide whether *Masanzu* Ltd. should make or buy the components.

Solution and Discussion

- The relevant costs are the differential costs between making and buying. They consist of differences in unit variable costs plus differences in directly attributable fixed costs. Subcontracting will result in some savings on fixed cost.

	W	X	Y	Z
	$	$	$	$
Unit variable cost of making	14	17	7	12
Unit variable cost of buying	12	21	10	14
	(2)	-4	2	2
Annual requirements in units	1,000	2,000	4,000	3,000
Extra variable cost of buying per annum	(2,000)	8,000	12,000	6,000
Fixed cost saved by buying	1,000	5,000	6,000	8,000
Extra total cost of buying	(3,000)	3,000	6,000	(2,000)

- The company would save $3,000/annum by sub-contracting component W, and $2,000/annum by sub-contracting component Z.
- In this example, relevant costs are the variable costs of in-house manufacture, the variable costs of sub-contracted units, and the saving in fixed costs.
- Other important considerations are as follows:
  - If components W and Z are sub-contracted, the company will have spare capacity. How should that spare capacity be profitably used? Are there hidden benefits to be obtained from sub-contracting? Will there be resentment from the workforce?
  - Would the sub-contractor be reliable with delivery times, and is the quality the same as those manufactured internally?
  - Does the company wish to be flexible and maintain better control over operations by making everything itself?
  - Are the estimates of fixed costs savings reliable? In the case of product W, buying is clearly cheaper than making in-house. However, for product Z, the decision to buy rather than make would only be financially attractive if the fixed cost savings of $8,000 could be delivered by management. In practice, this may not materialise.

Exercise Make or buy: The Pip, a component used by *Goya Manufacturing Ltd.*, is incorporated into a number of its completed products. The Pip is purchased from a supplier at $2.50 per component and some 20,000 are used annually in production.

The price of $2.50 is considered to be competitive, and the supplier has maintained good quality service over the last five years. The production engineering department at Goya Manufacturing Ltd. has submitted a proposal to manufacture the Pip in-house. The variable cost per unit produced is estimated at $1.20 and additional annual fixed costs that would be incurred if the Pip were manufactured are estimated at $20,800.

- Determine whether Goya Manufacturing Ltd. should continue to purchase the Pip or manufacture it in-house.
- Indicate the level of production required that would make Goya Manufacturing Ltd. decide in favour of manufacturing the Pip itself.

SHUTDOWN PROBLEMS

Shutdown problems involve the following types of decisions:

- Whether or not to close down a factory, department, product line or other activity, either because it is making losses or because it is too expensive to run.
- If the decision is to shut down, whether the closure should be permanent or temporary. Shutdown decisions often involve long term considerations, and capital expenditures and revenues.
- A shutdown should result in savings in annual operating costs for a number of years in the future.
- Closure results in release of some fixed assets for sale. Some assets might have a small scrap value, but others, e.g. property, might have a substantial sale value.
- Employees affected by the closure must be made redundant or relocated, perhaps even offered early retirement.

  There will be lump sums payments involved which must be taken into consideration. For example, suppose closure of a regional office results in annual savings of $100,000, fixed assets sold off for $2 million, but redundancy payments would be $3 million. The shutdown decision would involve an assessment of the net capital cost of closure ($1 million) against the annual benefits ($100,000 per annum).

It is possible for shutdown problems to be simplified into short run decisions, by making one of the following assumptions.

- Fixed asset sales and redundancy costs would be negligible.
- Income from fixed asset sales would match redundancy costs and so these items would be self-cancelling.

In these circumstances the financial aspects of shutdown decisions would be based on short run relevant costs.

Exercise: Adding or deleting products *Brass Ltd.* manu-factures three products, Swans, Ducks and Chicks.

The present net annual income from each item is as follows:

	Swans $	**Ducks $**	**Chicks $**	**Total $**
Sales	50,000	40,000	60,000	150,000 Variable costs
30,000	25,000	35,000	90,000	Contribution

20,000	15,000	25,000	60,000	Fixed costs
17,000	18,000	20,000	55,000	Profit/(loss)
3,000	(3,000)	5,000	5,000	

Brass Ltd. is concerned about its poor profit performance, and is considering whether or not to cease selling Ducks. It is felt that selling prices cannot be increased or lowered without adversely affecting net income. $5,000 of the fixed costs of Ducks are direct fixed costs which would be saved if production ceased. All other fixed costs will remain the same.

- Advise Brass Ltd. whether or not to cease production of Ducks.
- Suppose, however, it were possible to use the resources realised by stopping production of Ducks, and switch to produce a new item, Eagles, which would sell for $50,000 and incur variable costs of $30,000 and extra fixed costs of $6,000. What will the new decision be?

KEY TERMS

- Breakeven analysis
- Contribution/sales ratio
- Cost-volume-profit analysis
- Decision making
- Make or buy decisions
- Opportunity costs
- Profit-volume charts
- Relevant costs
- Shutdown

MANAGEMENT ACCOUNTING AND COST ACCOUNTING

FINANCIAL AND MANAGERIAL ACCOUNTING

Financial accounting reports are prepared for external parties such as shareholders and creditors, whereas managerial accounting reports are prepared for managers inside the organization.

This contrast in orientation results in a number of major differences between financial and managerial accounting, even though they often rely on the same under-lying financial data. Comparison of Financial and Managerial Accounting

Identify the major differences and similarities between financial and managerial accounting.

As shown in Exhibit 1-3, financial and managerial accounting differ not only in their user orientation but also in their emphasis on the past and the future, in the type of data provided to users, and in several other ways. These differences are discussed in the following paragraphs.

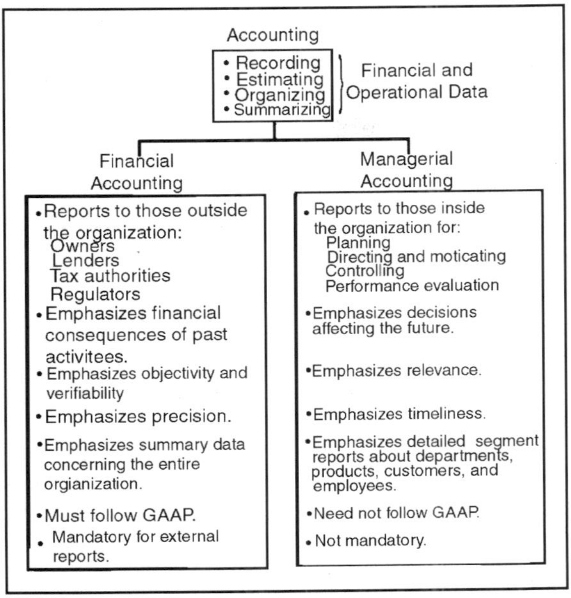

Emphasis on the Future

Since *planning* is such an important part of the manager's job, managerial accounting has a strong future orientation. In contrast, financial accounting primarily summarizes past financial transactions. These summaries may be useful in planning, but only to a point. The future is not simply a reflection of what has happened in the past. Changes are constantly taking place in economic conditions, customer needs and desires, competitive conditions, and so on. All of these changes demand that the manager's planning be based in large part on estimates of what will happen rather than on summaries of what has already happened.

Relevance of Data

Financial accounting data should be objective and verifiable. However, for internal uses managers want information that is relevant even if it is not completely objective or verifiable. By relevant, we mean *appropriate for the problem at hand.* For example, it is difficult to verify estimated sales volumes for a proposed new store at Good Vibrations, but this is exactly the type of information that is most useful to managers. Managerial accounting should be flexible enough to provide whatever data are relevant for a particular decision.

Less Emphasis on Precision

Making sure that dollar amounts are accurate down to the last dollar or penny takes time and effort. While that kind of accuracy is required for external reports, most managers would rather have a good estimate immediately than wait for a more precise answer later. For this reason, managerial accountants often place less emphasis on precision than financial accountants do. For example, in a decision involving hundreds of millions of dollars, estimates that are rounded off to the nearest million dollars are probably good enough.

In addition to placing less emphasis on precision than financial accounting, managerial accounting places much more weight on nonmonetary data. For example, data about customer satisfaction may be routinely used in managerial accounting reports.

Segments of an Organization

Financial accounting is primarily concerned with report-ing for the company as a whole. By contrast, managerial accounting focuses much more on the parts, or segments , of a company. These segments may be product lines, sales territories, divisions, departments, or any other categorization that management finds useful. Financial accounting does require some breakdowns of revenues and costs by major segments in external reports, but this is a secondary emphasis. In managerial accounting, segment reporting is the primary emphasis.

Generally Accepted Accounting Principles (GAAP)

Financial accounting statements prepared for external users must comply with generally accepted accounting principles (GAAP). External users must have some assurance that the reports have been prepared in accordance with a common set of ground rules.

These common ground rules enhance comparability and help reduce fraud and misrepresentation, but they do not necessarily lead to the type of reports that would be most useful in internal decision making. For example, if management at Good Vibrations is considering selling land to finance a new store, they need to know the current market value of the land. However, GAAP requires that the land be stated at its original, historical cost on financial reports. The more relevant data for the decision—the current market value—is ignored under GAAP.

Managerial accounting is not bound by GAAP. Managers set their own rules concerning the content and form of internal reports. The only constraint is that the expected benefits from using the information should outweigh the costs of collecting, analyzing, and summarizing the data. Nevertheless, as we shall see in subsequent chapters, it is undeniably true that financial reporting requirements have heavily influenced management accounting practice.

Managerial Accounting—Not Mandatory

Financial accounting is mandatory; that is, it must be done. Various outside parties such as the Securities and Exchange Commission (SEC) and the tax authorities require periodic financial statements. Managerial accounting, on the other hand, is not mandatory. A company is completely free to do as much or as little as it wishes. No regulatory bodies or other outside agencies specify what is to be done, or, for that matter, whether anything is to be done at all. Since managerial accounting is completely optional, the important question is always, "Is the information useful?" rather than, "Is the information required?"

ROLE OF FINANCIAL AND MANAGEMENT ACCOUNTING

Learning Objectives

- Outline to participants on the major differences between financial and management accounting
- Explaining to the participants on the role manag-ement accountant in an organization.
- Briefing the participants on the useful qualities of management information.

Important Terms

- Financial accounting
- Management accounting
- Data
- Information

Management accounting is the process of identification, measurement, accumulation, analysis, preparation, interpreta-tion and communication of information used by management to plan, evaluate and control within an entity and to assure appropriate use of and accountability for its resources. Management accounting also comprises the preparation of financial reports for non management groups such as shareholders, creditors, regulatory agencies and tax authorities.

The core activities of management accounting include:

- Participation in the planning process at both strategic and operational levels. This involves the establish-ment of policies and the formulation of plans and budgets which will subsequently be expressed in the financial terms.
- The initiation of and the provision of guidance for management decisions. This involves the generation, analysis, presentation and interpretation of appropriate information.
- Contributing to the monitoring and control performance through the provision of reports on organisational performance, including comparisons of actual with planned or budgeted performance, and their analysis and interpretation.*Financial accounting* is the periodic

reporting of accounting as required by statue for shareholders, government agencies and other parties external to the business. As such, various conventions and rules are necessary to ensure consistency between the sets of accounts.

Comparision

The following table summarises the main differences between management accounting and financial accounting.

Management Accounting	Financial Accounting
A management accounting system produces information that is used within an organization, by managers and employees creditors.	A financial accounting system produces information that is used by parties external to the organization, such as shareholders, bank and
Management accounting helps management to record, plan and aids an organization over a defined period and the state of affairs at the end of that period.	Financial accounting provides a record of the performance of and control activities the decision making process.
There are no legal law prepare financial accounts.	Limited companies must, by requirementsfor an organization to use management accounting.
Management accounting can organisation's activities.	Financial accounting Concentra-focus on specific areas of an tes on the organization as a whole, aggregating revenues
Information may aid a decision operation.	and costs from different making rather than be an end product of a decision. Financial accounts are an end themselves.
Management accounting information may be monetary or alternatively non monetary.	Most financial accounting information is of a monetary nature.
Management accounting and presents an a future planning tool.	Financial accounting provides both an historical essentially historical picture of record of the immediate past past operation.
No time span for producing financial Financial statements.	Financial statements are required to be produced for the period of 12 months.
No strict rules govern the way in which management accounting operates.	Financial accounting must operate within a framework determined by law and IASs.
The management accounts and	In principle the financial information are prepared

in a format that is of use to managers.	accounts of different organizations can be easily compared.
Management accounting has no specified format. There are no specific statements which should be produced.	Financial accounts are supposedto be produced in accordance with a specified format by IAS or law.

Feature of useful management accounting:

- It should be relevant for its purpose.
- It should be complete for its purpose.
- It should be sufficiently accurate for its purpose.
- It should be clear to the manager using it.
- The manager using it should have confidence in it.
- It should be communicated to the appropriate manager.
- Its volume should be manageable.
- It should be timely.
- It should be communicated through appropriate channel of communication.
- It should be provided at a cost which is less than the value of the benefits it provides.

Role of Management Accountant

Assistance in Planning

The management accountant assists planning by providing information. This information may be about pricing, capital expenditure projects, product costs or competition. In the short-term planning process of budgeting, the management accountant provides information on past costs and revenues which may be used as guidance. The management accountant is also involved in the budgeting process itself.

Assistance in Controlling

The management accountant supplies performance reports which compare actual performance with the planned performance and which therefore highlight those activities which are not conforming to plan.

Assistance in Organizing

By ensuring that the accounting system is tailored to the organisational structure, the management accountant reinforces the objectives of the organisational framework.

Assistance in Motivating

Budgets prepared by the prepared by the management accountant serve to motivate managers and subordinates to attempt to achieve the organisation's objectives. Formalized targets are more likely to motivate than vague comments. Performance reports produced by the management accountant for the control process also motivate by communicating performance information in relation to the targets which have been set.

Assistance in Decision Making

The management accountant is a vital cog in the organisation's decision making process. He or she collects and analyses data, and presents information to managers to help in the decision making.

COST ACCOUNTING

Uses of Cost Accounting

The main uses of cost accounting as follows:

- *Helps in Ascertainment of Cost*:Cost Accounting helps in the ascertainment of cost of each product, process, job, contract, activity etc. by using different methods of costing such as Job Costing and Process Costing.
- *Helps in Control of Cost*: It helps in the control of material costs, labour costs and overheads by using different techniques of control such as Standard Costing and Budgetary Control.
- *Helps in Decision making*: It helps the management in making various decisions such as.
  - Whether to make or buy a component
  - Whether to retain or replace an existing machine
  - Whether to process further or not
  - Whether to shut down or continue operations
  - Whether to accept orders below cost or not
  - Whether to expand or not
  - How much reduction in the selling price should
- *Helps in fixing Selling Prices*: It helps the management in fixing selling prices of products or services by providing detailed cost information.
- *Helps in Inventory Control*: It helps in inventory by using various techniques such as *ABC* analysis, Economic Order Quantity, Stock levels, Perpetual Inventory system and Continuous Stock Taking, Inventory Turnover Ratio etc.
- *Helps in Cost reduction*: It helps in the introduction of cost reduction programme and finding out new and improved method to reduce costs.
- *Helps in measurements of Efficiency*: It helps in measure-ments of efficiency of operations through establi-shment of standards and variance analysis.
- *Helps in preparation of Budgets*: It helps in the prepara-tion of various

budgets such as Sales Budget, Production Budget, Purchase Budget, Man-Power Budget, Overheads budget.

- *Helps in identifying Unprofitable Activities*: It helps in identifying unprofitable activities so that the nece-ssary correction action may be taken.
- *Helps in identifying Material Losses*: It helps in identifying material losses such as wastage, scrap, spoilage and defective through report on material losses so that the necessary corrective action may be taken.
- *Helps in identifying Idle Time and Labour Turnover:* It helps in identifying idle time and labour turnover through the report on idle time and labour turnover so that the necessary corrective action may be taken.
- *Helps in identifying Idle Capacity*: It helps in identi-fying idle capacity so that the necessary corrective action may be taken.
- *Helps in improving Productivity*: It helps in improving productivity of materials and labour.
- *Helps in Cost Comparison*: It helps in Cost Compari-sons such as.
  - *Comparison with Standard Figures*: Comparison of actual figures with standard of budgeted figures for the same period and the same firm;
  - *Intra-firm Comparison*: Comparison of actual figures of one period with those of another period for the same firm;
  - *Inter-firm Comparison*: Comparison of actual figures of one firm with those of another standard firm belonging to the same industry; and
  - *Pattern Comparison*: Comparison of actual figures of one firm with those of industry to which the firm belongs.
- *Helps in checking the accuracy of financial accounts*: It helps in checking the accuracy of financial accounts with the help of reconciliation statement prepared to reconcile the profit as per cost accounts with the profit as per financial accounts.

TYPES OF COST

LEARNING OBJECTIVES

After you have read and studied this chapter, you should be able to:

- Describe the five components of a cost accounting system.
- Define the concepts of pure historical, normal historical and standard cost systems.
- Discuss four types of inventory valuation methods.
- Describe and compare four types of cost accumula-tion methods.
- Discuss three types of cost flow assumptions.
- Explain the difference between perpetual and periodic systems.

- Describe four functions of information or cost accounting systems.
- Discuss the characteristics and requirements of the four functions referred to in objective.
- Describe the manner in which a full absorption costing income statement is developed.
- Describe the manner in which a direct (or variable) costing income statement is developed.
- Prepare a full absorption costing income statement.
- Prepare a direct (or variable) costing income statement.
- Relate the matching concept to the statements in learning objectives.
- Explain the difference between net income determined under full absorption costing and net income determined under direct costing.

FOUNDATION

This chapter builds a foundation for developing an operational cost accounting system by describing the main components of such a system. In addition, the chapter includes discussions of the various functions of information systems and illustrations of the basic types of financial results that are obtained from cost accounting systems.

More specifically, the purpose of this chapter is to:

- Describe the five major components of a cost accounting system, including the various alternatives associated with each component,
- Describe the four functions of information or cost accounting systems
- To illustrate the two major types of income statements that are generated from these systems. The chapter contains three main sections that are related to these three objectives. The emphasis in this chapter is still primarily conceptual, although several illustrations and practice problems require the preparation of income statements. While these illustrations and problems are mainly mechanical exercises, the objective is to build a foundation for our study of cost accounting systems that includes the necessary technical, as well as conceptual knowledge.

  An ability to prepare income statements is an important part of this foundation because these statements provide an overall summary of a company's financial performance. They are used frequently in subsequent chapters.

This is an important chapter because it provides a foundation for studying subsequent chapters. Developing an understanding of how and why cost accounting systems are developed and used is a cumulative process. We will build on these concepts throughout the text.

PARTS OF COST ACCOUNTING SYSTEM

A cost accounting system requires five parts that include:

- An input measurement basis,

- An inventory valuation method,
- A cost accumulation method,
- A cost flow assumption,
- A capability of recording inventory cost flows at certain intervals.

These five parts and the alternatives under each part are summarized in Exhibit 2-1. Note that many possible cost accounting systems can be designed from the various combinations of the available alternatives, although not all of the alternatives are compatible. Selecting one part from each category provides a basis for developing an operational definition of a specific cost accounting system.

Exhibit 2-1
The Five Parts Of A Cost Accounting System

INPUT MEASUREMENT BASES

The basis of a cost accounting system begins with the type of costs that flow into and through the inventory accounts.

There are three alternatives including:

- Pure historical costing
- Normal historical costing
- Standard costing

These concepts are illustrated in Exhibit 2-2 and discussed individually below.

Exhibit 2-2
Basic Cost Systems

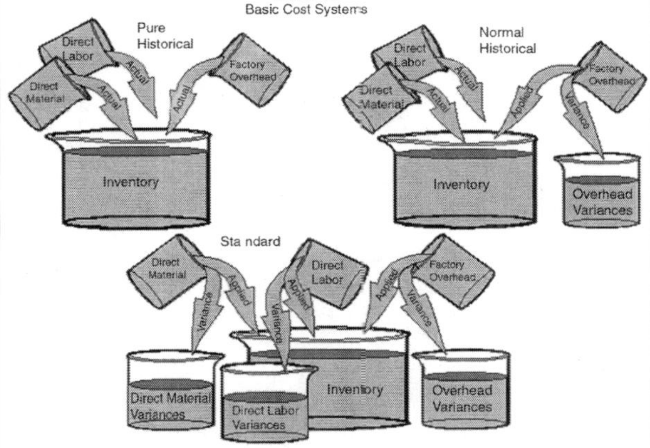

Pure Historical Costing

In a pure historical cost system, only historical costs flow through the inventory accounts. Historical costs refers to the costs that have been recorded. The term actual costs is sometimes used instead, but the term "actual" seems to imply that there is one true cost associated with a particular output.

But determining the cost of a product, or service requires many cost allocations, e.g., allocating the cost of fixed assets to time periods, and allocating indirect manufacturing costs, or overhead to products. Since there are many alternative alloca-tion methods. A pure historical cost system is symbolized in the enlarged view shown below.

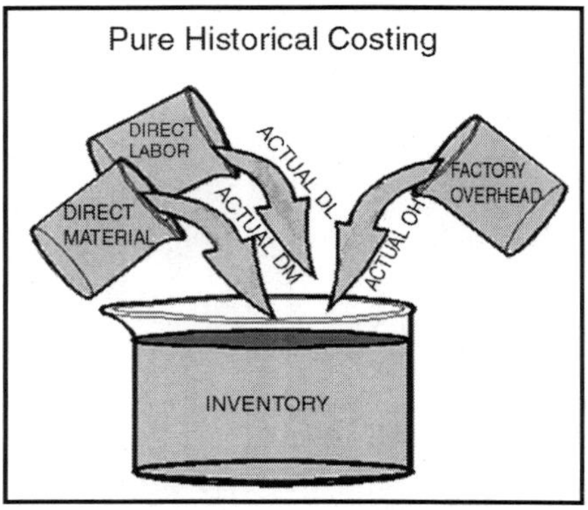

Normal Historical Costing

Normal historical costing uses historical costs for direct material and direct labour, but overhead is charged, or applied to the inventory using a predetermined overhead rate per activity measure. Typical activity measures include direct labour hours, or direct labour costs. The amount of factory overhead charged to the inventory is determined by multiplying the predetermined rate by the actual quantity of the activity measure.

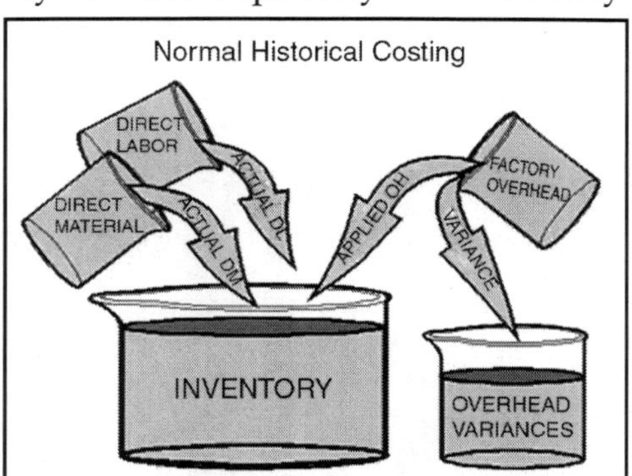

Standard Costing

In a standard cost system, all manufacturing costs are applied, or charged to the inventory using standard or predetermined prices, and quantities. The differences between the applied costs and the actual costs are charged to variance accounts as shown symbolically in the enlarged graphic below.

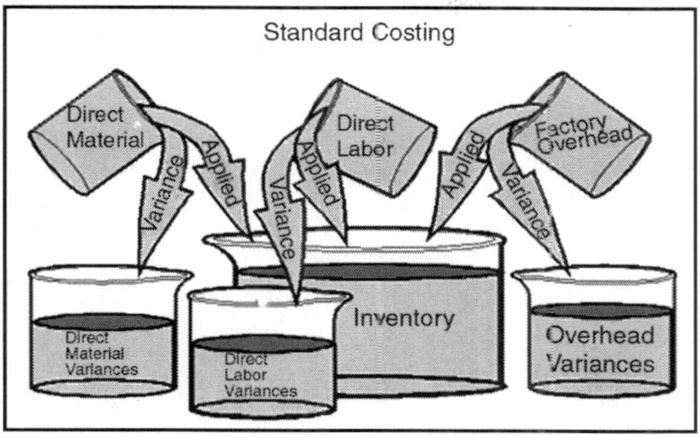

FOUR INVENTORY VALUATION METHODS

The four inventory valuation methods that appear in Exhibit 2-1 are arranged in the order of the amount of cost that is traced to the inventory. The throughput method involves tracing the least amount of cost to the inventory, while the activity based method includes tracing the greatest amount of costs to the inventory. In direct (or variable) costing, a greater amount of cost is traced than in the throughput method, but a lesser amount than in the full absorption method. Direct costing and full absorption costing are the traditional methods, while the throughput and activity based methods are relatively new. These inventory valuation methods are very important because they control the manner in which net income is determined. As we shall see is this chapter and subsequent chapters, the amount of net income can vary substantially for different inventory valuation methods. The four methods are described below. A symbolic overview of the four methods is provided in Exhibit 2-3.

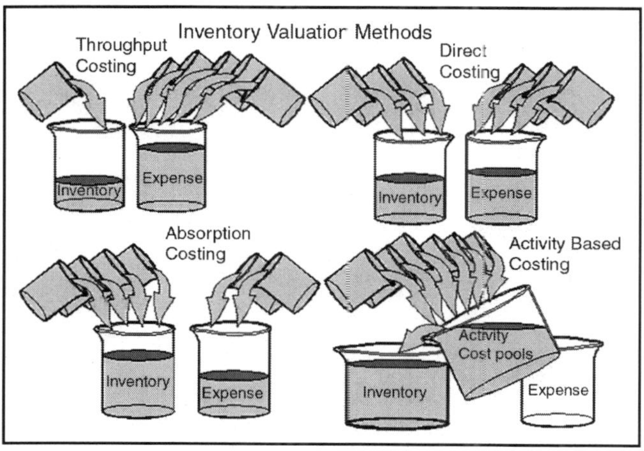

The Throughput Method

The throughput method was developed to complement a concept referred to as the theory of constraints. In this method only direct material costs are charged to the inventory. All other costs are expensed during the period. The concept is symbolized in the enlargement below. Sales, less direct material costs is referred to as throughput which reflects how the method got its' name. The throughput method does not provide proper matching (as defined by GAAP) because all manufacturing cost, other than direct material are expensed when incurred rather than capitalized in the inventory. Therefore, the throughput method is not acceptable for external reporting although advocates argue that it provides many advantages for internal reporting. The throughput method is described in more detail in along with the broader concept referred to as the theory of constraints.

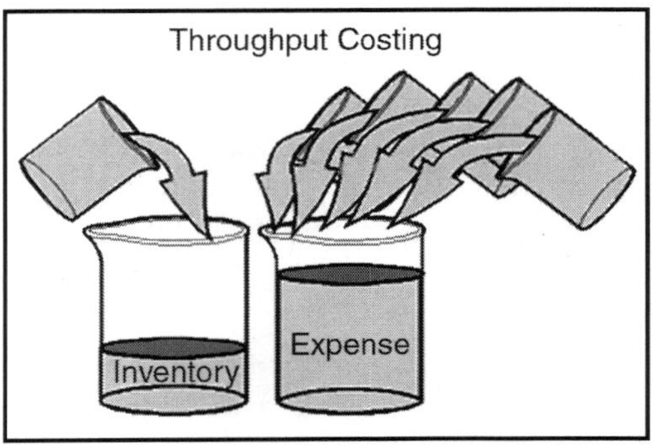

THE DIRECT OR VARIABLE METHOD

In the direct method, only the variable manufacturing costs are capitalized, or charged to the inventory. Fixed manufacturing costs flow into expense in the period incurred as illustrated in the enlargement.

This method provides some advantages and some disadvantages for internal reporting. However, it does not provide proper matching because the current fixed costs associated with producing the inventory are charged to expense regardless of whether or not the output is sold during the period. For this reason direct costing is not generally acceptable for external reporting.

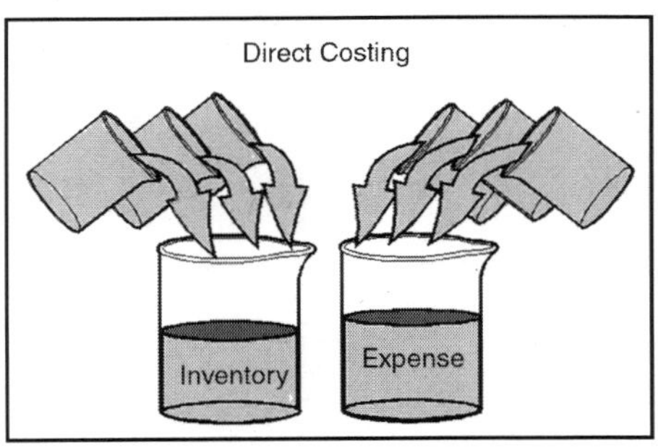

Full Absorption Method

Full absorption costing (also referred to as full costing and absorption costing) is a traditional method where all manufacturing costs are capitalized in the inventory, i.e., charged to the inventory and become assets. This means that these costs do not become expenses until the inventory is sold. In this way, matching is more closely approximated. All selling and administrative costs are charged to expense however, as indicated in the enlargement provided.

Technically, full absorption costing is required for external reporting, although many companies apparently use something less than a pure full absorption costing system. The full absorption method is also frequently used for internal reporting. The second major section of this chapter compares the income statements for full absorption costing with those used for direct costing because they are by far the dominant methods. Are based on full absorption costing. compare all four methods and discuss the behavioral implications of using the different methods.

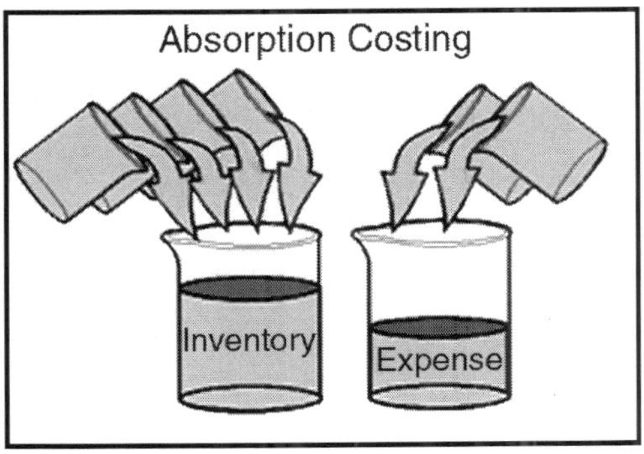

The Activity Based Method

Activity based costing is a relatively new type of procedure that can be used as an inventory valuation method. The technique was developed to provide more accurate product costs. This improved accuracy is accomplished by tracing costs to products through activities. In other words, costs are traced to activities (activity costing) and then these costs are traced, in a second stage, to the products that use the activities.

The concept of ABC is illustrated in the enlarged graphic below. Another way to express the idea is to say that activities consume resources and products consume activities.

Essentially, an attempt is made to treat all costs as variable, recognizing that all costs vary with something, whether it is production volume or some non-production volume related phenomenon. Both manufacturing costs and selling and administrative costs are traced to products in an ABC system. Note that treating selling and administrative costs in this way is not acceptable for external reporting.

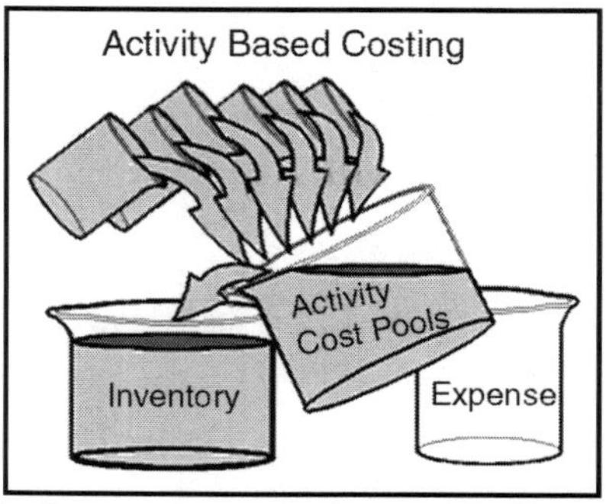

In traditional full absorption costing and direct (or variable) costing systems, indirect manufacturing costs are allocated to products on the basis of a production volume related measurement such as direct labour hours. Thus, the fundamental differences between traditional systems and activity based systems are:

- How the indirect costs are assigned (ABC uses both production volume and non-production volume related bases)
- Which costs are assigned to products (in ABC systems, an attempt is made to assign all costs to products including engineering, marketing, distribution and administrative costs, although some facility related costs may not be assigned).

At the present time, most of the companies that use the activity based method have developed stand alone, micro-computer based systems separate from the company's mainframe cost accounting system used for external report-ing. The idea is to develop more accurate product costs than the traditional cost accounting system provides so that management can make better strategic decisions such as product introduction, pricing, mix and discontinuance. In these systems, ABC is not used as an inventory valuation method. Activity based costs are not charged to the inventory accounts. However, it is used to determine product costs once per year, or more frequently when changes are made in the production process. The activity based method is described in and referred to frequently in other parts of the text.

COST ACCUMULATION METHODS

Cost accumulation refers to the manner in which costs are collected and identified with specific customers, jobs, batches, orders, departments and processes. The centre of attention for cost accumulation can be individual customers, batches of products that may involve several customers, the products produced within individual segments during a period, or the products produced by the entire plant during a period.

The company's cost accumulation method, or methods are influenced by the type of production operation and the extent to which detailed cost accounting information is needed by management.

Job Order

In job order costing, costs are accumulated by jobs, orders, contracts, or lots. The key is that the work is done to the customer's specifications. As a result, each job tends to be different. For example, job order costing is used for construction projects, government contracts, shipbuilding, automobile repair, job printing, textbooks, toys, wood furniture, office machines, caskets, machine tools, and luggage.

Accumulating the cost of professional services (e.g., lawyers, doctors and CPA's) also fall into this category. illustrates a cost accounting system that includes normal historical costing as the basic cost system, full absorption costing as the inventory valuation method and job order costing as the cost accumulation method.

Process

In process costing, costs are accumulated by departments, operations, or processes. The work performed on each unit is standardized, or uniform where a continuous mass production or assembly operation is involved. For example, process costing is used by companies that produce appliances, alcoholic beverages, tires, sugar, breakfast cereals, leather, paint, coal, textiles, lumber, candy, coke, plastics, rubber, cigarettes, shoes, typewriters, cement, gasoline, steel, baby foods, flour, glass, men's suits, pharmaceuticals and automobiles.

Process costing is also used in meat packing and for public utility services such as water, gas and electricity. Illustrates a cost accounting system that includes normal historical costing as the basic cost system, full absorption costing as the inventory valuation method and process costing as the cost accumulation method.

Back Flush

Back flush costing is a simplified cost accumulation method that is sometimes used by companies that adopt just-in-time (JIT) production systems. However, JIT is not just a technique, or collection of techniques. Just-in-time is a very broad philosophy, that emphasizes simplification and continuously reducing waste in all areas of business activity.

JIT systems were developed in Japan and depend on the communitarian concepts of teamwork and continuous improvement. In fact, many of the assumptions, attitudes and practices of communitarian capitalism are included in the JIT philosophy.

One of the many goals of JIT systems is zero ending inventory. In a backflush cost system, manufacturing costs are accumulated in fewer inventory accounts than when using the job order or process cost methods. In fact, in extreme backflush systems, most of the accounting records are eliminated. The production facilities are also arranged in self contained manufacturing cells that are dedicated to the production of a single, or similar products. In this way more of the manufactu-ring costs become direct product costs and fewer cost allocations are necessary. Thus, more accurate costing is obtained in spite of the fact that the cost accumulation method is simplified.

Hybrid, or Mixed Methods

Hybrid or mixed systems are used in situations where more than one cost accumulation method is required. For example, in some cases process costing is used for direct materials and job order costing is used for conversion costs, (i.e., direct labour and factory overhead). In other cases, job order costing might be used for direct materials, and process costing for conversion costs.

The different departments or operations within a company might require different cost accumulation methods. For this reason, hybrid or mixed cost accumulation methods are sometime referred to as operational costing methods.

FOUR COST FLOW ASSUMPTIONS

A cost flow assumption refers to how costs flow through the inventory accounts, not the flow of work or products on a production line. This distinction is important because the flow of costs is not always the same as the flow of work. The various types of cost flow assumptions include: specific identification (e.g., by job), first in, first out, last in, first out and weighted average. Costs flow through the inventory accounts by the job in a job order cost system which represents an example of specific identification. The requirements of the various jobs determines the timing of the cost flows.

Simple jobs tend to move through the system faster than more complex jobs. The first-in, first-out (FIFO) and weighted average cost flow assumptions are used in process costing. Since costs are accumulated by the process or department in a process cost environment, a cost flow assumption is needed to determine the treatment of the beginning inventory.

When FIFO is used, it is assumed that the units of product in the beginning inventory are finished first and transferred to the next department before any of the units that are started during the period. The group of units in the beginning inventory maintain their separate identity and prior period costs.

However, when the weighted average cost flow assumption is used, the beginning inventory units lose their separate identity because they are lumped together with the units of product started during the period. Process costing tends to be fairly challenging, therefore you may find these introductory concepts to be confusing.

Although last-in, first-out (LIFO) is frequently used for tax reporting purposes, it is not normally used in the accounting records. For this reason, we consider the FIFO and weighted average cost flow assumptions in, but leave the LIFO cost flow assumption for courses that emphasize financial and tax reporting.

RECORDING INTERVAL CAPABILITY

Inventory records can be maintained on a perpetual or a periodic basis. Conceptually, the perpetual inventory method provides a company with the capability of maintaining continuous records of the quantities of inventory and the costs flowing through the inventory accounts. The periodic method, on the other hand, requires counting the quantity of inventory before inventory records can be updated.

In the past, manufacturers tended to keep perpetual inventories, while retailers used the periodic method. However, today a variety of modern point of sale devices and dedicated microcomputer software are readily available to provide any company with perpetual inventory capability.

FUNCTIONS OF INFORMATION OR COST ACCOUNTING SYSTEMS

Now that you have an understanding of the components of a cost accounting system, we are ready to discuss the various purposes, or functions of information or cost accounting systems. The term information system is used to emphasize that although the accounting system is likely to be the organi-zation's major source of information, it is not the only source of information. In fact, for some purposes, accounting information is not as useful as other types of information.

Generally the purposes, or functions of an information or cost accounting system fall into four categories.

These include providing information for:

- External financial statements,
- Planning and controlling activities or processes,
- Short term strategic decisions
- Long term strategic decisions.

These four functions relate to different audiences, emphasize different types of information, require different reporting intervals and involve different types of decisions. These characteristics and requirements of the four functions are summarized in Exhibit 2-4 and discussed individually below.

EXTERNAL FINANCIAL STATEMENTS

General purpose financial statements are designed for outsiders in accordance with generally accepted accounting principles and the regulations of the Internal Revenue Service (IRS) and the Securities and Exchange Commission (SEC). Of course outsiders include investors and creditors as well as the IRS and SEC. These users generally require information concerning the overall financial performance of the company on a quarterly basis. The information is highly aggregated because these outside users do not require detailed information about the performance or profitability of specific segments of the company such as divisions, departments, activities, processes, products, services and customers. The inventory valuation method is the key component in satisfying the requirements of GAAP and other regulatory agencies.

PLANNING AND CONTROLLING ACTIVITIES AND PROCESSES

Plant, production and operating managers and workers need information for planning and controlling specific activities and processes. These users need dis-aggregated quantitative and qualitative non-financial information on a timely basis. In some cases, information is needed daily, hourly or even on a real time (continuous) basis. For example, the operating managers of a nuclear power plant, a computer integrated factory and a jumbo jet need continuous non-financial information to monitor performance.

Characteristic or Requirement	External Financial Statements	Planning & Controlling Activities or Processes	Short Term Strategic Decisions	Long Term Strategic Decisions
Audience.	1. Outside investors, creditors, IRS and SEC.	2. Plant, production and operating managers, and workers.	3. Marketing, product, business and senior managers.	4. Marketing, product, business and senior managers
Type of information required.	Aggregated quantitative overall financial results.	Disaggregated quantitative and qualitative non-financial information on specific activities and processes.	Disaggregated quantitative and qualitative financial and non-financial information on specific products, services, customers and suppliers.	Disaggregated quantitative and qualitative financial and non-financial information on specific aspects of the company's competitive strategy.
Reporting interval required.	Quarterly.	Real time, hourly or daily.	Annual or life cycle unless product design or process changes.	Special studies performed periodically.
DecisionExamples.	Should an investor purchase, or dispose of the stock or bonds of this company?	What resources are needed for the period? Are specific processes in control?	Should the company continue producing current products and services? What prices should be charged for products and services?	Should the company replace a machine, build a new plant, reengineer a product or process, convert to a JIT system?

Although standard costing was developed to aid in planning and measuring the financial consequences of performance variations, cost accounting reports and financial statements do not satisfy the requirements of these users. Cost accounting reports and financial statements are useful to plant managers for planning and measuring financial results, but they are not designed to control the activities, processes and work performed on a day to day basis. Many measurements that are considered more useful for this audience are discussed in the given table.

SHORT TERM STRATEGIC DECISIONS

Marketing, product, business and senior level managers require information to provide guidance for a variety of short term strategic decisions. Dis-aggregated, quantitative and qualitative information is needed on both the financial and non-financial aspects of specific products, services, customers and suppliers. For example, the life cycle costs associated with a product or service are needed for pricing products and services. Life cycle costs include design, production, promotion, distribution and service after the sale. Traditional cost accounting systems are frequently inadequate for short term strategic decisions because product costs are distorted and incomplete.

These two deficiencies of traditional cost accounting systems are given considerable attention by Johnson and Kaplan, the CAM-I sponsors and many other critics of accounting. The proposed solutions include activity based costing and activity based management. As mentioned earlier, these concepts are mainly discussed in.

LONG TERM STRATEGIC DECISIONS

Marketing, product, business and senior level managers also need information for a variety of long term strategic decisions. Decisions such as the replacement of a machine, building a new plant, re-engineering a product or process and implementing a JIT system require dis-aggregated quantitative and qualitative financial and nonfinancial information on a periodic basis.

These decisions usually require special studies that fall into the topical areas of relevant costing, capital budgeting and investment management. Special studies and analysis are needed because none of the cost accounting systems that can be designed from the components in Exhibit 2-1 are capable of providing forecasts of future cash flows for hypothetical situations. Some long term relevant cost decisions are discussed in under the heading of capital budgeting and investment management.

THE NEED FOR MULTIPLE SYSTEMS

Someone may eventually design a single information system that satisfies all of the requirements of the four functions discussed above. The continuing development of activity based accounting concepts is a movement in that direction. However, most companies will need multiple systems for the foreseeable future. The main point to grasp from this section is that the information generated for one purpose such as external reporting is not likely to be very useful for other purposes such as controlling activities, pricing products or decisions concerning competitive strategy. Recognition of this fact of business life is another important building block in the conceptual foundation of management accounting. It will help you understand many of the controversial issues that you are likely to encounter in practice. A number of these issues are discussed in subsequent chapters.

INCOME STATEMENTS

This section shifts the emphasis from a purely conceptual orientation to a mixed conceptual-practice orientation by discussing and illustrating the two main types of income statements. This topic is introduced in this chapter for several reasons. First, full absorption and direct costing income statements have traditionally been the major product of a management accounting system. In addition, the format of the income statement is controlled by the inventory valuation component of the system.

The throughput, direct, full absorption and activity based methods. This is an important consideration because the different formats can produce radically different financial results for a period when inventories are increasing or decreasing. Furthermore, these differences have very significant behavioral implications for management.

In addition, an understanding of the statement formats is needed in several other chapters of the text. For these reasons, full absorption and direct costing statements are emphasized in this section. The throughput and activity based formats are much less significant, at least in terms of the number of users. In addition, their introduction here might tend to confuse rather than enlighten before you internalize the conceptual foundation. For these reasons, a discussion of the throughput and activity based formats is postponed until

FULL ABSORPTION COSTING STATEMENTS

The symbols used to illustrate the relationships in a full absorption costing income statement are provided below:

Symbols used to Illustrate aBsorption

Costing income statement preparation:

B = Beginning merchandise inventory at cost.
P = Purchases of merchandise at cost.
E = Ending merchandise inventory at cost.
BM = Beginning direct materials inventory at cost.
PM = Cost of direct material purchased.
DM = Cost of direct material used.

EM	=	Ending direct material inventory at cost.
DL	=	Cost of direct labour used.
FO	=	Cost of factory overhead incurred.
TMC	=	Total manufacturing costs incurred during the period.
BWIP	=	Beginning inventory of work in process at cost.
EWIP	=	Ending inventory of work in process at cost, i.e., unfinished products still in production.
COGM	=	Cost of goods manufactured, i.e., the cost of the completed products transferred to finished goods.
BFG	=	Beginning finished goods at cost.
EFG	=	Ending finished goods at cost.
COGS	=	Cost of goods sold.
S	=	Sales dollars.GP = Gross profit.
S and A	=	Selling and administrative expenses.
NIBT	=	Net income before taxes.

CALCULATIONS FOR MERCHANDISING FIRM

In step 1, the cost of merchandise purchases (P) is added to the cost of the beginning inventory of merchandise for resale (B) to arrive at the cost of merchandise available for sale. Subtracting the cost of the ending inventory of merchandise (E) from the amount available for sale completes the step and provides the cost of goods sold (COGS). If the periodic recording interval is used, rather than the perpetual method, then the ending inventory (E) would have to be counted (i.e., taking a physical inventory) and then priced using a cost flow assumption. Step 2 involves subtracting cost of goods sold (COGS) from sales (S) to obtain the amount or gross profit (GP) for the period. In step 3 selling and administrative expenses (S&A) are subtracted from gross profit to determine the amount of net income before taxes (NIBT).

Table. Income Statement Algorithm for a Merchandising Firm

Step	Purpose	Equation
1	To find cost of goods sold.	B + P - E = COGS
2	To find gross profit.	S - COGS = GP
3	To find net income before taxes.	GP - S&A = NIBT

CALCULATIONS FOR A MANUFACTURING FIRM

A manufacturer requires several types of inventory including an inventory of raw or direct materials, an inventory of work in process, and a finished goods inventory. As a result, the procedure for calculating net income for a manufacturing organization is somewhat more involved than for a merchandising firm. An income statement algorithm for a manufacturing firm appears below:

Table. Income Statement Algorithm for a Manufacturing Firm

Step	Purpose	Equation
1	To find the cost of direct material used.	BM + PM– EM = DM
2	To find total manufacturing costs.	DM + DL + FO = TMC
3	To find the costs of goods manufactured.	TMC + BWIP – EWIP = COGM
4	To find cost of goods sold.	COGM + BFG– EFG = COGS
5	To find gross profit.	S– COGS = GP
6	To find net income before taxes.	GP– S&A = NIBT

In step 1 the beginning direct materials costs (BM) are added to the cost of direct material purchased (PM) to arrive at the cost of direct material available for use. Subtracting the cost of the ending inventory of direct materials (EM) provides the cost of direct material used (DM) and completes the step. Step 2 involves adding the cost of direct material (DM), the cost of direct labour used (DL) and factory overhead (FO) to provide the total manufacturing costs (TMC). Total manufacturing costs represents the factory costs charged to the work in process inventory during the period.

Adjusting for the change in the work in process inventory in step 3 provides the cost of goods manufactured (COGM). Adding the cost of the beginning inventory of work in process (BWIP) to the total manufacturing cost (TMC) and subtracting the cost of the ending inventory of work in process (EWIP) generates the cost of the products completed and charged to finished goods inventory. Adjusting for the change in finished goods inventory provides the cost of goods sold in step 4. Adding the cost of the beginning inventory of finished goods to the cost of goods manufactured provides the cost of goods available for sale. Then subtracting the cost of the ending finished goods inventory from the cost of the goods available provides the cost of goods sold. Gross profit and net income are determined in the same manner illustrated for a merchandising firm, therefore steps 5 and 6 are the same as steps 2 and 3 in Exhibit 2-6. Notice that although the costs must be separated by functional areas, i.e., factory and selling/administrative, the full absorption costing algorithm does not require separating these costs into fixed and variable elements.

Cost Flow Diagram

In full absorption costing, the costs flow through the inventory accounts in the manner illustrated in Exhibit 2-8.This exhibit builds on the abstract view of absorption costing provided in Exhibit 2-3 and reveals several important concepts. First, observe that all factory costs are charged to the inventory. Second, all inventory costs represent assets until the products are sold. Then these costs are charged to an expense account referred to as cost of goods sold. Cost of goods sold represents expired factory costs that are matched with sales revenue on the income statement. Also note from Exhibit 2-8 that all selling and administrative costs are charged to expense or period costs as incurred. Generally, this is because the quantities and timing of any future benefits associated with selling and administrative costs cannot be objectively measured.

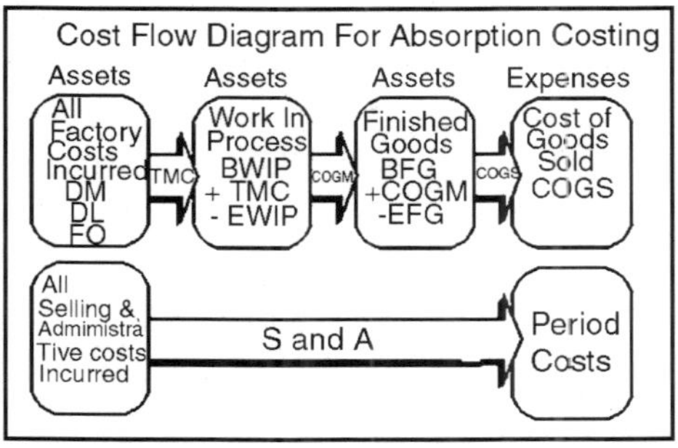

Now that you have a grasp of the concepts and algorithm for developing full absorption costing statements, consider the following example. The Hollow Company is a small manufacturer of leather products. The financial results needed to produce an income statement for January appear below:

Table. The Hollow Company Data

Account Or Cost Category	Amount	Account Or Cost Category	Amount
Beginning inventories:	$10,000	Indirect manufacturing costs:	$10,000
Direct materials	35,000	Indirect material	25,000
Work in process	24,000	Indirect labor	50,000
Finished goods		Depreciation	45,000
		Electric power	5,500
Ending	15,000	Property taxes &	20,000
inventories:	38,000	Insurance	4,500
Direct materials	26,000	Repair and maintenance	
Work in process			
Finished goods	70,000	Miscellaneous	10,000
			15,000
Direct materials purchased	80,000	Selling and Adm. costs:	5,000
			3,000
		Salaries	2,000
Direct labor used		Commissions	
		Depreciation	375,000
		Advertising	
		Miscellaneous	
		Sales	

Using the Income Statement Algorithm

The calculations that support the various parts of an absorption costing income statement appear here. Study and compare to insure that you understand these calculations.

Income Statement and Supporting Statements

An absorption costing income statement appears in Exhibit 2-11. Observe that the detailed calculations for cost of goods manufactured and selling and administrative expenses are provided in separate statements, or schedules.

This three statement approach is fairly common, although there are some alternatives. For example an even more abbreviated income statement can be prepared by combining the adjustment for the change in finished goods inventory with the statement of cost of goods manufactured.

Then the supporting statement becomes a statement of cost of goods sold rather than a statement of cost of goods manufactured. On the other hand, all of the calculations can be presented on a single detailed income statement. The specific approach adopted for internal purposes depends on the personal preferences and needs of internal users.

Income Statement Relationship to System Functions

Referring back to the four functions of an information system outlined in Exhibit 2-4, one might logically ask what part monthly internal income statements play in satisfying the requirements of internal users. Although the emphasis on financial results tends to vary somewhat from company to company, internal statements play a supporting roll for all of the decisions referred to in Exhibit 2-4. The supporting information comes mainly in the form of estimates of the effects each decision will have on future profitability.

Step	Purpose	Equation (See Exhibit 2-7)
1	To find the cost of direct material used.	DM = 10,000 + 70,000 - 15,000 = $65,000
2	To find total manufacturing costs.	TMC = 65,000 + 80,000 + 160,000 = 305,000
3	To find the costs of goods manufactured.	COGM = 305,000 + 35,000 - 38,000 = 302,000
4	To find cost of goods sold.	COGS = 302,000 + 24,000 - 26,000 = 300,000
5	To find gross profit.	GP = 375,000 - 300,000 = 75,000
6	To find net income before taxes.	NIBT = 75,000 - 35,000 = 40,000

Absorption Codting Income Statement for January

Although many other types of information are needed, (e.g., disaggregated, qualitative and non-financial) the effect on future profitability can never be ignored. In addition, internal income statements play an important roll in planning and monitoring the financial results of the various decisions after the decisions are made and implemented. Income Statement Algorithm Based On Absorption Costing

Sales		$375,000
Less Cost of Goods Sold:		
Beginning Finished Goods	$24,000	
Cost of Goods Manufactured	302,000	
Cost of Goods Available for sale	326,000	
Less Ending Finished Goods	26,000	
Cost of Goods Sold		
Gross Profit		300,000
		$75,000
Less Selling & Administrative		
Expenses		35,000
Net Income before Taxes		$40,000
		======

Statement Of Cost Of Goods Manufactured January 200x

Direct Materials:		
Beginning Inventory		$10,000
Purchases of Direct Materials		70,000
Cost of Direct Materials Available		80,000
Less Ending Inventory		15,000
Direct Materials Used		$65,000
Direct LaborIndirect		
Manufacturing Costs:		80,000
Indirect Material		
Indirect Labor		
Depreciation	10,000	
Electric power	25,000	
Property taxes & Insurance	50,000	
Repairs and maintenance	45,000	
Miscellaneous	5,500	
Total Indirect Manufacturing	20,000	
Costs	4,500	
Total Manufacturing Costs		
Add Beginning Work in Process		160,000
Manufacturing Costs to be		
Accounted For		$305,000
		35,000
Less Ending Work in Process		$340,000
Cost of Goods Manufactured		
		38,000
		$302,000
		=======

Statement Of Selling & Administrative Costs For January

Salaries	$10,000
Commissions	15,000
Depreciation	5,000
Advertising	3,000
Miscellaneous	2,000
Total	$35,000

DIRECT OR VARIABLE COSTING STATEMENTS

As indicated earlier in this Chapter, direct or variable costing is an inventory valuation method where only the variable manufacturing costs are charged to the inventory. Fixed manufacturing costs, i.e., fixed overhead costs, are charged to expense in the current period. In other words, all fixed costs are treated as period costs in direct costing. All other costs, including selling and administrative costs are treated in the same manner used in full absorption costing. Although this approach does not provide proper matching of cost and benefits, it is frequently used for internal reporting because it tends to be less confusing than full absorption costing. Advocates also argue that direct costing is more consistent with economic reality because fixed costs do not vary with production in the short run.

Need For Fixed and Variable Costs

Since only variable manufacturing costs are charged to the inventory in direct costing, this method requires separating all manufacturing costs into fixed and variable elements. To prepare a complete income statement based on this approach we must also separate the selling and administrative costs into fixed and variable elements.

New Symbols for Direct Costing

Some revised, as well as some new symbols are needed to illustrate direct costing and to emphasize the differences between the direct and absorption costing statement formats. In direct costing, factory overhead, total manufacturing cost, beginning and ending work in process, cost of goods manufactured and cost of goods sold are stated at variable manufacturing cost rather than full cost. To emphasize this difference, the letter V is added to the symbols used previously. These revised symbols are presented in the top section of Exhibit 2-14. In addition to these revisions, five new symbols are needed to represent the separation of the various costs into fixed and variable elements.

These new symbols are provided below:

- Symbols Used To Illustrate Direct
- Costing Income Statement Preparation

Revised Symbols:

- VFO = Variable factory overhead.
- TVMC = Total variable manufacturing costs.
- VCOGM = Variable cost of goods manufactured.
- VCOGS = Variable cost of goods sold.

New symbols needed to seoarate fuxed and variable costs:

- FFO = Fixed factory overhead.
- VS&A = Variable selling and administrative expenses.
- FS&A = Fixed selling and administrative expenses
- MM = Manufacturing margin.
- CM = Contribution margin.

CALCULATIONS FOR DIRECT COSTING

An algorithm for the preparation of direct costing income statements is presented below. The equations reflect the revised and new symbols are provided hereunder. Income Statement Algorithm Based On Direct Costing,

Step	Purpose	Equation
1	Find the costs of direct material used.	BM + PM - EM = DM
2	Find total variable manufacturing cost.	DM + DL + VFO = TVMC
3	Find variable cost of goods manufactured.	TVMC + BWIP - EWIP = VCOGM
4	Find variable cost of goods sold.	VCOGM + BFG - EFG = VCOGS
5	Find the manufacturing margin.	S - VCOGS = MM
6	Find the contribution margin.	MM - VS&A = CM
7	Find net income before taxes.	CM - FFO - FS&A = NIBT

Step 1 of the direct costing algorithm involves calculating direct materials costs and is the same as in absorption costing.

In step 2, the cost of direct labour used (DL) and the cost of variable factory overhead incurred (VFO) are added to the cost of direct material (DM) to arrive at the total variable manufacturing costs (TVMC). This is the amount charged to work in process.

Step 3 involves adjusting total variable manufacturing cost for the change in work in process inventory. This step generates the variable cost of goods manufactured (VCOGM).

Note that beginning work in process (BWIP) is added and ending work in process (EWIP) in subtracted in the same manner illustrated for full absorption costing, but of course, the beginning and ending inventories do not include fixed overhead costs in direct costing.

Arriving at variable cost of goods sold (VCOGS) in step 4 requires adjusting for the change in finished goods inventory. The cost of the beginning inventory of finished goods (BFG) is added to the variable cost of goods manufactured (VCOGM) to arrive at the cost of goods available for sale. Then the cost of the ending inventory of finished goods (EFG) is subtracted from this amount to produce the variable cost of goods sold (VCOGS). Note that the only difference between this calculation and step 4 in full absorption costing is that the finished goods inventory contains variable manufacturing costs rather than full costs.

Manufacturing Margin and Contribution Margin

Steps five and six include two new terms. In step 5, sales (S) less variable cost of goods sold (VCOGS) provides the manufacturing margin (MM), i.e., the revenue over and above the variable manufacturing costs.

Then, subtracting variable selling and administrative expenses from manufacturing margin (MM) in step 6 yields the contribution margin (CM). Contribution margin represents the revenue over and above the variable costs that contributes towards covering the fixed costs and, after the fixed costs are covered, providing a profit. Step seven is needed to arrive at the amount of net income before taxes. Note that all fixed costs are subtracted from contribution margin in this step, including fixed factory overhead (FFO) and fixed selling and administrative expenses (FS&A).

Cost Flow Diagram for Direct costing

In direct costing, the costs flow through the inventory accounts in the manner are shown in figure below. First, observe that only variable factory costs are charged to the inventory. This includes direct material, direct labour and variable factory overhead. This means that the beginning and ending inventories, total manufacturing costs, cost of goods manufactured and cost of goods sold contain only variable factory costs. The fixed factory costs are charged to expense during the period along with all of the selling and administrative costs. In direct costing, the fixed factory costs are viewed as the costs of maintaining the readiness to produce, rather than part of the costs of producing products.

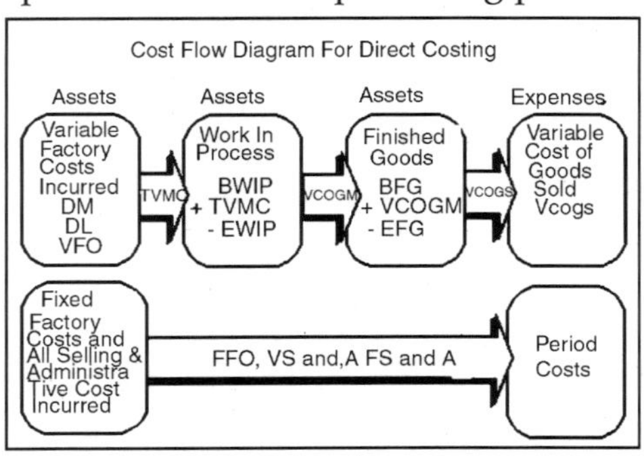

The economic reality, according to the advocates of direct costing, is that fixed costs are incurred during the period whether the company produces or not. Thus, these costs should be treated as expenses of the period, rather than costs of production. We will consider this controversy and other interesting issues concerning inventory valuation methods later in the text. *Example*: Direct or variable costing income statement. The Hollow Company costs have been separated into variable and fixed cost categories to facilitate the preparation of a direct costing income statement.

This revised set of data appears below:

Table. Revised Hollow Company Data

Account Or Cost Category	Amount	Account Or Cost Category	Amount
Beginning inventories:		Indirect manufacturing costs:	
Direct materials	$10,000	Indirect material (all variable)	$10,000
Work in process:		Indirect labor:	
Variable	16,100	Variable	15,000
Fixed	18,900	Fixed	10,000
Finished goods:		Depreciation (all fixed)	50,000
Variable	11,040	Electric power:	
Fixed	12,960	Variable	40,000
		Fixed	5,000
Ending inventories:		Property taxes & Insurance (all fixed)	5,500
Direct materials	15,000	Repair and maintenance:	
Work in process:		Variable	5,000
Variable	17,480	Fixed	15,000
Fixed	20,520	Miscellaneous (variable)	4,500
Finished goods:			
Variable	11,960	Selling and Administrative costs:	
Fixed	14,040	Salaries (fixed)	10,000
Direct materials purchased	70,000	Commissions (variable)	15,000
		Depreciation (fixed)	5,000
Direct labor used	80,000	Advertising (variable)	3,000
		Miscellaneous (variable)	2,000
		Sales	375,000

Using the Income Statement Algorithm

The calculations required to develop a direct costing income statement are presented in Exhibit 2-18. These calculations are based on the algorithm presented in Exhibit 2-15. Study and compare exhibits 2-15, 2-17 and 2-18 to insure that you understand the calculations. Observe that the fixed costs that appear in the beginning inventories (i.e., $18,900 for work in process and $12,960 for finished goods) are not included in the calculations that appear below. These fixed costs are omitted because they would have been charged to expense in the previous period under direct costing. While comparing the exhibits, also consider the fixed costs associated with the ending inventories in absorption costing (i.e., $20,520 for work in process and $14,040 for finished goods). These costs are included in the $85,500 fixed manufacturing costs incurred during the period and are charged to expense in step 7 shown below:

Table. Income Statement Algorithm for Direct Costing

Step	Purpose	Equation
1	Find the costs of direct material used.	DM = 10,000 + 70,000 - 15,000 = 65,000
2	Find total variable manufacturing cost.	TVMC = 65,000 + 80,000 + 74,500 = 219,500
3	Find variable cost of goods manufactured.	VCOGM = 219,500 + 16,100 - 17,480 = 218,120
4	Find variable cost of goods sold.	VCOGS = 218,120 + 11,040 - 11,960 = 217,200
5	Find the manufacturing margin.	MM = 375,000 - 217,200 = 157,800
6	Find the contribution margin.	CM = 157,800 - 20,000 = 137,800
7	Find net income before taxes.	NIBT = 137,800 - 85,500* -15,000 = 37,300

Income Statement and Supporting Statements

A direct costing income statement is presented and a supporting statements are provided for the cost of goods manufactured and selling and administrative expenses. The format of these statements follows the logic of the algorithm presented.

Hollow Company

Table. Direct Costing Income Statement for January 200x

Sales		$375,000
Less Cost of Goods Sold:		
Beginning Finished Goods	$11,040	
Cost of Goods Manufactured	218,120	
Cost of Goods Available for sale	229,160	
Less Ending Finished Goods	11,960	
Cost of Goods Sold		
		217,200
Manufacturing Margin		
Less Variable Selling &		
Administrative Expenses		157,800
Contribution Margin		
		20,000
Less Fixed Costs:		137,800
Manufacturing		
Selling & Administrative		-
Net Income before Taxes	85,500	
	15,000	
		100,500
		$37,300
		======

Table. Statement of Selling and Administrative Cost for January

Variable Costs:		
Commissions	$15,000	
Advertising	3,000	
Miscellaneous	2,000	$20,000
Fixed Costs:		
Salaries	10,000	
Depreciation	5,000	15,000
Total Selling & Administrative Costs		$35,000
		======

FULL ABSORPTION AND DIRECT COSTING

A comparison of the income statements in Exhibit's 2-11 and 2-19 indicates that net income for full absorption costing is $40,000, while net income for direct costing is only $37,300. The reason these amounts are different is that all of the current period fixed costs are charged to expense in direct costing, but $2,700 of the current period fixed costs remains in the ending inventories under full absorption costing.

Analyzing Fixed Costs In Absorption Costing

Examining the changes in the fixed costs in the inventory under full absorption costing reveals the difference between the two net income amounts.

Table. The Difference Between Net Income under Direct and Absorption Costing

Inventory	Fixed Costs	Totals	Net Income Difference	Explanation
Beginning Inventory:				It appears that the number of products produced is greater than the number of products sold. Since fixed factory costs are capitalized in the inventory under absorption costing, it is logical to assume that the $2,700 difference represents current period fixed costs deferred in the inventory with those extra products.
BWIP	$18,900			
BFG	12,960			
Total		$31,860		
Ending Inventory:				
EWIP	20,520			
EFG	14,040			
Total		34,560		
Increase			$2,700	
			=====	

What the analysis appears to show is that a greater number of products were produced than sold. This caused the inventory to increase. Since fixed overhead is charged to the products produced in full absorption costing, an increase in the inventory means that some of the current period fixed costs remain in the ending inventories. These costs will be released into expense when the inventory is sold in a subsequent period. However, this $2,700 is charged to expense in direct costing, along with all the other current period fixed costs.

Comparing total Inventory Changes

Another way to explain the difference between the two net income amounts is to examine the changes in the total inventory costs under the two methods. This information can be found in the previous exhibits, but for convenience consider. The diagram shows that the inventory increased by $5,000 under absorption costing, including a $3,000 increase in work in process and a $2,000 increase in finished goods. On the other hand, Exhibit 2-24 shows that the inventory increased by only $2,300 under direct costing including a $1,380 increase in work in process and a $920 increase in finished goods. The $2,700 difference between the total changes under the two inventory valuation methods (i.e., $5,000 - $2,300) is equal to the difference between the two net income amounts. Of course the difference between the inventory changes in Exhibits 2-23 and 2-24 is caused by the fixed costs that are deferred in the

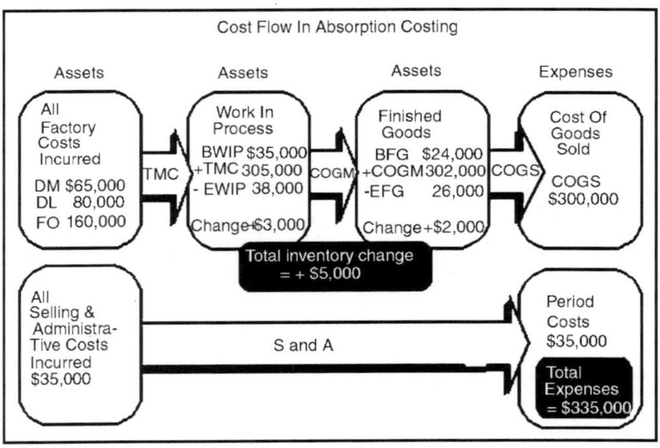

inventory under absorption costing. These include increases of $1,620 (i.e., $3,000 - $1,380) in work in process and $1,080 (i.e., $2,000 - $920) in finished goods. We know the differences between the increases in the two exhibits represents fixed costs because the variable costs are treated exactly the same in both exhibits. Although the terminology and format of the income statements is different under the two inventory valuation methods, the variable costs are treated the same in the accounting records.

Comparing the Total Expenses

A third way to explain the $2,700 net income difference is by comparing the total amount of expenses under the two inventory valuation methods. Notice from Exhibit 2-23 that the total expenses under absorption costing are $335,000 (i.e., $300,000 COGS + $35,000 S&A). However, in Exhibit 2-24, total expenses are $337,700 (i.e., $217,200 VCOGS + $120,500 for S&A and FFO). The $2,700 difference in total expenses explains the extra net income that appears in the full absorption costing income statement.

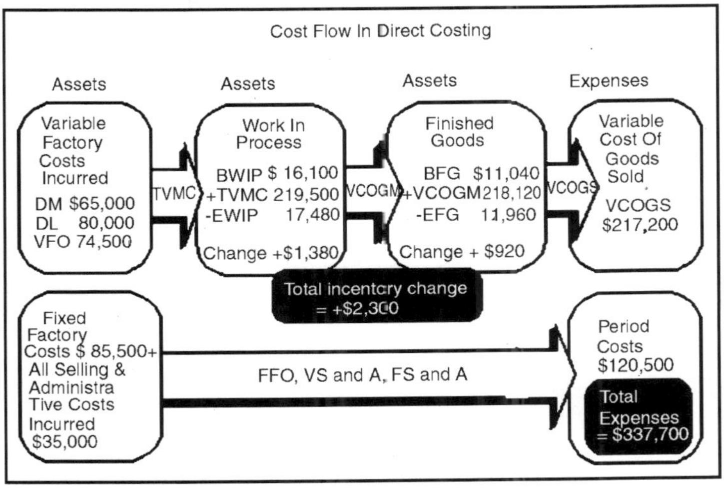

Generalizations Direct and Absorption Costing

There are three generalizations that are helpful in understanding the relationship between absorption and direct costing net income.

- When the number of units sold are equal to the number of units produced, net income under the two inventory valuation methods will usually be equal.
- When the number of units sold are less than the number of units produced, i.e., the inventories increase, absorption costing net income will usually exceed direct costing net income. This is because some of the current period's fixed manufacturing costs are capitalized (or deferred) in the inventory under absorption costing, while all fixed manufacturing costs are expensed under direct costing.
- When the number of units sold are greater than the number of units produced, i.e., the inventories decrease, direct costing net income will usually exceed absorption costing net income. This is because some prior period fixed manufacturing costs are expensed under absorption costing along with the current period's fixed manufacturing costs.

These three generalizations are valid as long as the fixed overhead per unit remains constant. Since this will not always be true, the generalizations are not always valid. Now you are probably confused.

COST CONCEPT

MARGINAL COST

Marginal, as always in economics, should be read as extra . Here, it is the extra cost of one more item of output; or the change in total cost divided by change in output .

Marginal cost is the type of cost to consider in short-run output decisions.

The rules to apply are:

- If MC < P, increase output.
- If MC > P, decrease output.
- If MC = P, leave output unchanged. The firm is in SHORT-RUN EQUILIBRIUM .

VARIABLE COST

Variable cost is the sum of marginal costs . It is the total expenditure on all variable factors of production, such as labour, raw materials and energy.

Variable cost is also known as operating cost. If the marginal cost of producing the first unit of output is 10, and the marginal cost of the second item of output is 20, then the variable cost of producing two items is 30.

FIXED COST

Fixed costs are costs which do not change per unit of output. Even if no crops are grown on a piece of land, the bank will insist on a mortgage payment from the farmer; even if no output is produced by a corporation, its bondholders will legally insist on payments of interest. The only way to avoid these payments is to go out of business; they are accordingly NOT considered in making a short-run operating decision, but ARE considered in making LONG-RUN, ENTRY or EXIT decisions

TOTAL COST

The sum of variable cost and fixed cost is TOTAL COST

AVERAGE COST

Average cost is total cost per unit of output, or

AC = TC/Q

Average cost plays a major role in long-run, entry and exit decisions.

The basic decision rules are parallel to those for marginal cost:

- If AC < P, the industry is profitable. ENTER
- If AC > P, the industry is unprofitable. EXIT
- If AC = P, the industry yields zero profit. Remain where you are; firms neither enter nor exit the industry, so this zero profit condition is characteristic of Industry Equilibrium .

Zero profit, incidentally, is not as bad as its sounds when costs are calculated to include opportunity costs . Firms always have the option of auctioning off their factory and machinery and putting the money in the bank or government bonds; if they decide to stay in business, they are incurring an opportunity cost equal to the interest they could have earned on a bank deposit or on bonds. This will not show up on an accountant's cost calculation today; since

Economic Cost = (Accounting + Opportunity)Cost

And

Economic Profit = (Revenue - Accounting -Opportunity) Cost

We could easily show an ACCOUNTING PROFIT of (say) per cent, and if the opportunity cost of NOT investing in bonds were per cent, we would have anECONOMIC LOSS of per cent.

COST PROBLEMS

Problem

Given that fixed costs are $100 throughout and that marginal costs are $5 for one unit of output and increase by $5 for each additonal unit of output,

- Construct a table showing for one to ten units of output, the marginal cost, variable cost, fixed cost, total cost and average cost.
- Translate the information on the table into a graph of marginal and average cost.
- Assuming the price of the good is $30, what is the best level of output in the short run? Should the firm exit its industry? Should other firms enter? Explain your answers.
- Graphically depict the price line of $ 30, the operating profit of the firm, and the total profit or loss of the firm.

Answer to Problem 1

The calculations are straightforward:

- Variable cost is the sum of marginal cost. Note that the third column is simply a running total of the second.
- Fixed cost, in column four, is fixed at $100.

Quantity	Marg. cost	Var. cost	Fixed cost	Total cost	Avg. cost
1	5	5	100	105	105.00
2	10	15	100	115	57.50
3	15	30	100	130	43.33
4	20	50	100	150	37.50
5	25	75	100	175	35.00
6	30	105	100	205	34.17
7	35	140	100	240	34.29
8	40	180	100	280	35.00
9	45	225	100	325	36.11
10	50	275	100	375	37.50

- Total cost = Variable Cost + Fixed Cost.
- Average cost = Total Cost/Quantity.

That at a price of $30, the output in the short run would be chosen at the level at which P = MC or 6 items of output.

At that level, REVENUE = PQ = $30 x 6 = $180. and while this is above the VARIABLE COST of $105, and leaves an Operating Profit of $75, it is below the TOTAL COST of $205. Total profit = REVENUE - TOTAL COST = $180 - $205, so there is a loss of $25 even at the best short run operating level. The AVERAGE COST of $34.17 is above the price of $30, leading to a loss of $4.17 (more exactly, $4 and 1/6) on each item, or multiplied by the quantity of 6, to a total loss of $25. The LONG RUN decision of this firm, if price does not improve, will be to EXIT the industry.

A graphical presentation of the problem: You should be able to identify all areas on the graph and explain what they mean.

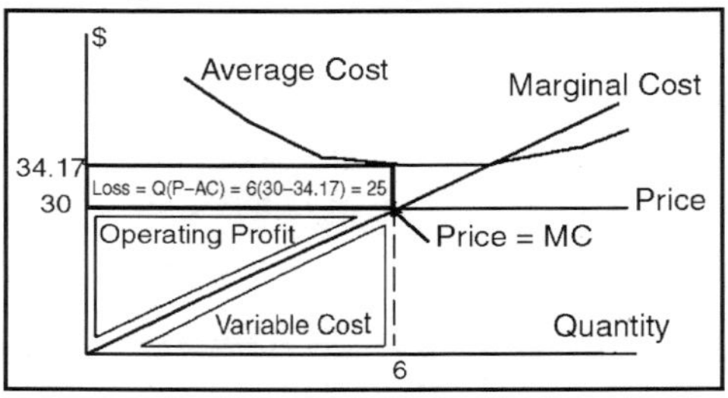

Problem

Repeat the above problem with a fixed cost of $50.

Answer to Problem

Table. Cost Table

Quantity	Marg. cost	Var. cost	Fixed cost	Total cost	Avg. cost
1	5	5	50	55	55.00
2	10	15	50	65	32.50
3	15	30	50	80	26.67
4	20	50	50	100	25.00
5	25	75	50	125	25.00
6	30	105	50	155	25.83
7	35	140	50	190	27.14
8	40	180	50	230	28.75
9	45	225	50	275	30.56
10	50	275	50	325	32.50

The calculations are straightforward:

- Variable cost is the sum of marginal cost. Note that the third column is simply a running total of the second.

- Fixed cost, in column four, is fixed at $100.
- Total cost = Variable Cost + Fixed Cost.
- Average cost = Total Cost/Quantity.

Note that at a price of $30, the output in the short run would be chosen at the level at which P = MC or 6 items of output.

At that level, revenue = PQ = $30 x 6 = $180. This is above the variable cost of $105, and leaves an operating profit of $75, it is above the total cost of $155. Total profit = revenue - total cost = $180 - $155, so there is a profit of $25 at the best short run operating level. The average cost of $25.83 is above the price of $30, leading to a profit of $4.17 (more exactly, $4 and 1/6) on each item, or — multiplied by the quantity of 6, to a total profit of $25.

The long run decision of this firm, if price does not improve, will be to expand. The long run decision of other firms, which notice that this industry offers above=normal profits, will be to enter the industry.

Note that the choice of operating level is NOT made at lowest possible average cost. The average cost is lowest at a quantity of 4 or 5, and if we choose to produce 4 units, we will get a larger profit per unit of $30 - $25 or $5 per unit, the total profit or profit per unit multiplied by quantity is only $5 x 4 = $20 rather than $25.

Problem 3

Given the following table, compute marginal and average costs. What is fixed cost?

Note that output goes up by 10-unit increments, not one-unit increments. What impact does this have on the computation of marginal costs?

Table. Cost Data

Output	Total cost	Average cost	Marginal cost
0	$ 1,000	--	--
10	$ 3,000	--	--
20	$ 8,000	--	--
30	$15,000	--	--
40	$24,000	--	--

Answer: At zero units of output, the firm incurs costs of $1000. These cannot be variable costs, since it is producing nothing; we therefore have FIXED COSTS of $1000. Note that output goes up by 10-unit increments, not one-unit increments. What impact does this have on the computation of marginal costs?

Answer: Since MC = Change in cost/Change in output, we must remember to divide by 10.

Note: The first row of the table cannot be filled in: Average cost = TC/Q, and we cannot divide by zero. Marginal cost depends on the change in costs, and we have no previous cost figure.

The rest of the calculations should be straightforward.

In the row with an output of 10, the total cost was $3000, a change in cost of $2000. We therefore compute:

AC = TC/Q = $3000/10 = $300

MC = Change in cost/Change in output = $2000/10 = $200.

In the row with an output of 20, the total cost was $8000, a change in cost of $5000. We therefore have

AC = TC/Q = $8000/20 = $400

MC = Change in cost/change in Q = $5000/10 = $500.

In the row showing output of 30, total cost is $15,000, an increase of $7000. Hence:

AC = TC/Q = $15000/30 = $500

MC = Change in cost/change in Q = $7000/10 = $700

Table. Cost Data

Output	Total cost	Average cost	Marginal cost
0	$ 1,000	——	——
10	$ 3,000	$300	$200
20	$ 8,000	$400	$500
30	$15,000	$500	$700
40	$24,000	$600	$900

Problem

Given the following table, fill in the blanks.

Hint: Are the costs at output = 0 variable costs or fixed costs?

Hint: Output is in 100 unit increments. Remember the definition of MARGINAL cost. The table should be read as stating that the marginal cost is 10 for EACH unit between 0 and 100, so that the variable cost is $10 × 100 units.

Table. Cost Table

Output	Marg.Cost	Var.Cost	Fixed Cost	Total Cost	Avg. Cost
0	—-	——	——	6000	—-
100	10	——	——	—-	—-
200	—-	2500	——	—-	—-
300	—-	——	——	10,500	—-
400	—-	——	——	—-	36.25
500	—-	——	——	—-	—-
600	70	20,000	——	—-	—-

Answer to Cost Problem

Given the following table, fill in the blanks.

Hint: Are the costs at output = 0 variable costs or fixed costs?

Hint: Output is in 100 unit increments. Remember the definition of MARGINAL cost = Change in cost/change in output. In computing marginal costs, rember to divide by 100. The table should be read as stating that the marginal cost is 10 for EACH unit between 0 and 100, so that the variable cost is $10 × 100 units, that is, the variable cost at Q = 200 is $1000.

Table.Cost Table

Output	Marg.Cost	Var.Cost	Fixed Cost	Total Cost	Avg. Cost
0	--	0	6000	6000	--
100	10	1,000	6000	7000	70
200	15	2,500	6000	8,500	42.50
300	20	4,500	6000	10,500	35.00
400	40	8,500	6000	14,500	36.25
500	45	13,000	6000	19,000	38.00
600	70	20,000	6000	26,000	46.67

Note that marginal cost increases throughout; average cost first declines, then increases.

Row-by-row explanation: Output 0. Since there is no output, there are zero variable costs. The $6000 total cost is entirely fixed cost. Marginal cost is not computable, since there is no previous total or variable cost figure; average cost is not computable since division by zero is not defined.

You can now fill in the FC column at $6000, since FC does not change with output. Output 100. MC is given at 10; this is to be read as 10 per unit for each of the extra 100 units. This means a total MC or variable cost of $1000.

The total cost is FC + VC = $6000 + $1000 = $7000.

The average cost is TC/Q = $7000/100 = $70.

Output 200. The variable cost is given as $2500. This is $1500 higher than the previous VC, and output is 100 units higher.

Since,

MC = Change in cost/Change in output we know that MARGINAL COST = $1500/100 = $15.

Note that we do not have to compute total cost to find change in cost; since variable cost is the only cost which changes, the change in cost and the change in variable cost are the same.

The total cost = FC + VC = 6000 + 2500 = $8500.

The AVERAGE COST = TC/Q = $8500/200 = $42.50

Note that AC falls from $70 to $42.50 despite a rise in MC from $10 to $15.

Output 300. The TOTAL COST is given at $10,500. Since TC = FC + VC, it must be the case that VC = TC - FC or VC = 10500 - 6000 = $4500.

The previous VC (at Output 200) was $2500, so that VC has increased by $2000 while output has increased by 100.

MC = Change in cost/change in output = $2000/100 = $20.

AC = Total cost/output = $10,500/300 = $35.

Output 400. The AVERAGE COST is given at 36.25. Since AC = TC/Q, we can find Total Cost by multiplying Average cost by Q.

Hence TC = 400 x 36.25 = $14,500.

As in the last problem, we can now find VC = TC - FC

or VC = $14,500 - $6,000 = $ 8,500. This is $4000 higher than the last VC of $4500, so that

MC = Change in VC/Change in output = 4000/100 = $40

Output 500. Looks impossible, since there are no costs whatsoever given. But go on the final row and then come back.

Output 600. We are given two cost figures — marginal cost is 70 and the variable cost is 20,000. Since

MC = Change in VC/Change in Q, and the change in Q is 100, we know that the change in the VC is $7000 — that is, that the previous value of VC was $13,000.

It is easy to complete the row for output of 600.

TC = VC + FC = $20,000 + $6,000 = $26,000.

AC = TC/Q = $26,000/600 = $46.67.

Output 500. We now have the figure of VC = $13,000. This is $4500 higher than the previous VC of $8500.

MC = Change in cost/change in output = $4500/100 = $45.

TC = FC + VC = 6000 + 13000 = 19,000.

AC = TC/Q = 19,000/500 = $38.00.

ELEMENTS OF COST

DEFINITION

Presented here are typical cost elements that must be considered when arriving at a total project cost estimate. These examples must be considered generic in nature. They are not definitive examples since the accounting practices of different firms and organizations may vary greatly. The definition of these cost parameters is usually not the responsibility of the engineering organization.

Rather, a financial or estimating organization is responsible for determining the cost data, which is combined with engineering (and fabrication, manufacturing, test & integration, purchasing, etc., as appropriate) estimates of the work to be performed. The point here is to give you some sense of the various components that may enter into the total project cost.

Direct Labour

Direct labour is the cost of all the time (hours) that people spend on a particular activity that is directly related to the contract objectives. This direct labour cost is the estimated number of hours spent by an individual on the job, times the dollars per hour that person is paid. These individual costs for all the people working on a job are then added up to get a total direct labour cost. Various techniques are used to determine the dollars per hour that are used to calculate the direct labour cost. A common approach is to use labour cost pool rates, where the average of the actual pay rates for all employees with the same job classification is used. These pool rates could be broken into categories such as Engineer, Senior Engineer, Foreman, Machinist I, Machinist II, etc. If your technical proposal names specific people to accomplish all or part of the proposed work, the actual pay of these individuals must be included in your cost estimates.

Another technique that is sometimes employed is to use the actual pay rate of all the individual(s) who will be working on the proposed job. The total direct labour cost is then determined by adding together the individual labour costs of all the people to be assigned to the project.

If the proposed project will last for a significant length of time, escalation factors must be applied to the current labour rates to account for future changes in these rates. This escalation will be due to items such as pay raises, attrition, and increases in starting pay for new hires. These escalation factors are often based on historical data.

Labour Overhead

The cost of an individual to a contract is more than just the pay that that person receives. There are expenses associated with employing that person that are referred to as labour overhead, or indirect, costs. Click here to see a number of these cost elements that may be included in the labour overhead. The estimated expense of these various items is usually based on historical data or expected future costs, or these expenses may be based on a combination of historical data and actual cost data.

These expenses are lumped together into a labour overhead factor that is multiplied by the direct labour cost to determine the overhead labour cost. This overhead represents costs related to people or labour working on the contract, and therefore this overhead cost follows the base or direct labour costs.

Facilities

This type of cost can be considered either direct or indirect, depending on the nature of the company. If a company's facility exists to serve only one contract, then the cost of facilities should be a direct cost to the contract. If space is used to house employees that work on several contracts, however, this type of cost should be an indirect that follows the direct labour of people working on the contract.

Materials

Included in this cost category are the expenses incurred in purchasing raw materials for use during the fabrication and assembly of hardware for testing and/or for delivery to the customer. For a test programme these material costs would be associated with the test hardware. For a test and hardware delivery project, the material costs would include materials required for both the test and for delivered hardware. These costs can include the purchase of metal stocks, bulk wire, screws and fasteners, and all parts that are used in the delivered product.

Other Costs

There are often other miscellaneous direct costs that will be charged to the contract, such as travel, postage, rentals, and insurance.

Subcontracts

Often another firm, under a subcontractor to your firm, will accomplish a portion of the work required by your contract, for example when a second organization has a special capability or product line that you require to accomplish the job. In this case you would have the potential subcontractor(s) respond to an RFP for the required services or hardware. If there are a number of potential sources, this would be a competitive situation and you would select the subcontractor whose participation would place your company in the most advantageous position for the overall project.

General and Administrative (G&A) Expenses

G&A expenses are other costs associated with doing business. These G&A expenses are expressed in terms of a factor that is applied to the total cost, less material and subcontracts. Click here to view the several elements that contribute to the total G&A expense. These expenses are associated with overall company management and the pursuit of new business opportunities. Historical data is often used to project these expenses into the future.

Fee

The fee is the amount you add to your bid that is the profit you hope your firm will make on the contract. A number of factors enter into determining the proposed fee for a specific contract. These include considerations such as:

- Required schedule performance and associated risk.
- Cost performance constraints and associated risk
- Personnel expertise required to accomplish the work.

In general, the higher the risk associated with the proposed work, the higher the fee that will be proposed.

Determining what fee to propose is a decision made collectively by the proposal management and by company management. Many considerations enter into determining this fee. If the project has a high risk associated with successful completion, you may choose to bid a higher fee than you would for a simpler project. Also, if winning the project is very important to your long-range business position, you may choose to propose a lower fee.

Unallowable Costs

As defined in the FAR, there are a number of costs that are deemed to be unallowable for federal government contracts. These costs should not be included in your proposal cost estimates, as they will not be reimbursable. Some of the major unallowable costs include:

- Airfare costs in excess of the lowest customary standard coach fare.
- Advertising and public relations.
- Alcoholic beverages.
- Bad debts.
- Entertainment costs.
- Fines and penalties.
- Goodwill.
- Lobbying.
- Losses on other contracts.

The FAR states that costs of amusement, diversion, social activities, and any directly associated costs such as tickets to shows or sports events, meals, lodging, rentals, transportation and gratuities are unallowable.

Unbillable hours are hours charged to a project that are costs to that project but are not reimbursable by the customer. Examples include hours charged above a contract ceiling, or hours related to project management that the customer is unwilling to reimburse. Costs that are for the benefit or convenience of the company such as the following may not be reimbursable. Care must be taken when including these type costs in your proposal.

- Relocation
- Travel and transportation incidental to employment
- Incentive awards
- Tools
- Uniforms
- Social functions, gifts, celebrations

In the preceding chapter the sources of income which are ordinarily open to a bank have been outlined, and one of them - the rate of interest or discount - has been analysed at some length. It is equally important to consider with care the various elements of cost which the bank is obliged to incur. Speaking generally, these elements of cost may be summarized as follows:

- Fixed expenses - rent (or the interest on invest-ment in building and equipment), insurance, surety bonds, taxes, light, heat, etc.
- Bad debts.
- Overhead expenses - salaries of president and general officers not assigned to any specific duty.

- Operating salaries.
- Stationery, printing, postage, etc.
- Allowance for interest on capital.
- Depreciation of equipment and building.

Most of these expenses are sufficiently obvious to require no description or explanation. The bank, of course, must have some definite quarters and it gets these either by hiring them from others or by purchas-ing or building them. In any case there is either an annual outlay or a capital sum on which interest must be allowed which represents the cost of the bank's quarters or offices. In the same way the fixed expenses for lighting, heating, and caring for the offices of the bank must be provided for, and may be regarded as a fixed sum in a degree independent of the total amount of business the bank has to do and in a large measure independent of the amount of its capital.

The overhead expenses are in somewhat the same class as these fixed or plant expenses. Every bank has a certain number of salaried officers whose work when well done is of utmost importance to the institution, but whose pay cannot be assigned to any particular undertaking. They are "overhead" in the sense that they belong to or must be charged against everything beyond bank debts in due proportion - that is to say, they are salaries which are practically incident to the doing of any business and which have only a secondary relationship to the amount of such business. We shall presently see how the cost of such salaries is usually distributed among the different factors or divisions of the organization.

IDENTIFYING COST ELEMENTS

The cost elements' classification of accounts is the very first structure in the internal accounting's chart of accounts.

From this first class of accounts (which will be identified with the number two), we shall begin. Consequently we must use great care to correctly identify the different amounts that will be incorporated in internal accounting, which then will help us to accurately establish the specific cost of production and the important appraisal of the cost of goods sold.

Let us start with a very basic first approach: We shall establish the code structure of our internal accounting's chart of accounts.

Class of Accounts: This is expressed by the first digit of the code. The cost elements class will be designated with the number two.

Group of Accounts: This is the identification by the next digit of the code. I recommend the use of only one digit in this position, for a total of nine groups in each class of accounts.

Main Accounts: These numbers should have only two digits, which will make it possible to create a total of roughly 90 main accounts. In my experience, I believe it is adequate to designate up to 90 main accounts within each group of accounts.

Sub Accounts: These should have a total of three digits. With a capacity of up to 900 sub accounts for each of the 90 main accounts within each group of accounts, we have created an adequate quantity of sub accounts for the code structure of the internal chart of accounts.

Sub-Sub Accounts: In case there is a need to increase the chart of accounts, we may allocate four digits for these sub-sub accounts, which would then increase the capacity of each sub account with some 9,000 accounts.

The code structure within the internal chart of accounts will be identified in following way.

Class	Group	Main	Sub	Sub-Sub
X	X	XX	XXX	XXXX

With this planned structure, we will now develop the following group of accounts.

- 2-1-00-000 Salaries and Wages
- 2-2-00-000 Benefits
- 2-3-00-000 Stores Withdrawal
- 2-4-00-000 Depreciation and Amortization
- 2-5-00-000 Adm. & Sales Costs
- 2-6-00-000 Utilities - Services
- 2-7-00-000 Financial Costs
- 2-8-00-000 General Costs

Let us now consider some main accounts that could be incorporated under some specific groups of accounts.

- 2-1-01-000 Salaries for Management and Professionals
- 2-1-05-000 Hourly Wages — Direct
- 2-1-11-000 Hourly Wages — Indirect
- 2-3-01-000 Stores Withdrawal of Direct Materials
- 2-3-11-000 Stores Withdrawal of Indirect Materials
- 2-3-41-000 Stores Withdrawal of Supplies
- 2-3-51-000 Stores Withdrawal of Spare-Parts
- 2-5-11-000 Administrative Costs of Professional Fees
- 2-5-12-000 Travel and Representation
- 2-5-13-000 Telephone and Fax
- 2-5-51-000 Sales Commissions
- 2-5-53-000 Advertising
- 2-6-11-000 Outside Services
- 2-6-15-000 Facility Services
- 2-8-06-000 Postage and Mailing Services
- 2-8-11-000 Employee Relations
- 2-8-21-000 Lease and Rentals

These main accounts can then be complemented with all necessary sub accounts to create an ideal information structure about all cost elements that the company may have. All of these cost elements are accrued costs. They are accrued or "matched" costs of this accounting period and the company's functional activities. We should not approve costs that do not belong to this accounting period and to the functional activities. Instead we shall proceed with the same attention as we do when matching expenses toward revenues. This matching procedure is very important. Since the newly developed internal chart of accounts will correctly establish the cost of goods sold and compare it with the corresponding sales revenues, there is no longer a need for accounts such as prepaid expenses in the general accounting structure. These prepaid accounts were developed for the purpose of matching the expenses toward the sales revenues. This approach of matching costs is only necessary in internal accounting.

This is a very important statement: We have created an absolutely new approach in our accounting philosophy.

Until now, there have been mixed definitions in general accounting (financial accounting) that actually correspond only to managerial accounting. We had to use these mixed definitions because there was not a separate internal accounting structure. Therefore we had to use prepaid accounts to prevent mistakes in income statement presentations. Amounts for prepaid rent, prepaid insurance, etc. had to be included in the assets. We now have internal accounting and the philosophy of matching expenses, which solves the cost elements accounts. We no longer need any prepaid accounts in our assets. An additional benefit to the internal accounting structure: Within the cost elements' class of accounts, we will open accounts that will register all necessary amounts regarding price, payment and efficiency variances. These new details will be included in the stores withdrawal group of accounts to show management a clear structure of the variances that exist between actual price and standard price, actual labour hours and standard labour hours. All these variations will be referring to the job orders that we worked with our new internal cost approach, we will be able to create absolutely new information that is as good as unthinkable with the old general accounting structure.

PREPARATION OF COST SHEET

BALANCE SHEET PREPARATION

The best way to determine if projected resources will cover academic year expenses is to prepare a cash flow balance sheet containing monthly expenses and resources. You can then compare expenses with the resources and income you project will be available during the academic year.

EXPENSES

- Begin by listing at the top of each column the months you are scheduled to attend school.

- Enter the exact amounts charged for tuition and fees in the appropriate column (month) when payment is to be made.
- *Books and Supplies*: List the required/recommended texts and instruments with appropriate charges. Talking with other students may give you a better estimate of probable expenses and help you determine at what time in the year it will be necessary to purchase the required books and equipment.
- *Rent/Mortgage*: Enter your monthly rent/mortgage charges. Do not forget to list deposits, escrow, and other charges.
- *Utilities - Include the obvious*: Gas, electric, water, phone, cable, etc. Some utilities vary over the course of a year. To get a knowledgeable estimate of what you may pay, consult your landlord and/or past tenants as to their experience with prior charges, or request figures from the various utility companies.
- *Food*: Consider this area very carefully. Plan conservatively but realistically. Carefully review the amounts you normally spend for food - at the supermarket, restaurants and for snacks. Consider whether this amount can be adjusted before entering this budget item.
- *Transportation*: Include travel to and from school, vacations and weekly trips to and from the places; you need to go. Also note car payments, insurance, upkeep, parking, etc.
- *Health Care*: Include the cost of student health insurance as well as unreimbursed visits to the physician and dentist plus the cost of prescriptions, etc.
- *Personal/Other*: This is a catch-all category. Sit down and do some brainstorming - laundry, clothing, debt repayment, entertaining, gifts, haircuts, health and beauty aids, postage, etc. Try to develop a realistic estimate of monthly needs.
- *Grand total*: Total each month. You may wish to make grand totals by both row and column. Now look over the totals. Do they seem high, low, accurate?

RESOURCES (INCOME)

- *Parental Support*: Such support may come in a variety of forms ranging from one lump sum to monthly allowances. Oftentimes parents provide assistance by covering such expenses as health or auto insurance.
- *Student Wages/Income*: This relates to both on and off-campus earnings. Place earnings in the appropriate monthly column on the basis of when monies will be earned.
- *Spouse Wages/Income*: Include your spouse's monthly net wages.
- *Savings*: Include any liquid assets. List total assets in the first month

of the academic year. Do not provide figures for any other month at this time.

- *Guaranteed Student Loan*: List the amount of assistance your state provides.
- *State/WICHE Contracts*: List the amount of assistance your state provides.
- *Institutional Financial Aid*: Review your award letter. Place the disbursement amounts of NDSL/HPSL in the month expected.
- *Other Resources*: This is a catch-all area for any other income or resources you may receive.

CASH FLOW ANALYSIS

Do not total the resource columns as you did with the expense columns. Instead, total the first month's expenses and subtract the sum from the first month's total resources. You should end up with a net positive balance (more resources than expenses). This net positive balance should be carried forward into the next month(s), probably in the form of increased savings. Continue this process until you either cover the entire academic year or end up with a net negative balance (expenses exceed resources). If a negative balance arises, continue to maintain the negative figure in the bottom net row. A negative balance is reduced or increased by the following month's balance. Continue the process until you reach the last month's net calculation. The exercise of developing your budget and your net worth will also prepare you for developing similar financial statements for a future practice situation. Such statements are important in preparation to borrow money for a practice or for a home.

METHOD OF COSTING

DEFINITION

Inventory valuation is an integral part of a business, especially when stocks are involved. It has direct effect on the cost of sales, which is the summation of initial stock and inventory purchase less final stock. Hence, it is a sensitive phenomenon because it impacts on your financial reports - Balance Sheet and Profit/Loss and even Tax reports. From the foregoing, it can be said that, inventory valuation is one of the metrics for determining the profitability of a business.

SAP Business One supports only three types of costing or inventory valuation methods namely: Moving Average, FIFO and Standard Price. The golden rule is that, continuous stock management must be activated before this functionality can be leveraged. Continuous stock system is defined under: Administration > System Initialization > Company Details > Check default valuation method box. Irrespective of the costing method leveraged, prices are calculated in local currency.

MOVING AVERAGE

Inventory is valued using the cost price of the items. On receipt of goods, the value is automatically updated. A stock receipt transaction that affects accounting, debits the stock account while a release transaction that affects accounting credits stock/sales return account based on the cost price of the item.

STANDARD PRICE

When standard price is used as the costing method, a static price is defined for each item. On stock receipt, it is not automatically updated. The standard price method is advantageous in cases where you produce the items yourself. A stock receipt transaction that affects accounting debits the stock account based on the standard price defined for the item. Very often than not, variance does occurs, thus the difference between the standard price and the receipt document price will be posted to a variance account. A stock release posting on the hand, credits the stock account according to the standard price defined for the item.

FIFO

The FIFO inventory valuation method uses a "First- In- First Out" methodology. This methodology ensures that when goods are received, a step-like arrangement or layer that is based on cost, quantities and entry date is created. And during goods release, the goods from the first layer (open) and their corresponding cost are used.

Thus, the choice of which of the costing method to use is a function of the objective to be achieved. Good enough, SAP Business One allows so much flexibility as it relates to costing system. Different costing method can be defined for different items and you can change the costing system of your items globally. However, it is important to note that continuous stock system cannot be deactivated after stock posting have been made.

In this posting, I have only given an Overview of the costing methods in SAP Business One. In my subsequent postings on the subject matter, I'd concisely analyse the journal implications of each of these methods for sales, purchasing, inventory and production transactions.

According to the FASB (Financial Accounting Standards Board), the cost method of accounting is a legitimate accounting method to account for investments. If the investment is such that there is no substantial influence of the investment holder over the company invested in, or if there is no readily determinable fair value of the investment, the cost method of accounting for investments is usually the one used.

Under this method, the investment is recorded in the balance sheet at historical cost. Here is a brief look into what the cost method of accounting for investments actually entails.

COST METHOD OF ACCOUNTING

The points below highlight the cost method of accounting for investments specifically and not the general method of cost accounting that are used in the internal firm product or service costing (accounting).

- The original cost of the investment, that is the historical cost which was paid for the investment, when it was first bought, is the one that is recorded in the balance sheet.
- Once the balance sheet entry has been made, no further adjustments and changes are required to be made, unless the fair market value of the investment drops to such an extent that there is doubt over any kind of possible recovery. Under such a circumstance, a permanent write off of the investment is made.
- If any dividends are declared on the investment in question, the dividends are recoredd like normal dividends and the usual accounting entries are passed for the same.
- Any undistributed earnings on the investments are not recorded in the owner's balance sheet and hence have no effect on the final balance sheet, per se.
- The consolidation process under the cost method of accounting requires that both, the investment account and the dividend account, be eliminated completely when the parent and the subsidiary consolidate their accounts. You can use accounting software to aid with the consolidation process.
- It is important to note here that no matter which method of accounting is used (cost or equity), the consolidated financial statements will be identical for both.

If the parent company uses the cost method of accounting for investments, the consolidation worksheet entries go in the following sequence. The consolidation starts with eliminating the book value of net assets at acquisition from the parent's balance sheet.

The second step is to record all excess costs incurred in or during the consolidation phase. The difference between the effect of prior periods on retained earnings and the current effects on the income statement and balance sheet are then amortized. A series of elimination entries then follow, namely, dividend income, accumulated depreciation at acquisition and other inter-company transactions.

EQUITY METHOD VS COST METHOD

Below are a few differences between the equity accounting method for investments and the cost accounting method for investments.

- The equity method of accounting is used when there is a significant influence or control, with the investment being between 20 to 50 per cent of the total stock of the firm invested in. The cost method, as mentioned earlier, is preferably used for lesser investment percentages.

- The cost method of accounting has an advantage over equity method of accounting when there is no fair, easily determinable value for the investment.
- It is easier to calculate the return on investment and do other financial analysis of figures when the equity accounting method is used. As the cost method uses working paper and not the general ledger, all figures must be tracked there first.
- The cost method of accounting includes less paperwork than the equity method. On the other hand, being more comprehensive, the financial statements done using the equity method are more useful to the internal management for facilitating analysis.
- The best scoring point of the equity method over the cost method of accounting is that it has an easy self-checking feature, i.e., the consolidated financial statements should tally with certain parent figures and when they don't, the problem can be easily identified and corrected. The cost method of accounting has no such self-check feature.

RECONCILIATION OF COST AND FINANCIAL ACCOUNTING

COST OF RECONCILIATION

How was it possible for 40 million South Africans to avoid a disastrous civil war and create a new society that raised the hope for peace among long-alienated peoples? Those familiar with the country believe that the answer is twofold: a rigorously negotiated constitution shaped around human rights and citizen participation in political decisions; and a Truth and Reconciliation Commission that walked the narrow boundary between exacting vengeance on the agents of the regime and granting them immunity.

It has become almost fashionable in South Africa to dismiss the TRC for failing to produce the "reconciliation" side of its announced mission. Can the word "reconciliation" be used with theological, ethical and political-empirical integrity? John de Gruchy and Puma Gobodo-Madikizela's books give strong answers to that question.

De Gruchy, a University of Cape Town theologian, looks at the roots of "reconciliation" in biblical and historical theology and measures its meaning against South African history. Nobody else has written so precisely and profoundly on this topic. Pumla Gobodo-Madikizela, an astute, sensitive young clinical psychologist, records and reflects on her 46 hours of prison interviews with Eugene de Kock, who headed the Vlakplaas prison as a secret police officer, and who more than earned the nickname "Prime Evil."

Gobodo-Madikezela was open to the possibility that underneath de Kock the murderer she might discover de Kock the human being. To read her book is to understand the cost in time and spiritual-moral struggle exacted of anyone who walks down the long road to reconciliation between the agents and the victims of gross, politically legitimated cruelty.

Gobodo-Madikezela served on the Human Rights Violations Committee of the TRC. To those who accuse the TRC of "healing the wound of my people lightly" (Jer.6:14) one has to say, with her, that remembering the awful wounds of genocide is a better beginning to reconciliation than is forgetting them. Members of the TRC know that reconciliation is a long-term, multigenerational project for South Africans. They know, too, that only growing economic justice will allow the ordinary South African to experience some tangible rectification of the economic exploitation that marked the colonial and apartheid eras.

De Gruchy takes a long look at the original uses of the Greek term for reconciliation, *katallage.* by Paul and subsequent theologians. His definition of the word is straightforward "a process in which there is a mutual attempt to heal and overcome enmities, build trust and relationships, and develop a shared commitment to the common good." De Gruchy believes, with Bonhoeffer and liberation theologians, that reconciliation is first "an action, praxis and movement before it becomes a theory or dogma, something celebrated before it is explained." It is first a gift of God and then a social task. God's gift of reconciliation in the life, death and resurrection of Jesus gives us the courage to struggle for human forgiveness and repentance in our relations with our neighbors.

Among modern neighbors the lack of reconciliation especially threatens Christians and Muslims. De Gruchy's chapter on "Reconciliation and the House of Abraham" alone is worth the price of the book. Though the three great Abrahamic religions have much in common, they also have non-negotiable differences. Christians believe that Jesus is the Word of God; Muslims say that only the Koran is. Notes De Gruchy, "For Muslims it is inconceivable that God, in any sense, could suffer on behalf of sinful humanity."

The test of social Justice is whether, despite profound differences, life-together triumphs over death-together. A Muslim in one of de Gruchy's UCT classes expressed surprise that Christians no longer celebrate the Crusades. It is time for all three of the Abrahamic religions to reject the idea of killing in the name of God.

De Gruchy's eloquent book is deeply grounded in both theology and South Africa's recent history. The power of the book lies in its sustained, intimate linking of concept and context just as Bonhoeffer once remarked that no one had the right to sing Gregorian chants without praying for Justice for the Jews. In Nazi Germany, de Gruchy insists that fellow Christians reflect on the connection between Pauline theology and the work of the TRC, whereby victims, perpetrators and bystanders in the apartheid era learned to listen to each other in many painful public hearings. Real empathetic hearing of a neighbor's story of officially imposed suffering is an indispensable step towards reconciliation.

A touching incident in de Gruchy's academic work underscores the role of empathy in healing. A doctoral student, Ginn Fourie, discussed with her committee her proposal for writing a dissertation on the 1993 Heidelberg Tavern Massacre. In that event, four young members of a militant wing of the Pan African Congress sprayed bullets around the tavern, killing and wounding many.

In a TRC hearing the four applied for amnesty on the grounds that their deed was politically motivated. Fourie wanted to research the motivations of the four. Why had she chosen this subject? She answered, "My daughter Lyndi was killed in the massacre, and I want to find out whether or not we can become reconciled to each other."

"There was a deathly silence in the seminar room by the time Ginn Fourie had completed her story." De Gruchy writes. "When at last the silence was broken a conversation began that took our hitherto academic inquiry to a deeper level than we had ever previously been. Our discussion about reconciliation was no longer theoretical, but neither was it purely emotional or 'romantic theologizing.'" Professors and student were forced to think about reconciliation "as a costly process and a painful journey"

A Human Being Died That Night is a moving documentation of that journey. Like Robert Lifton, who interviewed the Auschwitz medical doctors, Gobodo-Madlikizela approached de Kook with fear and trembling. She wondered whether it really was possible to empathize with someone who had killed and tortured hundreds of apartheid enemies. If she was able to touch the human being slumbering under the surface of "Prime Evil," could she resist being drawn into sympathy with him and then into excusing his behaviour?

Gobodo-Madikizela says that some of her friends and colleagues did not think that she should spend any time at all with de Kook. But the TRC had taught her that South Africa is a community "still learning to talk to itself, a community in which mistrust has become second nature." How could such a country approach genuine reconciliation if the alienated refused to talk to each other?

As her conversations with de Kock I proceeded she could see that he "was a desperate soul seeking to affirm to himself that he was still part of the human universe." On one occasion she Instinctively touched his hand. "you know, Pumla," De Kock remarked, "that was my trigger hand you touched." When she awoke the next morning, Gobodo-Madikizela found that her hand was paralyzed. "In touching de Kock's hand I had touched his leprosy and he seemed to be telling me that, even though I did not realise it at the time, I was from now on infected with the memory of having embraced in my heart the hand that had killed, maimed, and blown up lives." The experience taught her something about vulnerability and resistance to evil. Through repetition the psyche can get used to the doing of evil, but at the beginning, one's very body does not want to cooperate. I am struck by two particular contributions Gobodo-Madikizela makes to the ethics of political reconciliation: One is her conclusion from the TRC hearings that forgiveness and repentance must not be separated In theory or in practice. "Forgiveness usually begins with the person who needs to be forgiven. This means that there must be something In the perpetrator's behaviour, some 'sign,' that invites the victim's forgiveness. The most crucial sign is an expression of remorse," she writes.

De Kock's life sentence (220 years) gives him plenty of time to express remorse. But his sorrow for his life as an agent of his apartheid masters is laced with resentment at officials who denied that they authorized his atrocities. Their instructions to him often came in the smooth wrapping of words like "neutralize," "remove" and "eliminate." "How we did it was not important. The results were. They [officials] wanted to see results. They wanted to know that we were rooting out what at the time we called terrorism." He sees himself as the scapegoat of high-level politicians who never asked for amnesty from the TRC. Like a certain American Vietnam veteran, he was bitter that "my country sent me to do evil and then blamed me for it." Like de Gruchy, Gobodo-Madikizela knows that reconciliation, in both its theological and its messy political form, is a hard, complex, long-range process. De Gruchy would surely admire her conclusion:

The real subject of my visits to the C section of Pretoria Central Prison [was] to understand the inner mind of evil, to follow its thought processes, and to expose myself to its human face, stripped of media stereotypes and the easy distance of hatred. Connecting on a human level with a monster therefore comes to be a profoundly frightening prospect, for ultimately, it forces us to confront the potential for evil within ourselves.

FINANCIAL ACCOUNTING

WHAT IS FINANCIAL ACCOUNTING

Financial accounting is focused on providing accounting reports and analysis to other areas of the business. Financial accountants are responsible for the creation and issuing of the company's financial statements, providing accurate and timely information to management and ensuring that all regulatory reporting requirements are met. In financial accounting, the goal is to consistently provide the valuable, accurate and reliable information.

The issuing of the financial statements is the responsibility of the financial accounting department. These statements summarize the business's activities for the year and are used by shareholders, banks, employee bargaining units, and the general public to evaluate the financial worth of the company. The statements are audited by independent accountants to validate the information and provide assurance to readers.

The financial statements are comprised of five documents; balance sheet, income statement; cash flow and owners or shareholders equity and notes. Notes to the financial statement are written explanations of items in the financial statements. Any unusual items or change in procedure that has impact on the financial statements are detailed here. The balance sheet is a summary of all the assets and liabilities at year's end. The accounts reflect the total amount of cash and liquid assets on hand, the amount of debt the company is carrying, and how much money was spend in various categories. Financial accounting firms perform analysis of these values using ratios and other calculations to determine the financial health of the company.

An income statement is a critical component in financial accounting. It provides a clear list of all the sales for the year, the expenses and the net profit or loss of the firm. This statement provides insight into the sales performance for the year and the overall profitability of the firm.

A cash flow report provides details on funds received and disbursed. This section provides insight into the revenue values listed in the income statement. Funds received or lost from interest bearing investments are detailed here.

The statement of owners' or shareholders' equity shows the total net income from the year and how it will be distributed among the shareholders or reinvested in the business. Publicly traded companies must provide the number of shares issues, the type of share and the amount of divided to be paid on the shares, based on the articles of incorporation and the shareholder agreement.All certified public accountants have complete intermediate and advanced courses in financial accounting. There is no additional designation for a financial accounting specialty. The skill set for a financial accountant must focus on analysis and data manipulation software and tools.

DESCRIPTION OF THE EXAMINATION

The Financial Accounting examination covers skills and concepts that are generally taught in a first-semester undergraduate financial accounting course. Colleges may award credit for a one-semester course in financial accounting.

The exam contains approximately 75 questions to be answered in 90 minutes. Some of these are pretest questions that will not be scored. Any time candidates spend on tutorials or providing personal information is in addition to the actual testing time.

KNOWLEDGE AND SKILLS REQUIRED

Questions on the Financial Accounting examination require candidates to demonstrate one or more of the following abilities.

- Familiarity with accounting concepts and terminology

- Preparation, use, and analysis of accounting data and financial reports issued for both internal and external purposes
- Application of accounting techniques to simple problem situations involving computations
- Understanding the rationale for generally accepted accounting principles and procedures

2

Marginal and Absorption Costing

CHARACTERISTICS

Marginal costing is also termed as variable costing, a technique of costing which includes only variable manufacturing costs, in the form of direct materials, direct labour, and variable manufacturing overheads while determining the cost per unit of a product. Where as Absorption costing, is a costing technique that includes all manufacturing costs, in the form of direct materials, direct labour, and both variable and fixed manufacturing overheads, while determining the cost per unit of a product. It is also referred to as the full- cost technique. In the costing of product/service, a marginal costing technique considers the behavioural characteristics of costs (segregations of costs into fixed and variable elements), because per unit variable cost is fixed and total costs are variable in nature, where as total fixed costs are fixed and per unit fixed cost is variable in nature and furthermore variable costs are controllable in nature, while total fixed costs are un-controllable in nature.

Marginal costing is useful for short-term planning, control and decision-making, particularly in a business where multi-products are produced. In marginal costing technique, the contribution is calculated after deducting variable costs from sales value with reference to each product or service, in order to calculate the total contribution from all products/services which are made towards the total fixed costs incurred by the business. As the fixed costs are treated as period costs, are deducted from total contribution to arrive at net profit. In the context of costing of a product/service, an absorption costing considers a share of all costs incurred by a business to each of its products/ services. In absorption costing technique; costs are classified according to their functions. The gross profit is calculated after deducting production costs from sales and from gross profit, costs incurred in relation to other business functions are deducted to arrive at the net profit.

Absorption costing gives better information for pricing products as it includes both variable and fixed costs. Marginal costing may lead to lower prices being offered if the firm is operating below capacity. Customers may still expect these lower prices as demand/capacity increases.

Profit Statements

The net profit shown by marginal costing and absorption costing techniques may not be the same due to the different treatment of fixed manufacturing overheads. Marginal costing technique treats fixed manufacturing overheads as period costs, where as in absorption costing technique these are absorbed into the cost of goods produced and are only charged against profit in the period in which those goods are sold. In absorption costing income statement, adjustment pertaining to under or over-absorption of overheads is also made to arrive at the profit.

TERMS

Product and Period Costs

- *Product costs*: The costs of manufacturing the products;
- *Period costs*: These are the costs other than product costs that are charged to, debited to, or written off to the income statement each period.

A Case Example on Marginal and Absorption Costing:

Table. Data for a Quarter for a Manufacturing Company

Level of Activity	60%	100%
Sales and Production(Units)	36,000	60,000
	₹ ('000)	₹ ('000)
Sales	432	720
Production costs:		
(Variable and fixed)	366	510
Sales, distribution and administration costs (Variable and fixed)	126	150

The normal level of activity for the current year is 60,000 units, and fixed costs are incurred evenly throughout the year.

	Production Costs (Rs.)	**Sales etc costs (Rs.)**
Total costs of 60,000 units (fixed plus variable)	5,10,000	1,50,000
Total costs of 36,000 units (fixed plus variable)	3,66,000	1,26,000
Difference = variable costs of 24,000 units	1,44,000	24,000
Variable costs per unit	Rs.6	Re.1
	Production Costs (Rs.)	Sales etc. Costs (Rs.)
Total costs of 60,000 units	5,10,000	1,50,000
Variable costs of 60,000 units	3,60,000	60,000
Fixed costs	1,50,000	90,000

There were no stocks of the product at the start of the quarter, in which 16,500 units were made and 13,500 units were sold. Actual fixed costs were the same as budgeted. Then, various calculations regarding Absorption vs. Marginal costing can be worked out as under:

The rate of absorption of fixed production overheads will therefore be:

₹.1,50,000 ÷ 60,000 = ₹ 2.50 per unit.

- The fixed production overhead absorbed by the products would be 16,500 units produced × ₹ 2.50 = ₹ 41,250
- Budgeted annual fixed production overhead = ₹.1,50,000

	Rs.
Actual quarterly fixed production overhead = budgeted quarterly fixed production overhead (1,50,000 ÷ 4)	37,500
Production overhead absorbed into production [see (i) above]	41,250
Over -absorption of fixed production overhead	3,750

- Profit statement for the quarter, using Absorption Costing

	Rs.	Rs.	Rs.
Sales (13,500× Rs.12)			1,62,000
Costs of production (no opening stocks)			
Value of stocks produced (16,500 × Rs. 8.50)		1,40,250	
Less value of closing stock			
(3,000 units × full production cost of Rs. 8.50)		(25,500)	
		1,14,750	
Sales etc costs			
Variable (13,500 × Re. 1)	13,500		
Fixed (1/4 of Rs. 90,000)	22,500		
		36,000	
Total cost of sales		1,50,750	
Less over-absorbed production overhead		3,750	
			1,47,000
Profit			15,000

– Profit statement for the quarter using Marginal Costing

	Rs.	Rs.
Sales (13,500×Rs.12)		1,62,000
Variable costs of production (16,500 × Rs. 6)	99,000	
Less value of closing stocks (3,000 × Rs. 6)	18,000	
Variable production cost of sales	81,000	
Variable sales etc. costs (13,500 × Re.1)	13,500	
Total variable cost of sales (13,500 × Rs. 7)		94,500
Contribution (13,500 × Rs. 5)		67,500
Fixed Costs: Production	37,500	
Sales etc.	22,500	
		60,000
Profit		7,500

ABSORPTION AND MARGINAL COSTING SYSTEMS

A popular topic for examination at Foundation Level has been the preparation of profit statements in both absorption and marginal costing formats, and the reconciliation of the profits reported by the two systems.

Example: A company sells a single product at a price of £14 per unit. Variable manufacturing costs of the product are £6.40 per unit. Fixed manufacturing overheads, which are absorbed into the cost of production at a unit rate (based on normal activity of 20,000 units per period), are £92,000 per period. Any over-absorbed or under-absorbed fixed manufacturing overhead balances are transferred to the profit and loss account at the end of each period, in order to establish the manufacturing profit.

Sales and production (in units) for two periods are as follows:

	Period 1	**Period 2**
Sales	15,000	21,600
Production	18,000	21,000

Required:

- Prepare a trading statement to identify the manufacturing profit for Period 2 using the existing absorption costing method.
- Determine the manufacturing profit that would be reported in Period 2 if marginal costing was used.
- Explain, with supporting calculations, why the manufacturing profit in.

ABSORPTION COSTING PRINCIPLES

In product/service costing, an absorption costing system allocates or apportions a share of all costs incurred by a business to each of its products/ services. In this way, it can be established whether, in the long run, each product/service makes a profit. This can only be a guide. Arbitrary assumptions have to be made about the apportionment of many of the costs which, given that some costs will tend to remain fixed during a period, will also be dependent on the level of activity.

An absorption costing system traditionally classifies costs by function. Sales less production costs (of sales) measures the gross profit (manufacturing profit) earned. Gross profit less costs incurred in other business functions establishes the net profit (operating profit) earned.

Using an absorption costing system, the profit reported for a manufacturing business for a period will be influenced by the level of production as well as by the level of sales. This is because of the absorption of fixed manufacturing overheads into the value of work-in-progress and finished goods stocks. If stocks remain at the end of an accounting period, then the fixed manufacturing overhead costs included within the stock valuation will be transferred to the following period.

ABSORPTION COSTING PROFIT STATEMENT

The first stage in the preparation of absorption costing profit statements is the measurement of the gross profit (manufacturing profit) earned. This requires the calculation of unit production costs, including the establishment of absorption rates for manufacturing overheads. Referring to the example being used for illustration in this article, variable manufacturing costs per units are given in the question (at £6.40 per unit).

Fixed manufacturing overheads of £92,000 per period are to be absorbed at a unit rate (based on normal production activity of 20,000 units per period). The fixed manufacturing overhead absorption rate is therefore £4.60 per unit (£92,000 ¸ 20,000 units) giving a total manufacturing cost of £11.00 per unit (£6.40 + £4.60).

The use of normal activity as the basis for overhead absorption is similar to the use of budgeted activity. It is to be expected that actual activity (and indeed actual expenditure also) will be different to normal/budget thus giving rise to overhead over or under absorption. It is important that this is highlighted in profit statements. The use of normal (or budgeted) activity and expenditure to establish the absorption rate not only helps to focus attention on overhead recovery but also has the effect of 'normalising' per unit product/ service costs.

Referring again to the example, fixed manufacturing overheads will be over-absorbed in Period 2 because the actual production of 21,000 units exceeds the normal activity, the basis used to establish the absorption rate, by 1,000 units. The extent of the over-absorption (the balance remaining in the fixed manufacturing overhead account) is, therefore, £4,600 (1,000 units at £4.60 per unit). This amount will be transferred to the profit and loss account in order to establish the manufacturing profit. It will have a positive effect (i.e., it will be added to profit) because more manufacturing overhead has been absorbed into stock in the period than has been incurred.

The Examiner's Report for the June 2000 Paper 3 noted that the over-absorption of fixed manufacturing overhead caused problems for many candidates. It was frequently not identified. Where it was calculated, it was at times described as 'under-absorbed' or was at least treated as such in terms of its impact on the manufacturing profit. Other candidates wrongly calculated the over/under- absorption based upon the difference between sales and production quantities, rather than upon the difference between actual production and normal production.

Preparation of the remainder of the trading statement (to identify the manufacturing profit for Period 2 using absorption costing) should be straightforward. The manufacturing cost of sales (the transfer out of the finished goods stock account) is simply the 21,600 units sold in the period (which at a selling price of £14.00 per unit yields total sales for the period of £302,400) multiplied by the unit manufacturing cost of £11.00.

Example:

Period 2 Trading Statement:	£000	
Sales	302.4	(21,600 units at £14.00 per unit)
Manufacturing cost of goods sold	237.6	(21,600 units at £11.00 per unit)
Manufacturing profit (before adjustment)	64.8	(21,600 units at £3.00 per unit)
Fixed manufacturing overhead over-absorbed	4.6	(1,000 units at £4.60 per unit)
Manufacturing profit (after adjustment)	69.4	

The Examiner's Report noted that there were many examples (in the examination scripts marked) of candidates matching the cost of the goods produced in the period (not the manufacturing cost of the goods sold) with sales. Many examination candidates also got into difficulty because they attempted to introduce stock into the profit statement.

There is generally no requirement to do this (unless opening and closing stocks are valued at a different rate per unit) but such an approach should (but often did not) lead to the same profit result.

In this example, no details of stock are provided in the question, but it could be assumed, for example, that 3,000 units were in stock at the end of Period I (production of 18,000 units less sales of 15,000 units). Finished goods stock at the end of Period 2 would then be 2,400 units due to the excess of sales over production of 600 units in that period.

Example:

A trading statement including stock would be.		
Period 2 Trading Statement	£000	
Sales	302.4	
Manufacturing cost of goods sold:		
Opening stock of finished goods	33.0	(3,000 units at £11.00 per unit)
Cost of goods produced	231.0	(21,000 units at £11.00 per unit)
Closing stock of finished goods	(26.4)	(2,400 units at £11.00 per unit)
	237.6	
Manufacturing profit (before adjustment)	64.8	
Fixed manufacturing overhead over-absorbed	4.6	

In the adapted question used for illustration is no information provided about costs incurred in other business functions (selling, administration, distribution) and thus it is not possible to complete the profit statement. If information on other costs was available, the costs incurred in the period would simply be deducted from the adjusted manufacturing profit to arrive at net profit.

MARGINAL COSTING PRINCIPLES

In product/service costing, a marginal costing system emphasises the behavioural, rather than the functional, characteristics of costs. The focus is on separating costs into variable elements (where the cost per unit remains the same with total cost varying in proportion to activity) and fixed elements (where the total cost remains the same in each period regardless of the level of activity). Whilst this is not easily achieved with accuracy, and is an oversimplification of reality, marginal costing information can be very useful for short-term planning, control and decision-making, especially in a multi-product business. In a marginal costing system, sales less variable costs (regardless of function) measures the contribution that individual products/ services make towards the total fixed costs incurred by the business.

The fixed costs (regardless of function) are treated as period costs and, as such, are simply deducted from contribution in the period incurred to arrive at net profit.

MARGINAL COSTING PROFIT STATEMENT

Referring back to Example 1, as there is no information regarding non-manufacturing costs, it may be assumed that sales less variable manufacturing costs measures contribution. NB.

If any variable costs are incurred in non-manufacturing functions then they would also be deducted from sales in the measurement of contribution. The trading statement for Period 2, assuming that a marginal costing system was in place instead.

Example:

Period 2 Trading Statement:	£000	
Sales	302.40	
Variable cost of goods sold	138.24	(21,600 units at £6.40 per unit)
Contribution	164.16	(21,600 units at £7.60 per unit)
Fixed manufacturing overhead	92.00	
Manufacturing profit	72.16	

Costing approach is more straightforward. The Examiner's Report noted that candidates generally had rather more success with the marginal costing statement in part (b) than with the absorption costing statement in part (a), although some confusion between the two was demonstrated.

In practice, the marginal costing profit statement would be completed by the further deduction of fixed costs incurred in other functions.

PROFIT RECONCILIATION

The net profit reported by absorption and marginal costing systems may not be the same owing to the differing treatment of fixed manufacturing overheads. As has been demonstrated above, whilst marginal costing systems treat fixed manufacturing overheads as period costs (i.e. a charge against profit in the period incurred), in absorption costing systems they are absorbed into the cost of goods produced and are only charged against profit in the period in which those goods are sold.

As a result, if quantities produced and sold in a period are not the same (i.e., if the levels of work-in-progress or finished goods stock change) a different profit will be reported by the two systems.

The differing profits can be reconciled, and the difference explained, by an analysis of the product of the stock change and the fixed manufacturing overhead absorption rate. Thus, in answer to part (c) of Example 1:

Period 2 finished goods stock reduction 600 unitsx fixed manufacturing overhead absorption rate, £4.60 per unit =£2,760 difference in profit i.e., the difference between the absorption costing manufacturing profit of £69,400 and the marginal costing manufacturing profit of £72,160.

Absorption costing has a lower profit because more goods are being taken out of stock (including a charge for fixed manufacturing overhead) than are going into stock. This is demonstrated by the entries in the respective cost accounting systems.

Example: In the absorption costing system.

Table. Fixed Manufacturing Overhead Account

Incurred	£92,000	Absorbed into finished goods	£96,600 —
Over-absorbed – to P&L A/c (1,000 units at £4.60/unit)	£4,600	(21,000 units at £4.60/unit) £96,600	£96,600

Table. Finished Goods Stock Account

Fixed mfg o'hd absorbed	£96,600	Cost of sales £99,360 (fixed mfg o'hd only) (21,600 units at£4.60/unit)

Table. The Total Fixed Manufacturing Overhead Charged against Profit in the Period =

Overhead in cost of sales	£99,360
Less over-absorption	£4,600
£94,760	

Table. In the marginal costing system.

	Fixed Manufacturing	Overhead Account
Incurred	£92,000	P&L A/c-period cost £92,000

Absorption costing £94,760 less marginal costing £92,000 =£2,760 more fixed manufacturing overheads and less profit in absorption costing.

The difference in profit between absorption and marginal costing systems is nothing to do with overhead over/under absorption, a popular misconception amongst examination candidates.

Despite an over-absorption of £4,600, which is a positive adjustment to the absorption costing profit, the profit was nevertheless less than the marginal costing profit.

To emphasise again: The difference in reported profit demonstrated above, which can only be a timing difference, is due to changes in the level of finished goods stock which in an absorption costing system moves overhead, and therefore profit, from one period to another.

As a general rule: If production quantity > sales quantity then absorption costing profit > marginal costing profit. If production quantity < sales quantity then absorption costing profit <marginal costing profit.

Many candidates, when answering examination questions on this topic, do appreciate that the different treatment of fixed manufacturing overhead is the reason for profit differences but they are rarely able to reconcile the profits.

COST VOLUME PROFIT ANALYSIS

LEARNING OBJECTIVES

After you have read and studied this chapter, you should be able to:

- Discuss the assumptions underlying the conventional linear cost-volume-profit (CVP) model.
- Explain the implications of relaxing each of these assumptions in terms of the theoretical cost- volume-profit model.
- Explain the meaning of a series of graphic illustrations for both the linear and nonlinear CVP models including production functions, revenue functions and cost functions.
- Discuss the difference between performing a "what-if" analysis and converting from the linear model to the theoretical nonlinear model.
- Solve a variety of linear CVP problems for single product companies in either units or sales dollars.
- Define and use the margin of safety.
- Solve a variety of linear CVP problems for multiproduct companies in either units or sales dollars.
- Solve similar problems on a cash flow basis.
- Discuss the controversy concerning the compatibility of the contribution margin approach with activity based costing and the lean enterprise concepts of just in time and the theory of constraints.

ANALYSIS OF CVP

Conceptually, conventional linear cost-volume-profit (CVP) analysis is a simplified, short term planning technique that evolved as a practical version of the theoretical model of the firm described in economics textbooks. From an accounting perspective it is compatible with the direct, or variable costing method of inventory valuation. To use the CVP model, a company must separate total costs into fixed and variable categories using one of the methods. Recall from our earlier discussions of these terms that variable costs are those costs that vary with changes in the level of activity. The only activities that are allowed to affect variable costs in traditional cost-volume-profit analysis are production output and sales. Remember that fixed costs are those costs that do not vary with changes in the activity level. Conceptually, fixed costs are not constant. By definition, fixed simply means that these costs are not driven by short run changes in production or sales volume. Although explicit recognition of non production volume related cost drivers is a key concept in activity based costing, the idea is ignored in the conventional linear CVP model. Finally, it is important to recognize that the concept of fixed and variable costs is a short run concept.

All costs tend to vary in the long run as the company adds to its' capacity to produce and distribute products and services. Therefore, the short run emphasis of CVP analysis tends to conflict with the long run emphasis of activity based costing and the lean enterprise concepts of JIT and TOC. This creates another thought provoking controversial issue.

The purpose of this chapter is to describe the assumptions and techniques of the conventional linear cost-volume-profit approach as well as the controversy concerning the compatibility of CVP analysis with ABC and the continuous improvement concepts. The chapter is divided into five main sections. The first section addresses the underlying assumptions of the conventional linear model and the implications of relaxing these assumptions. This section is mainly conceptual and is illustrated with a series of graphs.

The second section illustrates the basic planning techniques for a single product company that provide the foundation for more realistic problems. The third section extends the basic analysis to multiproduct companies. Both sections two and three are more mechanical than conceptual and are mainly illustrated with a series of related equations. The fourth section is fairly short, but illustrates how to convert the analysis to a cash flow basis. The last section introduces the controversy associated with the CVP approach as it relates to the newer concepts of ABC, JIT and TOC. Since the CVP methodology is closely related to direct or variable costing, this chapter helps provide a better foundation for the more detailed comparison of direct and absorption costing presented in.

ASSUMPTIONS OF CONVENTIONAL LINEAR CVP ANALYSIS

Conventional linear cost volume profit analysis is based on five assumptions as follows:

- Constant sales price.

- Constant variable cost per unit.
- Constant total fixed cost.
- Constant sales mix.
- Units sold equal units produced.

Note that these are the same assumptions that are applicable to the master budget, with the exception of number five. Now we will examine the implications of each assumption.

Constant Sales Price

To assume that the sales price is constant implies that the company is facing a horizontal demand function as illustrated in Figure below. The implications of a horizontal demand function are that the company can sell any number of units at a constant sales price. Another way to describe this is to say that consumers are willing and able to buy any quantity the company offers for sale at a constant price. Average revenue (AR) is constant and equal to the sales price, (i.e., AR = PX÷X = P) as illustrated in Figure.

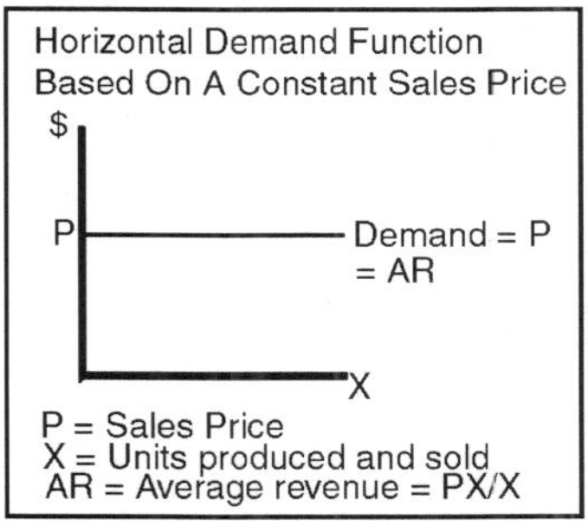

The slope of the total revenue function is equal to the sales price. When the company sells one additional unit, total revenue increases by an amount equal to the sales price of that unit. The fact that the sales price is constant causes the slope of the total revenue function to be constant which results in a linear total revenue function. Another way to describe this is to say that total revenue increases at a constant rate as additional units are sold.

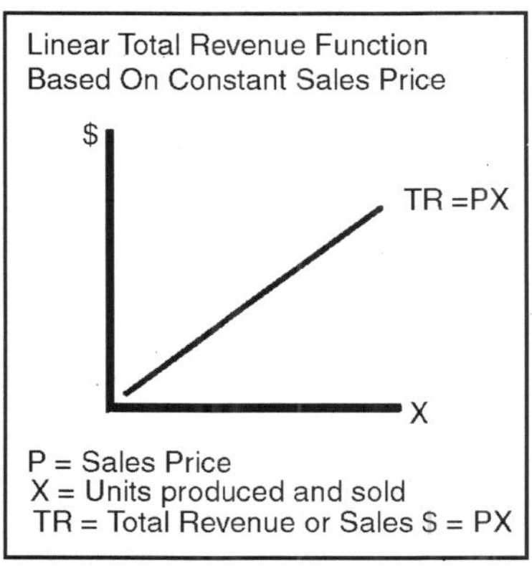

A more realistic down sloping demand function illustrates what economists refer to as the law of demand. This law describes the fundamental idea that consumers are willing and able to buy more at a lower price than a higher price.

When the price is decreased from P1 to P2, the quantity purchased, or demanded, increases from X1 to X2. The total revenue function based on the law of demand is nonlinear as illustrated in Figure. Total revenue increases at a decreasing rate as additional units are sold. This is because the sale of additional units requires that the company reduce the sales price. Each price corresponds to a specific sales quantity. Thus, average revenue (AR) will be decreasing, rather than constant.

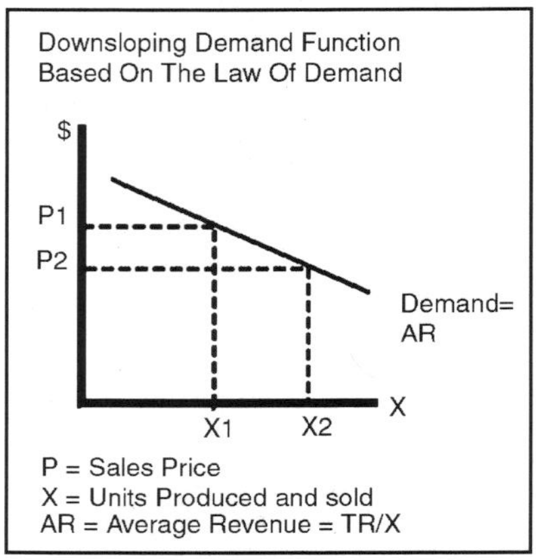

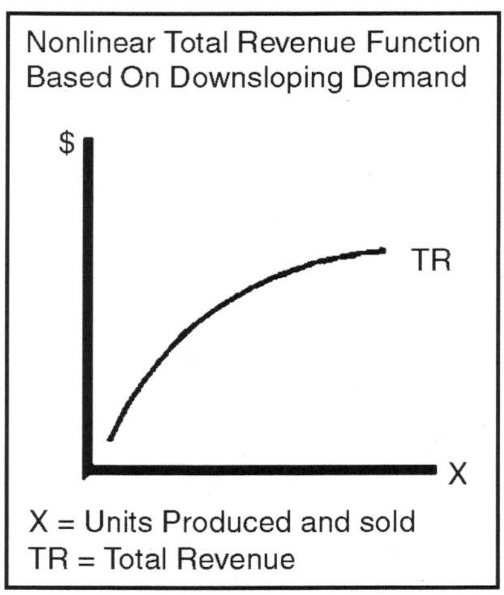

Although the assumption of a constant sales price is not realistic, it is defended as a practical way to expedite the planning process within a fairly narrow range of sales activity. The idea that most products are subject to a down sloping demand curve is intuitively obvious, but applying the concept is simply not practical. Most companies sell too many products in a constantly changing economic environment. Today's demand curve is very likely to be obsolete tomorrow.

Constant Variable cost per unit

The second assumption of the conventional linear cost-volume-profit approach is that the variable cost per unit of output is constant. This includes two important underlying assumptions: a) input prices are assumed to be constant for all variable inputs such as direct material, direct labour, and the various types of indirect resources represented by variable factory overhead costs and variable selling and administrative expenses, and b) the firm experiences constant productivity, i.e., constant output per variable input.

Constant productivity is illustrated in Figure. When productivity is constant, each new unit of output requires an equal amount of input and thus each unit of output will cost the same amount. This causes both the production function to be linear and the average variable cost function to be horizontal. Output (X) is placed on the vertical axis because output is the dependent variable, i.e., inputs drive outputs. Output is on the horizontal axis in the other graphs because cost is the dependent variable, i.e., output drives cost.

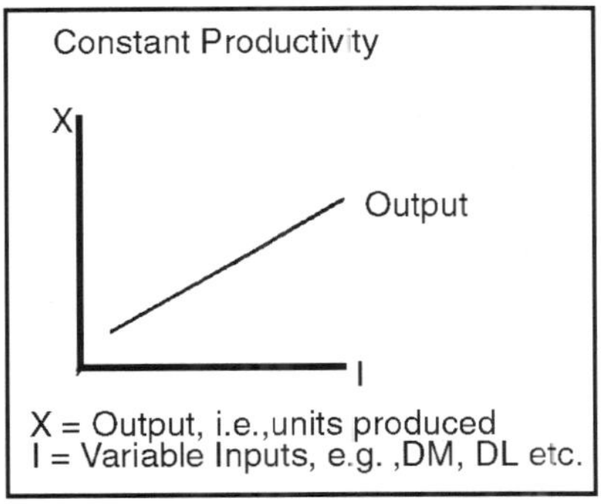

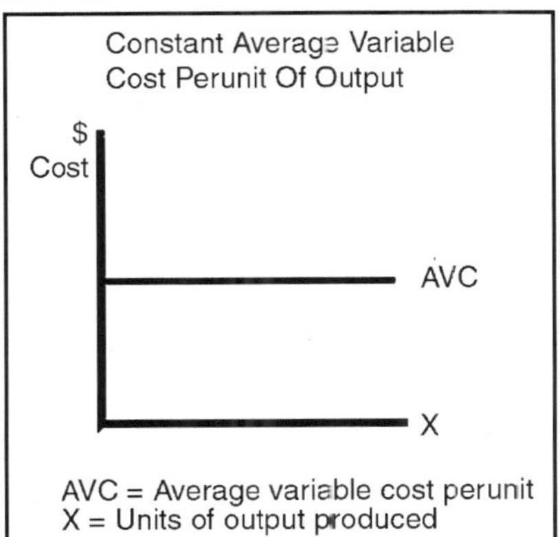

Although it is convenient to assume constant productivity for short run planning purposes, other types of production functions are more realistic when the whole range of production possibilities is considered. When a company begins to expand output from a low volume startup level to a medium volume level, productivity might be expected to increase due to the effects of increased specialization, experience and learning.

When productivity is increasing, output increases at an increasing rate. As variable inputs are added to production, each input generates more output than the previous input. When productivity is increasing, average variable cost per unit will be decreasing.

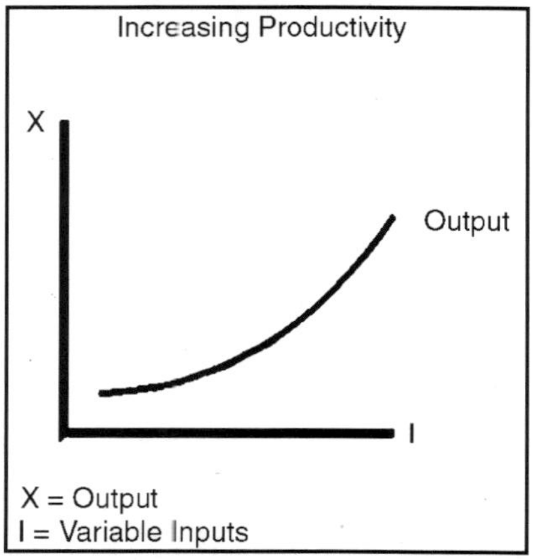

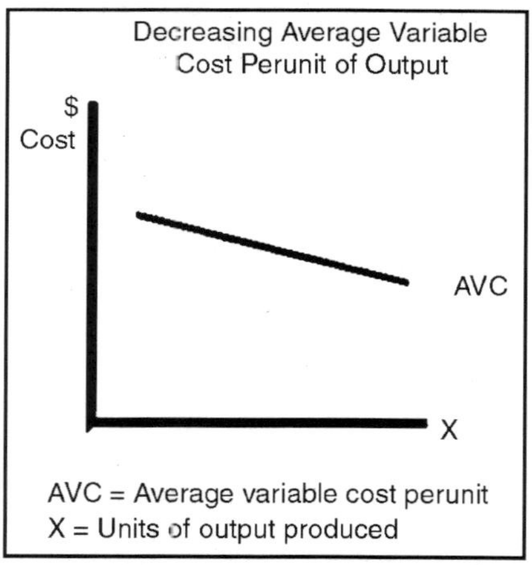

If the company increased production from a medium volume level to a high volume level by continuing to add variable inputs to a fixed size facility, productivity would be expected to decrease as indicated in Figures. This is because at high volume production levels, the inputs (labour, materials etc.) would become excessive relative to the size of the fixed facility. In the case of decreasing productivity, average variable cost per unit will be increasing as illustrated in Figures. Each unit will cost more because it requires more inputs to produce.

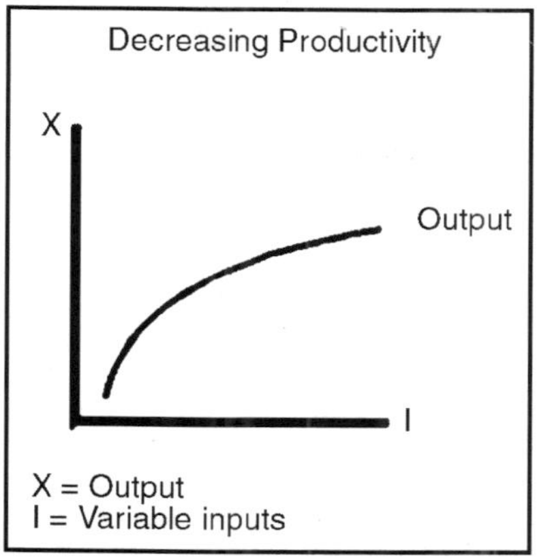

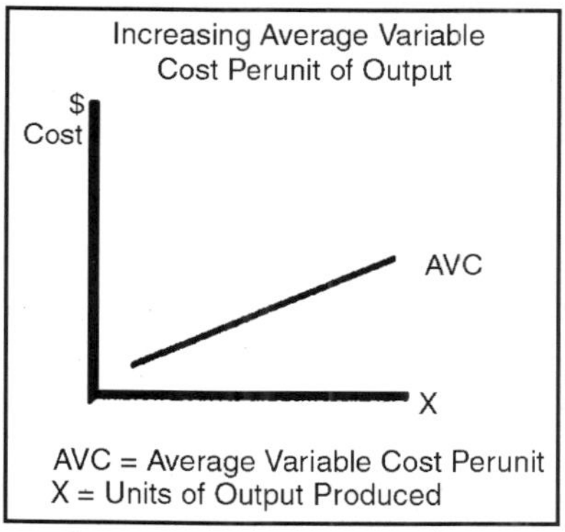

Theoretically, the production and average variable cost functions for the entire range of short run production possibilities will be similar to those illustrated in Figures.

The point where the production function changes directions from increasing to decreasing productivity and the average variable cost function changes from decreasing to increasing cost per unit is referred to as the point of diminishing returns. Output continues to increase beyond this point, but at a decreasing rate.

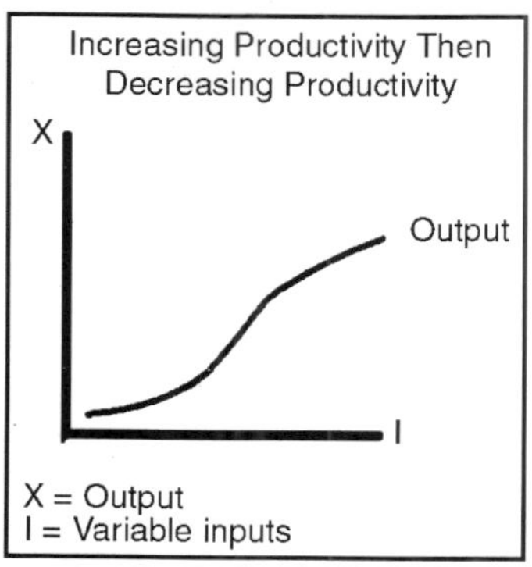

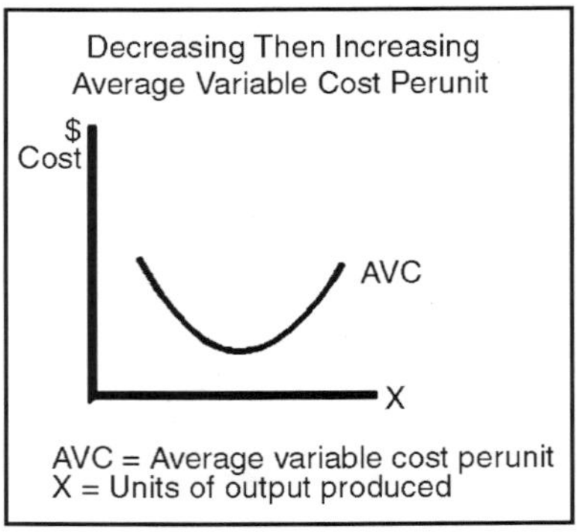

Constant Fixed Costs

A family of total cost functions for the conventional linear model is presented in Figures. The total variable cost and total cost functions are linear, i.e., they increase at a constant rate, because productivity is assumed to be constant. The total fixed cost function is represented by a horizontal line because of assumption three which eliminates the possibility of a non-output related change in fixed costs during the planning period. No changes in the company's fixed factors of production can occur. The total cost and total variable cost functions are vertically parallel and separated by the amount of total fixed costs.

A comparable family of total cost functions for the theoretical economic model appears in Figures below. The total variable cost and total cost functions increase at a decreasing rate at first in response to increasing productivity. When the inputs are becoming more productive, additional outputs cost less per unit because they require less input.

However, when productivity begins to decrease, the total cost and total variable cost functions begin to increase at an increasing rate. In the case of decreasing productivity, the inputs are generating less output per input, thus the unit cost of additional outputs is increasing. The total cost functions are also parallel and separated vertically by the amount of total fixed costs.

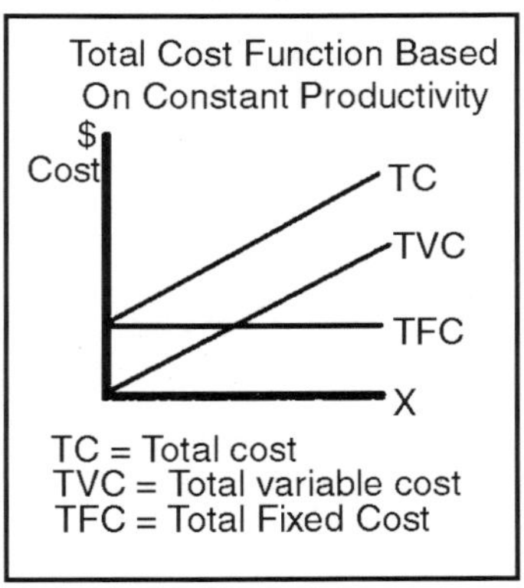

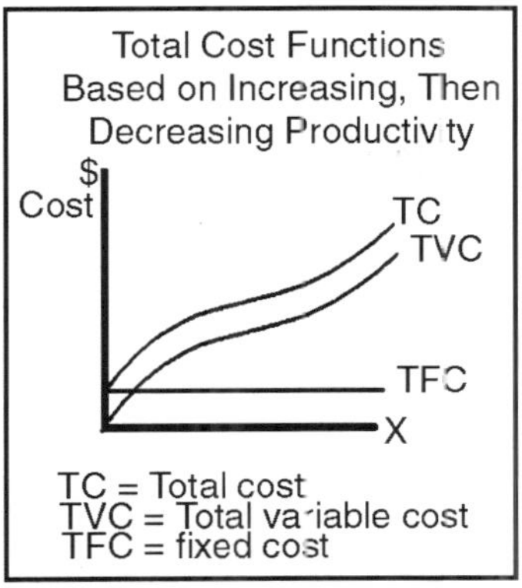

Constant Sales Mix and Inventory Level

The last two assumptions of the conventional linear cost-volume-profit model are more easily understood than the previous assumptions. The fourth assumption is that the sales mix will remain constant during the planning period for a multiproduct company. Sales mix proportions may be stated in terms of either units or dollars as explained in the illustrations below.

The fifth and last assumption is that units produced are equal to units sold. This means that there will be no changes in beginning or ending inventory levels to complicate the analysis.

This assumption along with the assumption concerning constant fixed cost will be relaxed in the following chapter where we will use the conventional linear CVP model to consider the differences between direct costing and full absorption costing.

CONVENTIONAL AND THEORETICAL MODELS

Graphic summaries of the two models are presented in Figures below. In the linear model there is one break-even point (BEP) where total revenue is equal to total cost. Since the total revenue and total cost functions are linear, the profit function is also linear. This is because the slope of the profit function is equal to contribution margin per unit which is automatically constant when the sales price and variable cost per unit are constant.

The theoretical model summarized in Figure above conveys a very different picture. There are two break-even points where total revenue and total cost are equal.

The theoretical profit function intersects the horizonal axis at the two break-even points and reaches a maximum level at the point where the vertical distance between TR and TC is the greatest. In the linear model illustrated in Figure, the area to the left of the break-even point represents a loss area and the area to the right of this point represents a profit area that continuously grows larger as additional units are produced and sold.

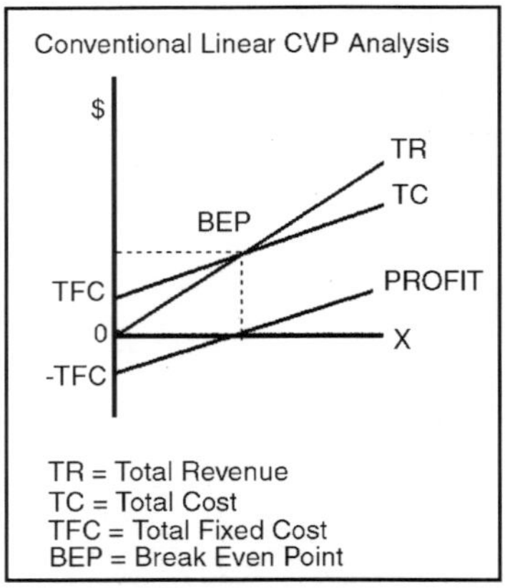

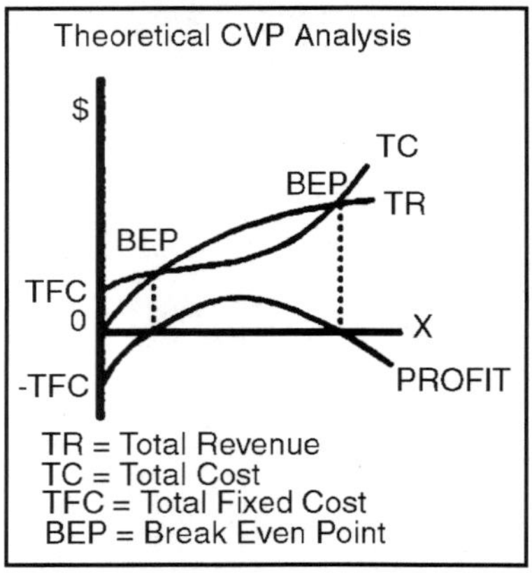

In the linear model the company maximizes profit where production and sales are at maximum capacity. However, in the theoretical model, there are two loss areas, one to the left of the first BEP and one to the right of the second BEP. The profit area is between the two break-even points, thus trying to achieve the maximum level of production and sales will produce losses rather than increased profits. For this reason, some critics of the conventional linear model argue that it represents a naive and dangerous view of a firm's economic environment.

On the other hand, advocates of the linear model contend that short term planning does not require a theoretical model of the entire range of production possibilities. Although the concepts underlying the theoretical model are important, the model does not provide a practical approach for short term planning. However, the linear model is a practical and adequate alternative for planning within the normal relevant range of production and sales alternatives.

Analysis Versus Changing the Model

For any given linear CVP analysis, we can ask a whole set of "what-if" questions about how increases and decreases in the sales price, unit variable costs, sales mix and fixed costs would affect the outcome. However, when we do that we are simply changing from one set of static assumptions to another set. This means that we are changing from one conventional linear problem to a somewhat different conventional linear problem. If the first two assumptions are relaxed to allow the sales price and unit variable costs to change continuously in response to the forces of supply and demand, we are not asking a "what if" question, we are changing the analysis from the practical linear approach to the theoretical nonlinear approach.

TECHNIQUES FOR SOLVING CVP PROBLEMS

The following symbols are used below to illustrate the various techniques used in cost-volume-profit analysis.

P = Sales price.

V = Variable costs per unit.

Note: This is not inventory cost because it includes both variable manufacturing costs as well as variable selling and administrative expenses.

X = The number of units produced and sold. A unit is a common way to describe an output, but an output may be expressed in pounds, gallons, board feet, cubic feet, etc.

TR = S = Total revenue, or sales dollars.

TVC = Total variable costs = VX

TFC = Total fixed costs.

TC = Total costs = TFC + TVC.

P-V = Contribution margin per unit. This is the amount of sales revenue that each unit provides towards covering the fixed costs and providing a profit, i.e., what's left over after the variable costs associated with the unit have been covered.

TCM = Total c ontribution margin = (P-V)(X).

CMR = (P-V)÷P = (TR-TVC)÷TR = (PX-VX)÷PX = 1-(V÷P). These are just different ways to define the contribution margin ratio. They all work because the functions are linear.

There are many algebraic equations illustrated on the next several pages that may appear to require memorization. However, every equation is simply a variation of the following basic concepts:

Total Revenue = Total Cost + Profit

TR = TC + NIBT

TR = TFC + TVC + NIBT

TR - TVC = TFC + NIBT

TCM = TFC + NIBT

Total revenue, or sales dollars, less total variable costs equals total contribution margin. Contribution margin is the revenue over and above the variable costs that contributes towards covering the fixed costs and also towards providing a profit after the fixed costs have been covered. Practically any cost-volume-profit problem can be solved with the last equation stated above and an understanding of the concepts involved.

SOLVING SINGLE PRODUCT CVP PROBLEMS IN UNITS

A summary of the cost volume profit equations for single product problems is presented below. All five equations are variations of the basic conceptual equation stated above. To reinforce the concept, each equation is developed and illustrated below.

Single product cvp problems in units number equation used to determine:

- (P-V)X = TFC Units needed to break-even.
- (P-V)X = TFC + NIBT Units needed to generate a target net income before taxes.
- (P-V)X = TFC + [NIAT ÷ (1-T)] Units needed to generate a target net income after taxes.
- (P-V)X = TFC + (R)(PX) Units needed to generate a target NIBT stated as a proportion (R) of sales dollars (PX).
- (P-V)X = TFC + [(R)(PX) ÷ (1-T)] Units needed to generate a target NIAT stated as a proportion (R) of sales dollars (PX).

UNITS NEEDED TO BREAK-EVEN

We can derive the break-even equation by starting with the fact that total revenue equals total cost at the break-even point. Then the equation is restated in terms of unit sales, unit prices and unit cost and then rearranged into the more convenient format presented in Equation.

TR = TC

TR = TFC + TVC

PX = TFC + VX

PX - VX = TFC

[1] (P-V)X = TFC or TCM = TFC

X = TFC ÷ (P-V)

Equation above shows that the break-even point is where total contribution margin (P-V)(X) is equal to total fixed costs, i.e., this level of production and sales provides just enough revenue to cover all the cost.

UNITS NEEDED FOR TARGET NET INCOME BEFORE TAXES

This equation can be derived from scratch in the same manner used to develop Equation 1. Notice however that Equation 2 may be obtained by simply adding the desired amount of net income to the right hand side of Equation.

TR = TFC + TVC + TARGET NIBT

PX = TFC + VX + NIBT

PX - VX = TFC + NIBT

[2] (P-V)X = TFC + NIBT

X = (TFC+NIBT) ÷ (P-V)

Equations simply indicates that total contribution margin is equal to the total fixed costs plus the desired net income before taxes. These relationships are illustrated graphically in Figure below which is similar to present.

Figure below shows that the break-even point is where the two lines representing total revenue and total cost intersect. To the left of this intersection, the vertical difference between the total revenue and total cost functions represents a net loss. To the right of the break-even point, the vertical difference between the two functions represents net income before taxes. The lower part of the graph shows that the break-even point can also be found by plotting the before tax profit function.

When the number of units produced and sold equals zero, the loss is equal to total fixed costs. When the firm produces a positive number of units, the loss is reduced by an amount equal to the contribution margin per unit multiplied by the number of units produced and sold. The slope of NIBT is contribution margin per unit. When enough units are produced and sold to cover the fixed costs, the company reaches the break-even point. This is the point on the graph where the profit function intersects the horizontal axis and it is directly below the point where the total revenue and total cost functions intersect.

Graphic and Equation Relationships

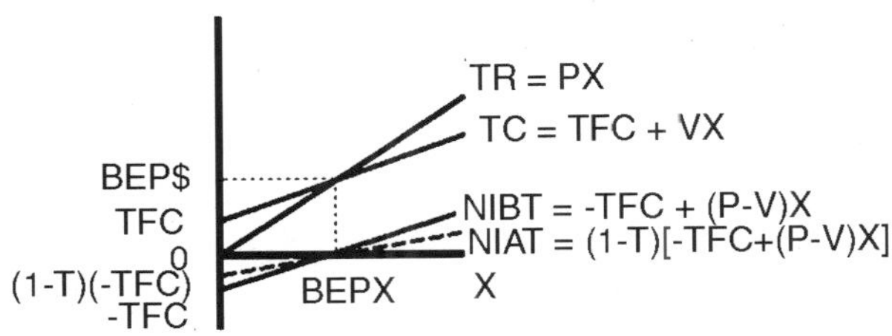

BEPS = Break even point in dollars.
BEPX = Break even point in units.

UNITS NEEDED FOR NET INCOME

If T = the tax rate, and NIAT = desired net income after taxes, then

(1-T)(NIBT) = NIAT therefore NIBT = NIAT ÷ (1-T)

Substituting NIAT÷(1-T) for NIBT in Equation 2, provides Equation 3, which allows us to solve for units needed to generate a desired amount of net income after taxes.

[3] (P-V) X = TFC + [NIAT ÷ (1-T)]

X = [TFC + [NIAT÷(1-T)]] ÷ (P-V)

The after tax relationships are also illustrated graphically in Figure above. The after tax profit function begins at a point equal to (1-T)(-TFC) assuming the tax benefits of a loss can be used in a prior period or perhaps in some other segment of the company. The slope of the after tax profit function is (1-T)(P-V), therefore the function is not as steep as the before tax profit function. The break-even point is the same however, and the vertical difference between the two profit functions is equal to the amount of the tax involved.

When target net income before taxes is stated as a % of sales $

If we use R to define the desired rate of return on sales, i.e., R = NIBT/TR, then we can substitute R(PX) for the desired net income before taxes in Equation. This provides Equation 4.

[4] $(P-V)X = TFC + (R)(PX)$

$X = [TFC + (R)(PX)] \div (P-V)$

Since PX equals sales dollars, then R multiplied by PX will provide the desired profit before taxes.

Although the desired profit is often stated as a percentage, R is a proportion, i.e, it ranges from 0 to 1.

When target net income after taxes is stated as a percentage of sales $

If the target rate of return is stated as an after tax rate, i.e., R = NIAT/TR, then the following approach is used. Substituting R(PX)÷(1-T) for R(PX) in Equation 4 provides Equation.

[5] $(P-V)X = TFC + [(R)(PX) \div (1-T)]$

$X = [TFC + [(R)(PX) \div (1-T)]] \div (P-V)$

When solving CVP problems, it is less confusing visually and more convenient for computational purposes to leave (P-V) on the left-hand side of the equations initially. It is best to simplify the expressions on both sides of the equation first, rather than attempt to divide every element on the right-hand side by P-V. The Cal Company produces pocket size calculators that are sold for $10 per unit.

The costs associated with each unit are as follows:

- Direct material = $3.00,
- Direct labour = $.25,
- Variable overhead = $2.00,
- Variable selling and administrative cost = $.75.

Total fixed costs are $100,000 for manufacturing and $20,000 for the selling and administrative functions. The company's tax rate is 40%.

In a recent meeting, the board of directors asked the following questions. How many calculators do we need to produce and sell to accomplish each of the following requirements?

- Break-even.
- Earn net income before taxes of $40,000.
- Earn net income after taxes of $24,000.

- Earn a 20% return on sales before taxes.
- Earn a 12% return on sales after taxes.

To answer these questions, we start by calculating the contribution per unit as follows:

Contribution margin per unit,

$$= P - V = 10 - (3 + .25 + 2 + .75) = 10 - 6 = 4.$$

Then, the five questions are answered by using the equations in Exhibit 11-1.

- Break-even.
  Using Equation [1] $4X = 120{,}000$
  $X = \$120{,}000 \div 4 = 30{,}000$ units.
- Earn net income before taxes of $40,000.
  Using Equation [2] $4X = 120{,}000 + 40{,}000$
  $X = 160{,}000 \div 4 = 40{,}000$ units.
- Earn net income after taxes of $24,000.
  Using Equation [3] $4X = 120{,}000 + [24{,}000 \div (1-.4)]$
  $4X = 120{,}000 + 40{,}000$
  $X = 160{,}000 \div 4 = 40{,}000$ unit.

  A graphic solution to Example is illustrated in Figure below.

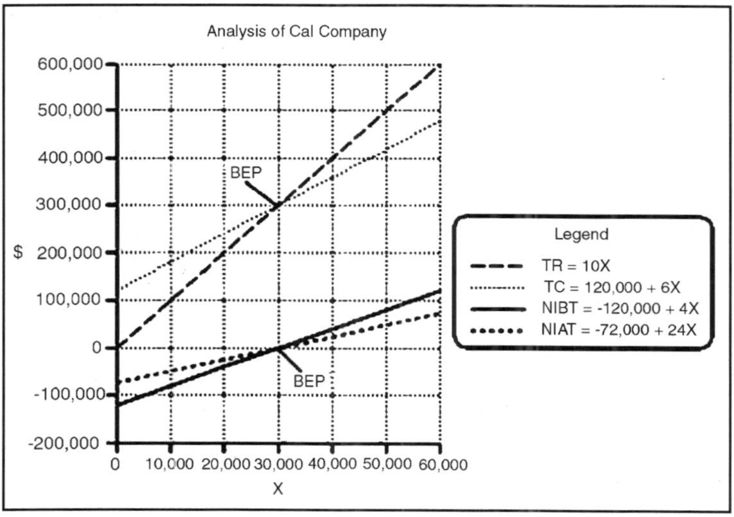

- Earn a 20% return on sales before taxes.
  Using Equation [4] $4X = 120{,}000 + .2(10X)$
  $4X = 120{,}000 + 2X$
  $2X = 120{,}000$
  $X = 120{,}000 \div 2 = 60{,}000$ units.
- Earn a 12% return on sales after taxes.
  Using Equation [5] $4X = 120{,}000 + [.12(10X) \div (1-.4)]$
  $4X = 120{,}000 + .2(10X)$
  $4X = 120{,}000 + 2X$

$2X = 120{,}000$
$X = 120{,}000 \div 2 = 60{,}000$ units.

After Tax Equations

The equation for NIAT that appears in the graph is found by multiplying the equation for NIBT by (1-T), i.e., (1-.4)(-120,000 + 4X) = -72,000 + 2.4X. Rearranging this equation we have 2.4X = 72,000 + NIAT. This revised equation indicates that the contribution margin after taxes ($2.4X) is equal to fixed costs after taxes ($72,000) plus the desired after tax income. It provides an alternative way to find the answers to questions 3 and 5 as illustrated below.

- Earn net income after taxes of $24,000.
  - 2.4X = 72,000 + NIAT desired
  - 2.4X = 72,000 + 24,000
  - 2.4X = 96,000
  - X = 96,000 ÷ 2.4 = 40,000 units.
- Earn a 12% return on sales after taxes.
  - 2.4X = 72,000 + NIAT desired
  - 2.4X = 72,000 +.12(10X)
  - 2.4X = 72,000 + 1.2X
  - 1.2X = 72,000
  - X = 72,000 ÷ 1.2 = 60,000 units.

Checking the Solutions

The accuracy of linear cost-volume-profit calculations can be verified easily. For example, the answers to the questions above can be verified as follows:

- Is 30,000 units the break-even point? Yes, since total contribution margin is equal to total fixed cost of 120,000, i.e., (4)(30,000) = $120,000.
- Will 40,000 units generate a before tax profit of $40,000? Yes, because total contribution margin is (4)(40,000) = $160,000 and this amount is 160,000 - 120,000 = $40,000 above total fixed costs.
- Will 40,000 units generate an after tax profit of $24,000? Yes, since (1-.4)($40,000 NIBT) = $24,000.
- Will 60,000 units provide a 20% return on sales before taxes? Yes, since the NIBT is TCM - TFC or (4)(60,000) - 120,000 = $120,000. Sales equals PX or ($10)(60,000) = $600,000. R = 120,000 ÷ 600,000 =.20 or 20%.
- Will 60,000 units provide a 12% return on sales after taxes. Yes, (1-.4)(.2) =.12 or 12%. For an alternative check (1-.4)(120,000) = $72,000 NIAT. Therefore, the after tax rate of return is 72,000 ÷ 600,000 =.12 or 12%.

SINGLE PRODUCT CVP PROBLEMS

A summary of the cost volume profit equations for solving single product problems in dollars is presented. These five equations are also variations of the basic conceptual equation stated in the first part of this chapter. Each of these equations is developed and illustrated below.

Table. Single Product Cvp Problems In Dollars

Number	Equation	Used To Determine
[1]	(CMR)(S) = TFC	Sales $ at break-even point
[2]	(CMR)(S) = TFC + NIBT	Sales $ for target NIBT
[3]	(CMR)(S) = TFC + [NIAT ÷ (1-T)]	Sales $ for target NIAT
[4]	(CMR)(S) = TFC + (R)(S)	Sales $ for target NIBT stated as a proportion (R) or sales $
[5]	(CMR)(S) = TFC + [(R)(S) ÷ (1-T)]	Sales $ for target NIAT stated as a proportion (R) of sales $

BREAK-EVEN POINT

The equation for the break-even point in sales dollars may also be derived by equating total revenue and total cost. It is more convenient to use the single symbol S for sales dollars, rather than TR for total revenue.

TR = TC

S = TFC + TVC

Since the variable cost ratio (V÷P) multiplied by sales dollars (S) equals total variable cost, we can substitute (V÷P)(S) for variable cost in the equation above as follows.

S = TFC + (V÷P)(S)

Then subtracting variable cost from both sides of the equation provides the basic break-even point equation in sales dollars.

S - (V÷P)(S) = TFC

Stated in words, the equation indicates that total revenue, less total variable costs, equals total contribution margin, and the break even point is where total contribution margin is equal to total fixed cost. Since the contribution margin ratio (CMR = 1- V÷P) multiplied by total revenue equals total contribution margin, it is more convenient for computational purposes to state the equation in the following manner.

(1- V÷P)(S) = TFC

[1] (CMR)(S) = TFC

S = TFC ÷ CMR

Total revenue needed for target net income before taxes: Although we could derive this equation from scratch, the fact that total contribution margin must be equal to the total fixed costs plus the desired net income before taxes allows us to develop.

[2] (CMR)(S) = TFC + NIBT

S = (TFC+NIBT) ÷ CMR

Total revenue needed for target net income after taxes: Solving for total revenue needed to generate a target net income after taxes involves substituting NIAT ÷ (1-T) for NIBT in the equation for Sales dollars needed before taxes (i.e., Equation). This provides Equation 3.

[3] (CMR)(S) = TFC + [NIAT ÷ (1-T)]

S = [TFC + [NIAT ÷ (1-T)]] ÷ CMR

Total revenue needed when target nibt is stated as a percentage of sales $: To solve a problem in sales dollars, when the desired net income is stated as a percentage of sales dollars, substitute (R)(S) into Equation for NIBT as follows.

[4] (CMR)(S) = TFC + (R)(S)

S = [TFC + (R)(S)] ÷ CMR

Total revenue needed when target niat is stated as a percentage of sales $: When the desired net income is stated as an after tax rate (R), the equation needed is developed by simply dividing (R)(S) in Equation by (1-T).

[5] (CMR)(S) = TFC + [(R)(S) ÷ (1-T)]

S = [TFC + [(R)(S) ÷ (1-T)]] ÷ CMR

To emphasize a point made earlier, it is less confusing visually and also more convenient for computational purposes to leave CMR on the left-hand side of each of the 5 equations initially.

Simplify the expressions first, rather than attempting to divide every element on the right-hand side by CMR.

The Cal Company example can be restated in the following manner. Variable costs (including both manuf-acturing and selling and administrative costs) represent sixty per cent of sales dollars. Total fixed costs are $120,000.

Assume the board of directors wants the answers to their questions provided in sales dollars rather than units. What amount of sales in dollars does the company need to accomplish each of the following requirements? 1. Break-even. 2. Earn net income before taxes of $40,000. 3.

Earn net income after taxes of $24,000. 4. Earn a 20% return on sales before taxes. 5. Earn a 12% return on sales after taxes. To answer these questions, we need the contribution margin ratio.

The ratio is,

$$CMR = 1- V/P = 1-.6 =.4$$

Then, the answers to the five questions are easily obtained as follows:

- Break even.

  Using Equation [1].4S = 120,000

  S = 120,000 ÷.4 = $300,000
- Earn net income before taxes of $40,000.

Using Equation [2].4S = (120,000 + 40,000)
S = 160,000 ÷.4 = $400,000

- Earn net income after taxes of $24,000.
Using Equation [3].4S = 120,000 + (24,000 ÷.60)
.4S = 120,000 + 40,000
S = 160,000 ÷.4 = $400,000
- Earn a 20% return on sales before taxes.
Using equation [4].4S = 120,000 +.2S
.2S = 120,000
S = 120,000 ÷.2 = $600,000
- Earn a 12% return on sales after taxes.
Using equation [5].4S = 120,000 – (.12S ÷.6)
.4S = 120,000 +.2S
.2S = 120,000
S = 120,000 ÷.2 = $600,000

A graphic analysis of this example is also illustrated in Figure since we are simply solving the problem in dollars rather than units. The graph is also useful for comparing the two approaches. Example 11-1 places emphasis on the horizontal axis (units) while Example 11-2 places emphasis on the vertical axis (dollars).

MARGIN OF SAFETY

Before we move on to multiproduct companies, there is a handy concept referred to as the margin of safety that you might find useful. The margin of safety (MS) for any sales level represents the amount of sales dollars above or below the break-even point. Mathematically, the margin of safety is:

MS = Sales$ - Break-even sales$

When sales are above the break-even point, the margin of safety is positive. When sales are below the break-even point, the margin of safety is negative. After determining the MS for a particular sales level, Equations 6 and 7 can be used to make some quick calculations.

NIBT = (MS)(CMR)

Solving Equation 6 provides the amount of contribution margin above the break-even point (when MS is positive) and this amount represents the net income (or loss if the MS is negative) before taxes.

Why? Because after the total fixed costs have been covered, additional contribution margin represents the before tax profit. Before the fixed cost have been covered the additional contribution needed represents the before tax loss.

The equation for after tax profit is,

NIAT = (MS)(CMR)(1-T)

EXAMPLE 11-3

Suppose we are in a board of directors meeting and a board member asks how much income would Cal Company generate at a particular sales level.

For convenience let's say $1,000,000. Using the margin of safety we can answer this question quickly. Since we already know the break-even point is $300,000, then the margin of safety is 1,000,000 - 300,000 = $700,000.

Using Equation [6] NIBT = (700,000)(.4) = $280,000.

Using Equation [7] NIAT = (700,000)(.4)(.6) = $168,000.

To show that the margin of safety calculations work on either side of the break-even point, consider another example. Suppose someone ask, how much income would Cal Company generate when total revenue is only $200,000?

MS = 200,000 - 300,000 = -100,000, i.e., $100,000 below the BEP.

Using Equation [6] NIBT = (-100,000)(.4) = -40,000 net loss before taxes, or Using Equation [7] NIAT = (-40,000)(.6) = -24,000 net loss after taxes. Solving Multiple Product Cvp Problems In Units Some additional symbols are needed to illustrate the algebraic techniques applicable to multiple product problems.

The following symbols are used below:

- i = The number designating a particular product.
- Pi = The price of product i.
- Vi = The variable cost per unit of product i.
- X = Total mixed units sold, i.e., includes all products.
- Xi = Units of product i sold.
- Mi = The mix ratio for product i, i.e., the proportion that product i represents out of the total number of units sold.
- E = Sigma or summation sign which means "the sum of".
- W = Weighted average contribution margin per unit = E [(Pi-Vi)(Mi)]
- Y = The weighted average price = E (Pi)(Mi)

A summary of the cost volume profit relationships for multiproduct problems is presented in Exhibit 11-3.

The five equations are comparable to the single product equations presented in Exhibit 11-1, but are somewhat more involved.

Each equation is developed and illustrated below,

EXHIBIT 11-3

Summary Equations For Solving

Multiple Product Cvp Problems In Units

Number	Equation	Used To Determine
[1]	WX = TFC	Total mixed units at the BEP.
[2]	WX = TFC + NIBT	Total mixed units for target NIBT.
[3]	WX = TFC + [NIAT ÷ (1-T)]	Total mixed units for target NIAT.
[4]	WX = TFC + (R)(YX)	Total mixed units for target NIBT stated as a proportion (R) of sales $.
[5]	WX = TFC + [(R)(YX) ÷ (1-T)]	Total mixed units for target NIAT stated as a proportion (R) of sales $.
	Xi = X(Mi)	The number of units of each product after X is obtained.

BREAK-EVEN POINT FOR MULTIPLE PRODUCTS

The same logic used to solve single product problems is applicable to multiple product problems. At the break-even point, total contribution margin is equal to total fixed costs. However, in multiple product situations, total contribution margin is found by multiplying the weighted average contribution margin per unit by the total number of mixed units produced and sold.

The weighted average contribution margin per unit is calculated by multiplying each product's contribution margin per unit (Pi-Vi) by the mix ratio applicable to that product (Mi) and then summing the results. The mix ratios (Mi's) represent the weights. The equation is,

W = E [(Pi-Vi)(Mi)]

The break-even equation for mixed units (X) is stated in the following manner.

[1] WX = TFC

After the total mixed units (X) have been determined, then the number of units of the individual products are found by multiplying the total mixed units by each product's mix ratio.

Xi = X(Mi)

Units Needed For Target Net Income Before Taxes: The equation for mixed units needed to generate a desired amount of net income before taxes is developed by simply adding NIBT to the right hand side of Equation 1.

WX = TFC + NIBT

Units needed for target net income after taxes: The equation for mixed units needed to generate a desired after tax profit is developed by substituting NIAT ÷ (1-T) for NIBT.

WX = TFC + [NIAT ÷ (1-T)]

When Target Net Income Before Taxes Is Stated As A Percentage Of Sales $

Using R to represent the target rate of return on sale dollars before taxes, i.e., R = NIBT÷TR, the following equation can be used to find the mixed units needed.

WX = TFC + (R)(YX)

Sales dollars are represented by the term YX. Since total sales dollars are mixed, we must multiply the total mixed units (X) by a weighted average price (Y) to find the total mixed sales dollars. Then, multiplying the term YX by R represents the desired NIBT.

The weighted average price (Y) is found by multiplying the price of each product (Pi) by the product mix ratios (Mi) and then summing the results, i.e., Y = E (Pi)(Mi).

When Target Net Income After Taxes Is Stated As A Percentage Of Sales $

The appropriate equation for after tax net income is found by dividing the term [(R)(YX], in Equation 4, by 1-T.

WX = TFC + [(R)(YX) ÷ (1-T)]

Remember that it is usually best for computational purposes to leave the amount represented by W on the left hand side in each of the equations until the expression on the right hand side has been simplified. Also remember that the units for individual products (Xi) are always found by multiplying the total mixed units (X) by the mix ratios (Mi) for each product.

The Sandlot Cap Company produces baseball caps in two categories referred to as regular logo and special logo. Caps in the regular logo category are high volume products that display familiar names of universities and professional sports teams. Caps in the special design category are typically created for a particular customer to promote special events such as the Olympics, or the opening of a unique museum exhibit. For convenience we will refer to the regular logo caps as product X1 and the special logo caps as product X2. Sales prices and variable costs are provided below.

Product	Price	Variable Cost PerUnit	Mix Ratio Based on Units
X1	$4	$3	.75
X2	8	5	.25

The variable costs for each product include direct materials and conversion costs of $2. Marketing costs account for an additional $1 for regular logo caps and $3 for special logo caps. As indicated above, three quarters of the company's unit sales are represented by regular logo caps, while the other one quarter represents special logo caps. The company's total fixed costs are $300,000. Sandlot Cap Company management wants to know how many caps need to be produced and sold to accomplish the following:

- Break even.
- Earn desired net income before taxes of $60,000.
- Earn desired net income after taxes of $36,000 given the tax rate is 40%.
- Earn desired net income before taxes equal to 15% of sales dollars.
- Earn a desired net income after taxes equal to 9% of sales dollars.

To solve this problem we need to calculate the weighted average contribution margin per unit, i.e., the contribution margin per mixed unit.

$$W = (4-3)(.75) + (8-5)(.25) = 1.5$$

The mix ratios (.75 and.25) are used as the weights to reflect the fact that the company normally sells three times as many X1's as X2's. After obtaining the weighted average contribution of $1.50, then 1.5X represents the total contribution margin on the lefthand side of each equation.

1. To break-even.
   - Using Equation [1] 1.5X = 300,000
   - X = 300,000 ÷ 1.5 = 200,000 Total mixed units.
   - X1 = (200,000)(.75) = 150,000 units
   - X2 = (200,000)(.25) = 50,000 units

2. To earn $60,000 net income before taxes.

- Using Equation [2] 1.5X = 300,000 + 60,000
- 1.5X = 360,000
- X = 360,000 ÷1.5 = 240,000 mixed units
- X1 = (240,000)(.75) = 180,000 units
- X2 = (240,000)(.25) = 60,000 units

3. To earn $36,000 net income after taxes.
   - Using Equation [3] 1.5X = 300,000 + (36,000 ÷.6)
   - 1.5X = 300,000 + 60,000
   - X = 360,000 ÷1.5 = 240,000 mixed units
   - X1 = (240,000)(.75) = 180,000 units
   - X2 = (240,000)(.25) = 60,000 units

In the last two requirements, income is stated as a percentage of sales dollars. Therefore, we need the YX measure of total mixed sales dollars to indicate the desired amount of income. Total mixed sales dollars is the weighted average price Y, multiplied by the mixed units X. To calculate Y we must use the unit mix ratios as weights to reflect the importance of each product in the price.

$$Y = 4(.75) + 8(.25) = \$5$$

Then, $5 represents the weighted average price and 5X represents the total mixed sales dollars.

4. To earn before tax net income equal to 15% of sales dollars, we substitute.15(5X) in the equation for desired income, i.e., R(YX).
   - Then using Equation [4]
   - 1.5X = 300,000 +.15(5X)
   - 1.5X = 300,000 +.75X
   - .75X = 300,000
   - X = 300,000 ÷.75 = 400,000 mixed units
   - X1 =.75(400,000) = 300,000 units
   - X2 =.25(400,000) = 100,000 units
5. To earn after tax net income equal to 9% of sales dollars, the desired income is,
   - (R)(YX) ÷ 1-T, or (.09)(5X) ÷ (1-.4).
   - Then using Equation [5]
   - 1.5X = 300,000 + [(.09)(5X) ÷ (1-.4)]
   - 1.5X = 300,000 + [.45X ÷.6]
   - 1.5X = 300,000 +.75X
   - .75X = 300,000
   - X = 300,000 ÷.75 = 400,000 mixed units
   - X1 =.75(400,000) = 300,000 units
   - X2 =.25(400,000) = 100,000 units

After Tax Equations As An Alternative

A graphic analysis of the Sandlot Cap Company example appears in Figure.

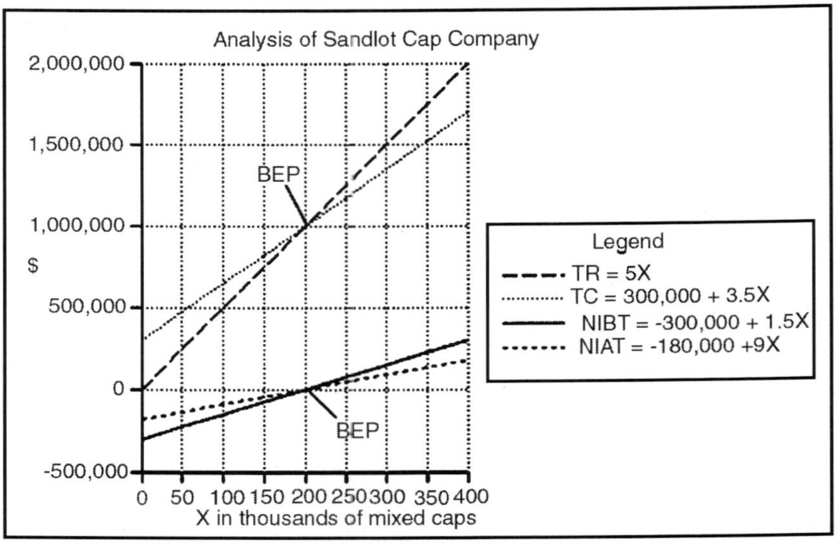

The equation for NIAT illustrated in the graph is found by multiplying the equation for NIBT by (1-T), i.e., (1-.4)(-300,000) + (1-.4)(1.5X) = -180,000 +.9X.

Rearranging this equation we have.9X = 180,000 + NIAT where.9X is the weighted average contribution margin after taxes. We can use this equation as an alternative way to find the answers to question 3 and 5 as follows.

3. Earn desired net income after taxes of $36,000.
   - .9X = 180,000 + 36,000
   - .9X = 216,000

   X = 216,000 ÷.9 = 240,000 mixed units
5. Earn desired net income after taxes equal to 9 per cent of sales dollars.
   - .9X = 180,000 +.09(5X)
   - .9X = 180,000 +.45X
   - .45X = 180,000
   - X = 180,000 ÷.45 = 400,000 mixed units

Solving Multiple Product Cvp Problems In Dollars

The following additional symbols are used to develop this section.

- S = Total mixed sales dollars.
- Si = Sales dollars for product i.
- CMRi = Contribution margin ratio for product i.
- M$i = The mix ratio for product i based on sales dollars. Note, these ratios are not equal to the mix ratio based on units.
- WCMR = The weighted average contribution margin ratio = E(CMRi)(M$i)

Number	Equation	Used To Determine
[1]	WCMR(S) = TFC	Sales $ at break-even point.
[2]	WCMR(S) = TFC + NIBT	Sales $ for target NIBT.
[3]	WCMR(S) = TFC + [NIAT ÷ (1-T)]	Sales $ for target NIAT.
[4]	WCMR(S) = TFC + (R)(S)	Sales $ for target NIBT stated as a proportion (R) of sales $.
[5]	WCMR(S) = TFC + [(R)(S) ÷ (1-T)]	Sales $ for target NIAT stated as a proportion (R) of sales $.
	Si = S(M$i)	Sales dollars for each product after S is obtained.

Break-even Point In Sales Dollars For Multiple Products: The same basic conceptual logic used in the previous sections is used to develop the equations in this section. The firm breaks even when total contribution margin is equal to total fixed costs.

$$(WCMR)(S) = TFC$$

The difference between the equations for single product and multiproduct situations is that we must use a weighted average contribution margin ratio, WCMR = E(CMRi)(M$I) to find the total mixed sales dollars. Then sales dollars for the individual products are found by multiplying the total mixed sales dollars (S) by the mix ratios for each product, Si = (S)(M$I)

Total Revenue Needed For Target Net Income Before Taxes Equation is developed in the usual manner by simply adding the desired amount of NIBT to the right hand side of Equation.

$$(WCMR)(S) = TFC + NIBT$$

Total Revenue Needed For Target Net Income After Taxes

Revising the previous equation to include after tax profit we have:

$$(WCMR)(S) = TFC + [NIAT \div (1-T)]$$

When Target Net Income Before Taxes Is Stated As A Percentage Of Sales $

If R is used as the before tax target rate of return on sales, i.e., NIBT÷S, then the equation needed to achieve the target return before taxes is:

$$(WCMR)(S) = TFC + (R)(S)$$

When Target Net Income After Taxes Is Stated As A Percentage Of Sales $

If R is used as the after tax target rate of return on sales, i.e., NIAT÷S, the equation becomes,

$$(WCMR)(S) = TFC + [(R)(S) \div (1-T)]$$

Suppose the Sandlot Cap Company information is provided to you in the following format.

Product	**Contribution Margin Ratios**	**Mix Ratios Based on sales dollars**			
X1	.25	.6	X2	.375	.4

TFC = $300,000.

Sandlot Cap Company management wants to know the amount of sales dollars needed for each product to accomplish the same five objectives.

- Break even.
- Earn desired net income before taxes of $60,000.
- Earn desired net income after taxes of $36,000. Assume the tax rate is 40%.
- Earn desired net income before taxes equal to 15% of sales dollars.
- Earn a desired net income after taxes equal to 9% of sales dollars.

To find the answers we need to start by calculating the weighted average contribution margin ratio.

WCMR = (.25)(.60) + (.375)(.40) =.30

The mix ratios stated in dollars are used as the weights.

Then the solutions are obtained as follows:

1. To break even. Using Equation [1].3S = 300,000
    - S = 300,000 ÷.3 = $1,000,000
    - S1 = (1,000,000)(.6) = $600,000
    - S2 = (1,000,000)(.4) = 400,000
2. To earn $60,000 before taxes. Using Equation [2].3S = 300,000 + 60,000
    - S = 360,000 ÷.3 = $1,200,000
    - S1 = (1,200,000)(.6) = $720,000
    - S2 = (1,200,000)(.4) = 480,000
3. To earn $36,000 after taxes. Using Equation [3].3S = 300,000 + (36,000 ÷.6)
    - S = 360,000 ÷.3 = $1,200,000
    - S1 = ($1,200,000)(.6) = $720,000
    - S2 = ($1,200,000)(.4) = 480,000
4. To earn desired NIBT of 15% of sales dollars. Using Equation [4]
    - .3S = 300,000 +.15S
    - .15S = 300,000
    - S = 300,000 ÷.15 = $2,000,000
    - S1 = ($2,000,000)(.6) = $1,200,000
    - S2 = ($2,000,000)(.4) = 800,000
5. To earn desired NIAT of 9% of sales dollars. Using Equation [5]

- .3S = 300,000 + (.09S ÷.6)
- .15S = 300,000
- S = 300,000 ÷.15 = $2,000,000
- S1 = ($2,000,000)(.6) = $1,200,000
- S2 = ($2,000,000)(.4) = 800,000

The solutions to these five questions are also illustrated in Figure since we simply changed our emphasis from the horizontal axis (units) to the vertical axis (dollars). The mix ratios determine whether the emphasis is on units or dollars and the manner in which the answers must be obtained. If the mix ratios are stated in units, as in Example 11-4, then the solutions must be obtained in units. If the mix ratios are stated in dollars, as in Example 11-5, then the solutions must be obtained in dollars. Why? To see why we cannot use the mix ratios interchangeably, suppose the Sandlot Cap Company data were stated in the following manner.

Product	Price	Variable Cost per Unit	Mix Ratios Based on Sales Dollars
X1	$4	$3	.6
X2	8	5	.4

Total fixed costs = $300,000. Now, find the break-even point in units. Try this, at least mentally before you look at the solution in the footnote below.

Now suppose Sandlot Cap Company management gave you following information and asks for the break-even point. TFC is still $300,000. What would you do?

Product	Contribution MarginRatios	Mix Ratios Based on Units
X1	.25	.75
X2	.375	.25

Think about it and then consult the footnote below.

The Cash Flow Break-even Point: Since some of the fixed costs do not require cash payments (e.g., depreciation), the cash flow break-even point will be below the conventional accrual accounting break-even point. The following

Cash Flow Break-even Before Taxes: The cash flow break-even point is where the cash inflows before taxes are equal to the cash outflows before taxes. This is presented in equation form below.

PX = TFC + VX - Non cash Fixed Costs

PX - VX = TFC - Non cash Fixed Costs

(P-V) X = TFC - Non cash Fixed Costs

The equation above is based on the assumption that all other costs are paid for during the period and that all sales dollars are collected during the period.

Cash Flow Break-even After Taxes: The cash flow break-even point after taxes is where the cash inflows after taxes are equal to the cash outflows after taxes. We simply convert the contribution margin and total fixed costs to an after tax basis by multiplying by 1-T.

The equation is as follows:

(1-T)(P-V)X = (1-T)(TFC) - Non cash Fixed Costs

Example: Cal Company's specifics from Example 11-1 are P = $10, V = $6, total fixed costs = $120,000 and the tax rate is 40%. If depreciation is $24,000 and there are no other non cash fixed costs, then the cash flow break-even point after taxes is:

(1-.4)(4X) = (1-.4)(120,000) - 24,000

2.4X = 72,000 - 24,000

X = 48,000 ÷ 2.4 = 20,000 units

The solution is verified in Figure below.

Income Statement Showing Cal Company's Cash Flow Break-even Point

Sales	
(20,000)($10)	$200,000
Variable Costs (20,000)($6)	120,000
Contribution Margin	80,000
Less Total Fixed Costs	120,000
Net Loss	(40,000)
Add Tax Reduction(.4)(40,000)	16,000
Add back Depreciation	24,000
Cash Flow after taxes	0
	======

We can also use the equation above to calculate the number of units needed to generate a desired amount of net cash inflow after taxes. Just add the desired amount and solve for X.

For example, suppose management desires a net cash inflow after taxes of $36,000.

2.4X = 48,000 + 36,000

X = 84,000 ÷ 2.4 = 35,000 units

Check: (35,000units)($4) = 140,000 contribution margin. Subtract fixed cost of $120,000, then multiply by.6 and we have $12,000 NIAT. Add back depreciation of 24,000 to obtain $36,000.

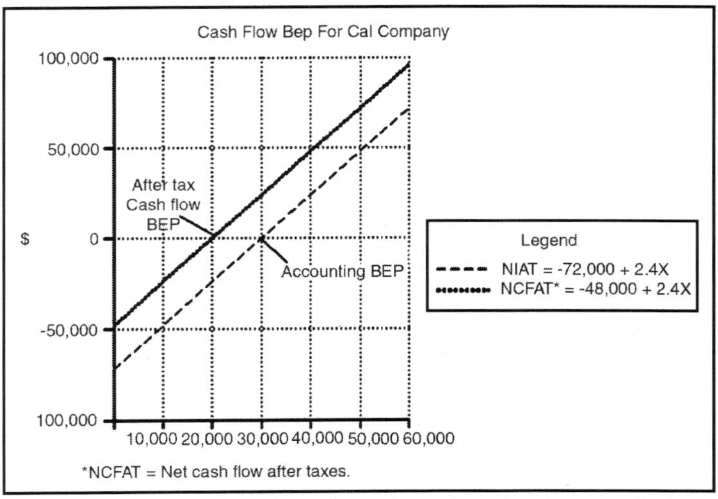

The Controversy Over The Contribution Margin Approach. There are two issues that involve the contribution margin approach and the closely related direct (or variable) costing inventory valuation method. The first issue is a

relatively old controversy over whether direct costing or full absorption costing is the most useful way to present accounting information. The second issue questions the compatibility of the contribution margin approach to activity based costing and the lean enterprise concepts of just-in-time and the theory of constraints.

The second issue questions the wisdom of separating costs into fixed and variable categories. The following discussion concentrates on the second controversy. We will return to the first issue in the next chapter.

The Case Against

From the activity based costing perspective, critics of the contribution margin approach argue that the costs traditionally defined as fixed costs have been increasing faster than the costs traditionally defined as variable costs. As a result, the CVP model does not reflect the cost structure of complex, multiproduct organizations.

Although the CVP model may be useful for some short term forecasting and optimization decisions, it is misleading for decisions such as product introduction, product pricing, product mix and make versus buy. The so-called fixed costs are not explained by output volume, but by the diversity and complexity of the company's products, services, customers, distribution channels and product lines.

The CVP approach is flawed because it assumes that the volume of production is the only cost driver. As a result, the model motivates managers to produce as much as possible to lower total unit cost. It encourages managers to add new products and services ignoring the "overhead creep" that inevitably results It supports the misguided view that the company should never drop a part of the business as long as that part generates a positive contribution margin.

But this signal to constantly expand is a trap because the costs that are assumed to be constant, increase rapidly instead, in response to the greater demands that are placed on the various support activities. As the so-called fixed costs rise, the manager attempts to add more volume to lower unit cost again. The process is somewhat analogous to a dog chasing it's tail.

From the lean enterprise, or continuous improvement perspective, the contribution margin approach emphasizes maximizing output with a static set of constraints, rather than emphasizing the continuous improvement of the company's value creating processes and activities. The contribution margin approach has the same basic defect as any other constrained optimization technique. It promotes short run optimization within a static system.

However, from the viewpoint of the lean enterprise concepts of just-in-time and the theory of constraints, becoming competitive and maintaining competitiveness in the long run requires a dynamic learning organization. The emphasis should be on relentlessly eliminating waste, removing constraints, re-engineering processes when necessary and increasing customer value, not on maximizing output in an attempt to minimize short run unit costs.

THE CASE FOR

Defenders of the contribution margin approach argue that the concepts of contribution margin and related techniques are useful for short term planning and for performing a variety of special relevant cost studies. Although production volume is not the only cost driver, it is still the major cost driver.

Production volume based systems and techniques such as direct costing and CVP analysis still provide reasonably accurate information for a fraction of the cost of elaborate ABC systems. Another advantage of these methods is that income statements based on the contribution margin approach (i.e., direct costing) are much easier for managers to understand than statements based on either traditional full absorption costing or activity based costing.

In addition, direct costing reduces the full cost behavioral bias towards over production by eliminating the production volume variance and the inventory change effect that increases net income when production exceeds sales. The contribution margin approach is neutral, or nearly neutral, because it does not encourage management to produce anything that cannot be sold.

The argument that the contribution margin approach promotes overproduction is not warranted. In fact, full absorption costing creates a much stronger motivation to overproduce and ABC is just an expanded form of that same methodology. In addition, CVP analysis does not discourage continuous improvement. It is just a quantitative tool that can be used or misused like any other tool.

The CVP approach can complement the plan-do-check-action (PDCA) continuous improvement cycle by providing a way to estimate the financial consequences of proposed changes in the system.

A Possible Reconciliation With Abc

A possible reconciliation between ABC and the contribution margin approach is provided by Robin Cooper's levels of cost variability. The idea is to combine ABC with the contribution margin approach to reveal contributions at the unit, batch, product, distribution and customer levels to review these terms). This expanded information will indicate which products, distribution channels and customers really are profitable and perhaps help avoid the potential trap set by the contribution margin logic that keeps companies from ever dropping anything.

- The economic, or theoretical cost-volume-profit model was developed by a number of theorist between 1800 and 1930. The classical economists (e.g., Adam Smith, David Ricado, Thomas Malthus, Jeremy Bentham and Jean Baptiste Say) believed that the cost of production (supply) determined the market price. The marginalist (e.g., Herman Gossen, William Jevons) believed that demand was the primary determinant of market price. Around 1890, the neoclassical economist, Alfred Marshall argued that the interaction of supply and demand determines the price using his famous scissors analogy (i.e., both supply and demand are needed, just as both blades of a pair of scissors are needed to cut a piece of paper). Later, around 1930, Edward Chamberlin and others developed the theoretical model described in this chapter. Joel Dean presented the linear model as a practical alternative. See Marshall, A. 1890. *Principles of Economics*. The Macmillan Company; Chamberlin, E. H. 1946. *The Theory of Monopolistic Competition*. Harvard University Press; and Dean, J. 1951. *Managerial Economics*: Prentice-Hall, Inc.: 326-347. for some examples of non-production volume related drivers and measurements.

- In the theoretical model, profits are maximized where marginal revenue is equal to marginal cost. Solving for this point requires using calculus. Marginal revenue is the rate of change in total revenue and can be found by taking the first derivative of the total revenue function. Marginal cost is the rate of change in total cost and can be determined by taking the first derivative of the total cost function. Upper level microeconomics textbooks show this in considerable detail using quadratic and cubic equations.

- Although you may be tempted to multiply P-V for each product by the mix ratios to obtain the weighted average contribution margin per unit, that step will produce the wrong answer. Note that (1)(.6) + (3)(.4) = 1.8 and we know from Example 11-4 that W is 1.5 not 1.8. We must solve the problem in dollars first and then convert to units. Therefore, we need to calculate the contribution margin ratios (4-3)÷4 =.25 and (8-5)÷8=.375 and then solve for sales dollars as in Example 11-5, question 1 above. We calculate the weighted average contribution margin ratio, i.e., (.25)(.60) + (.375)(.4) =.30. Then solve for mixed sales dollars at the break-even point, i.e., S= $300,000 ÷.30 = $1,000,000. Find the sales dollars for each product, S1 = (1,000,000)(.6) = $600,000 and S2 = (1,000,000).4) = $400,000. Then we divide by the sales prices to find the break-even point in units, i.e., X1 = $600,000 ÷ $4 = 150,000 caps and X2 = $400,000 ÷ $8 = 50,000 caps.

- Multiplying the contribution margin ratios by the mix ratios and summing the results we get.28125. Comparing this number to W and WCMR (1.50 and.30 from examples 11-4 and 11-5) reveals that.28125 is not a recognizable piece of information. Any attempt to use it will produce the wrong answer. Since there is no way to find the contribution margin per unit for each product, or the mix ratios in dollars, you would need to ask for additional information to answer the question.

- The first issue started back around 1936. See Harris, J. 1936. What did we earn last month? *NACA Bulletin* (January 15): 501-526. Harris used the term direct costing rather than variable costing.
- A long list of references could be provided here, but the edited version of a 1989 panel discussion by Robert Kaplan, John Shank, Charles Horngren and Germain Boer provides the best single reference. See
- This is essentially an argument that any model that recognizes the distinction between fixed and variable costs will create a bias towards overproduction. This is because total unit cost decreases as the average fixed cost per unit decreases when additional units are produced, i.e., unit fixed cost = TFC÷ X.
- The theoretical economic model is also flawed for the same reason. Although changes in productivity are considered in the model, the problem referred to as "overhead creep" is not considered. In other words, in the theoretical model, productivity affects the rate of change in variable costs, but fixed costs remain constant.
- The controversy over the usefulness of constrained optimization techniques is a broader issue since a long list of techniques fall into this category. The economic order quantity and economic batch size models, linear programming and standard costing provide a few examples.
- See Johnson, H. T. 1989. Professors, customers and value: Bringing a global perspective to management accounting education.*Proceedings* of the Third Annual Management Accounting Symposium.

P/V RATIO ANALYSIS

RATIO ANALYSIS

The Profit Volume (PV) Ratio is the ratio of Contribution over Sales. It measures the Profitability of the firm and is one of the important ratios for computing profitabilty. The Contribution is the extra amount of sales over variable cost. Contribution is also Fixed cost plus profit.

Profit = Sales - Variable Cost - Fixed Cost.

Thus Contribution is:

Profit + Fixed Cost = Sales - Variable Cost.

Therefore PV Ratio = (Contribution/Sales)X100. (This as a percentage of sales) Inventory ratio analysis model is easy to follow financial template to calculate vital Inventory ratios for current year.

***The model includes*:**

- Roll forward Inventory Balance Sheet Schedule;
- 12 mo Cost of Goods Sold;
- 12 mo Inventory additions;
- 12 mo Avg Inventory additions
- 12 mo Avg Net Inventory

INVENTORY TURNOVER RATIO

How many times Inventory is over during 12 months period; the ratio is activity ratio that shows company effectiveness in managing its inventory levels; A low turnover ration may indicate overstocking, obsolescence, or low market demand for the product. High turnover ration may indicate inadequate inventory level and potential inability to answer customer depend on time. However, you always need to compare your company Inventory Turnover ration to that of the industry that your company is in.

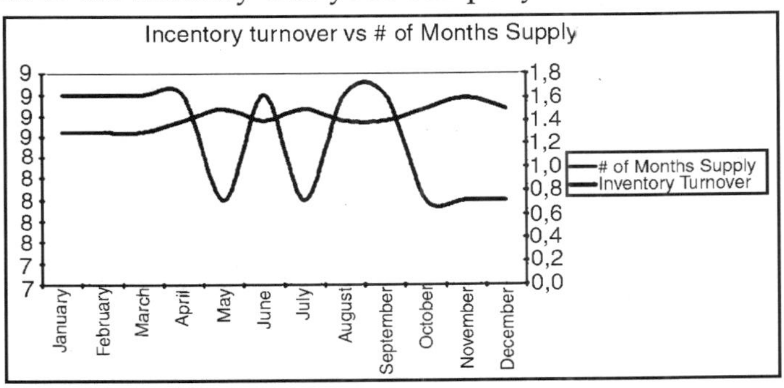

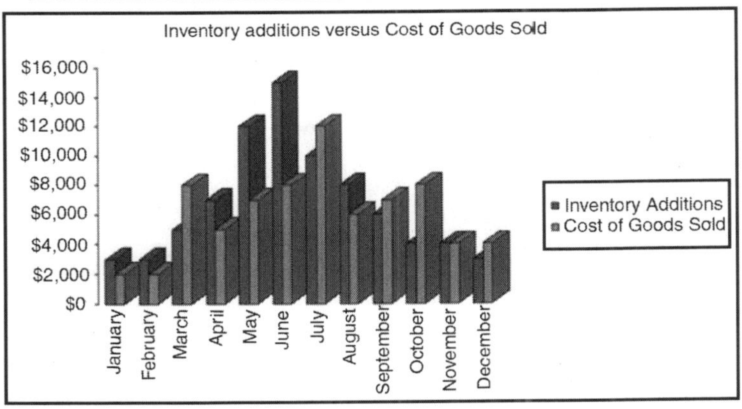

PV LOSS RATIO

This column represents the Present Value of the Loss Ratio to date at the end of the policy year. The definition of the Loss Ratio is controlled by the Loss Ratio Definitionswitch in PRICING ASSUMPTIONS.

The rate that is used for the PV calculation is specified in the cell in the Rate for PV of loss ratio field in PRICING ASSUMPTIONS.

All Loss Ratio calculations are done on a Gross basis, i.e. before reinsurance. The PV of the loss ratio is calculated by first determining the PV of the numerator values to date and then dividing by the PV of the denominator values to date. The calculation is demonstrated in the following example:

Example:

Assume:

- Loss Ratio Definition switch is set to (paid claims + change in DLR)/ premium
- Rate for PV of loss ratio is set to 6%

Policy Year	Premium	Paid Claim	Increase in DLR	Loss Ratio	PV Loss Ratio
1	435.38	31.750	68.063	22.92517	22.92517
2	368.30	48.363	34.909	22.60974	22.78517
3	323.390	49.362	28.838	24.18139	23.16050

Policy Year 1

PV Loss Ratio = Loss Ratio = (Paid claim + Inc in DLR)/Premium = 22.925%

Policy Year 2

$$\text{PV Loss Ratio} = \frac{\begin{array}{c}(\text{Paid claim Y2}/1.06 + \text{Inc in DLR Y2}/1.06\\ + \text{Paid claim Y1} + \text{Inc in DLR Y1})\end{array}}{(\text{Prem Y2}/1.06 + \text{Prem Y1})}$$

$= (48.363/1.06 + 34.909/1.06 + 31.750 + 68.063)/(368.301/1.06 + 435.388)$

$= 22.785\%$

IMPLICATION

DEFINITION

In any discipline one seeks to establish facts and to draw conclusions based on observations and theories. One can do so deductively or inductively. In inductive reasoning, one starts with many observations and formulates an explanation that seems to fit.

In deductive reasoning, one starts with premises and, using the rules of logical inference, draws conclusions from them. In disciplines such as mathematics, deductive reasoning is the predominant means of drawing conclusions. In fields such as psychology, inductive reasoning predominates, but once a theory has been formulated, it is both tested and applied through the processes of deductive thinking. It is in this that logic plays a role. Basic to deductive thinking is the word "implies," symbolized by "=>." A statement p⇒q means that whenever p is true, q is true also. For example, if p is the statement, "x is in Illinois," and q is the statement "x is in the United States," then p⇒q is the statement, "If x is in Illinois, then x is in the United States."

In logic as well as in ordinary English, there are many ways of translating p⇒q into words: "If p is true, then q is true" "q is implied by p;" "p is true only if q is true;" "q is a necessary condition for p;" "p is a sufficient condition for q."

The implication p ⇒q has a truth table some find a little perplexing:

p	q	p=>q
T	T	T
T	F	F
F	T	T
F	F	T

The perplexing part occurs in the next to last line where a false value of p seems to imply a true value of q. The fact that p is false does not imply anything at all. The imolication says only that q is true whenever p is. It doesn't say what happens when p is false. In the example given earlier, replacing x with Montreal makes both p and q false, but the implication itself is still true.

Implication has two properties which resemble the reflexive and transitive properties of equality. One, p⇒p, is called a "tautology." Tautologies, although widely used, do not add much to understanding. "Why is the water salty?" asks the little boy.

The other property, "If p⇒q and q⇒r, then p=>r," is also widely used. In connecting two implications to form a third, it characterizes a lot of reasoning, formal and informal. "If we take our vacation in January, there will be snow. If there is snow, we can go skiing. Let's take it in January." This property is called a "syllogism."

A third property of equality 1 "If a = b, then b = a," called symmetry may or may not be shared by the implication p=>q. When it is, it is symbolized by the twoheaded arrow used earlier, "p q." p q means (p⇒q) Ë (q⇒p). It can be read "p and q are equivalent;" p is true if and only if q is true;" "p implies and is implied by q;" "p is a necessary and sufficient condition for q;" and "p implies q, and conversely."

In p⇒q, p is called the "antecedent" and q the "consequent." If the antecedent and consequent are interchanged, the resulting implication, q⇒p, is called the "converse." If one is talking about triangles, for example, there is a theorem, "If two sides are equal, then the angles opposite the sides are equal." The converse is, "If two angles are equal, then the sides opposite the angles are equal." If an implication is true, it is never safe to assume that the converse is true as well. For example, "If x lives in Illinois, then x lives in the United

States," is a true implication, but its converse is obviously false. In fact, assuming that the converse of an implication is true is a significant source of fallacious reasoning. "If the battery is shot, then the car won't start." True enough, but it is a good idea to check the battery itself instead of assuming the coverse and buying a new one.

Implications are involved in three powerful lines of reasoning. One, known as the Rule of Detachment or by the Latin *modus ponendo ponens,* states simply "If p⇒q and p are both true, then q is true."

This rule shows up in all sorts of areas. "If x dies, then y is to receive $100,000." When x dies and proof is submitted to the insurance company, y gets a check for the money. The statements p⇒q and p are called the "premises" and q the "conclusion." A second rule, known as *modus tollendo tollens,* says if p=>q is true and q is false, then p is false. "If x ate the cake, then x was home." If x was not at home, then someone else ate the cake. A third rule, *modus tollerdo ponens,* says that if p V q and p are true, then q is true.

Mary or Ann broke the pitcher. Ann did not; so Mary did. Of course, the validity of the argument depends upon establishing that both premises are true. It may have been the cat. Another type of argument is known as *reductio ad absurdum,* again from the Latin. Here, if one can show that ~p⇒(q Ë ~q), then p must be true. That is, if assuming the negation of p leads to the absurdity of a statement which is both true and false at the same time, then p itself must be true.

TAX IMPLICATION

The interest of the "Aam Aadmi" was taken care of in the Budget 2010-11. The finance minister in order to provide impetus to consumption has proposed a new personal income tax slab, which will result in higher savings and simulta-neously higher disposable income at the hands of individuals.

Table. Tax Implication for Individual Asessee

Income Slab	Old tax rate	Tax computed	New tax rate	Tax computed	Cumulative benefit
Upto Rs 160000	0%	-	Nil	-	-
Rs 160001-300000	10%	14,000.00	10%	14,000.00	-
Rs 300001-500000	20%	40,000.00	10%	20,000.00	20,000.00
Up to Rs.800000	30%	90,000.00	20%	60,000.00	50,000.00
Above Rs.800000	30%	60,000.00	30%	60,000.00	50,000.00
Total Tax Liability for					
Income upto Rs.10lac	**20%**	**204,000.00**	**15%**	**154,000.00**	**50,000.00**

Table. Tax Implication for Women Asessee v

Income Slab	Old tax rate	Tax computed	New tax rate	Tax computed	Cumulative benefit
Upto Rs 190000	0%	-	Nil	-	-
Rs 190001-300000	10%	11,000.00	10%	11,000.00	-
Rs 300001-500000	20%	40,000.00	10%	20,000.00	20,000.00
Up to Rs.800000	30%	90,000.00	20%	60,000.00	50,000.00
Above Rs.800000	30%	60,000.00	30%	60,000.00	50,000.00
Total Tax Liability for					
Income upto Rs.10lac	**20%**	**201,000.00**	**15%**	**151,000.00**	**50,000.00**

Table:Tax implication for Senior Citizen

Income Slab	Old tax rate	Tax computed	New tax rate	Tax computed	Cumulative benefit
Upto Rs 240000	0%	-	Nil	-	-
Rs 240001-300000	10%	6,000.00	10%	6,000.00	-
Rs 300001-500000	20%	40,000.00	10%	20,000.00	20,000.00
Up to Rs.800000	30%	90,000.00	20%	60,000.00	50,000.00
Above Rs.800000	30%	60,000.00	30%	60,000.00	50,000.00
Total Tax Liability for					
Income upto Rs.10lac	20%	**196,000.00**	15%	**151,000.00**	**50,000.00**

This we believe will help boosting consumption and will be beneficiary for Auto's, FMCG, Consumer Durables, Hotels & Hospitality

3

Concept and Uses of Contribution

CONCEPT

The concept of the group contribution using Kihara intermolecular potentials with a spherical core is extended to perfluorinated *n*-alkanes ($n = 1$–6). The effective Kihara parameters for groups (CF_2, CF_3, CF_4) are estimated by fitting second virial coefficient B and dilute gas viscosity ç together. The assumption of regarding CF_4 molecule as a single group is preferable to other two approaches based on the principle of group additivity: a combination of F–(CF_3) and CF_3–(F) groups; a single C–$(F)_4$ group and four F–(C) groups.

Application of the model shows that second virial coefficients are represented with better results than those of the Tsonopoulos correlation, and are comparable to the correlation of Dymond's group and the Hohm correlation. Feasibility of the present method to calculate dilute gas viscosities is proved by comparison with the Lucas method, the Hohm correlation, the correlation of Yaws, and the Simsci Data Bank.

Mixture property calculations of the model are enhanced by including binary group interaction coefficients $k_{ij,gc}$, determined from second cross virial coefficient data, and are more reliable than other correlations for second cross virial coefficients and mixture viscosities.

Prediction results of binary diffusion coefficients, not supplied to the parameter evaluations, are in significant agreement with experimental data and are compared well with values obtained by means of the Fuller method. Results studied here would be of use when extended to halogenated paraffins and their mixtures.

The methods based on the Group Contribution Concept usually fail when one attempts to estimate the physico-chemical properties of different branched isomers of a given compound. We present a new concept, the Group-Interaction Contribution Approach (GIC) which considers the contribution of the different interactions between groups present in a molecule instead of the contribution of structural groups.

This approach allows differentiation between branched isomers, thus leading to different values of the physico-chemical properties. The GIC

Approach can be easily implemented in current correlations based on the group contribution concept. The estimates of enthalpy of formation, normal boiling temperature and critical temperature of a series of 51 saturated hydrocarbons showed clearly that the GIC concept leads to very good estimations for branched isomers.

Earlier this year, I spent an intense half-day closeted in a room with the top 70 executives at Intuit. Our aim was to come up with ways that people outside the company could volunteer their time, energy, and expertise to make life better for our customers.

Sound odd? Well, if you're not conducting an exercise like that at your organization, you risk missing the boat on a sea change that's transforming business. Every day, millions of people make all kinds of vountary contributionsto companies–from informed opinions to computing resources – that create tremendous value for those firms' customers and, consequently, for their shareholders. When I first encountered this idea, several years ago, it struck me as unfathomable: Volunteerism was for charities, not for red-blooded, profit-making firms. That was just my first surprise. I also began to see that user contributions are fueling some of the world's fastest-growing and most competitively advantaged organizations – in some cases revolutionizing the economics of entire industries by radically shrinking their cost structures. Think of eBay, which opened as an online store with no inventory, leaving it up to customers to fill its "shelves" with goods to sell. Or Wikipedia, which gutted the value proposition of 230-year old *Encyclopaedia Britannica* by offering a free encyclopedia written and updated frequently by unpaid amateurs.

In other cases, the contribution is not as obvious but just as central to the value proposition. Skype incursalmost no capital costs because its internet-based phone system is built on the unused processing capacity of its customers' personal computers.

Google, too, is built on user contributions: Its search engine relies on thealgorithmic aggregation of links created by others between websites, and its ad placement system relies ondata from people's click behaviour.

OK, I'm not saying you can or should transform your company into a Google or a Skype whose business model is primarily based on user contributions. But you should understand the power of the phenomenon and, as I have, learn from the growing number of companies in traditional industries – firms like Honda, Procter & Gamble, Best Buy, and Hyatt – that are tapping user contributions to improve products, better serve customers, generate new business, reduce costs, boost employee performance, and more.

Contribution-driven results like those are achievable for pretty much any business. The concept of user contribution isn't new. But the companies I've just mentioned – both the internet highfliers and the old-economy behemoths

– have actively created something I call a *user contribution system*. That is, they've created methods for aggregating and leveraging people's contributions or behaviors in ways that are useful to other people. The *users* can be customers, employees, sales prospects – or even people with no previous connection to the company. Their *contributions* can be active (work, expertise, or information) or passive and even unknowing (behavioral data that is gathered automatically during a transaction or an activity). The *system* is the method, usually internet-based, by which contributions are aggregated and automatically converted into something useful to others.

Although the company retains control of the system and may choose to modify its design, the system converts inputs into useful outputs in real time with little or no intervention by the company. Such a system creates value for a business as a consequence of the value it delivers to users – personalized purchase recommendations, connections between buyers and sellers of hard-to-find items, new personal or business relationships, lower prices, membership in a community, entertainment, information of all kinds.

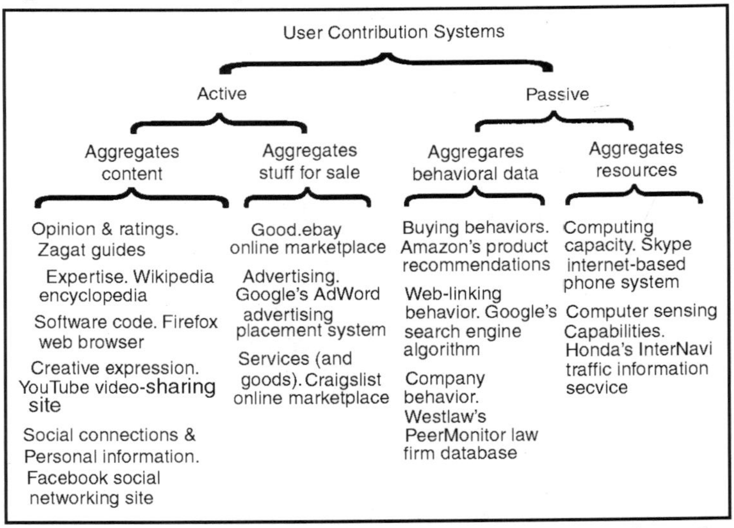

The challenge for executives is twofold. First, you must learn how to spot opportunities for creating value from user contributions. Second – and here's the difficult part – in acting on these opportunities, you must overcome natural organizational resistance to the idea of relinquishing significant control to people outside the company.

The advice I offer here is based on my personal experience at Intuit – the successes and failures, the moments of exhilaration and the times when I had to conquer my own fear of putting so much power in the hands of users.

REVOLUTIONARY POTENTIAL

Though I didn't know it at the time, my interest in user contribution systems began in the early 1990s with a series of slim red books. The Zagat guides offered reviews with quantitative ratings based on sustained performance rather than on a single visit or two by one reviewer. And those recommendations originated not with paid experts but with regular diners like me. It was a decade, though, before I recognized the significance of the method to my own company. That "aha" came from watching the winners on the web.

The success of the leading internet firms has admittedly been touted ad nauseam by the media and business experts. Yet for better and for worse, the internet is a reflection of society and the preferences of hundreds of millions of people around the world. Like book best-seller lists, rankings of the most popular websites reflect what's winning the battle for people's attention.

The companies joining the list of most popular websites in recent years include Wikipedia, YouTube, Facebook, Craigslist, and MySpace.

They have joined such older sites as Amazon, eBay, and Google. At first glance, these sites seem to have little in common, targeting unrelated areas of human endeavor: the cataloguing of information, video entertainment, social interaction, classified advertising, retail shopping, internet search. Some of the sites charge users; others are free. One's a nonprofit; another has one of the highest profit marginsamong public companies.

Despite their differences, all these winning sites rely on – or are themselves – user contribution systems. Much of their success flows from inherent characteristics of contribution systems that create advantages, detailed here, of a magnitude rarely known in traditional business.

WHY CONTRIBUTORS CONTRIBUTE

Most contribution systems offer no financial compensation to contributors. In fact, payment can destroy participation by undermining a sense of collaboration and trust. Rather, they rely on motivations intrinsic to humanity – or involve contributions that require no motivation at all, because the user contributes without realizing it.

Contributing

Some systems collect participants' resources or data as a by-product of things people are doing for other purposes. As shoppers buy from Amazon, they automatically contribute toits recommendation engine, which suggests products based on the ratings and purchase decisions of other customers.

Practical Solutions

In some systems, participants contribute in order to get reasonably immediate rewards.

For example, the site del.icio.usenables users to organize their bookmarks of websites. A byproduct of this activity is that, when aggregated, the bookmarks produce an index to the web that is valuable to others.

Social Reward

Many systems provide the benefits of interaction with others: being part of a community with a common interest, generating business prospects, getting a date – the drivers behind social networks like Facebook and LinkedIn.

Reputation

Contribution can be sparked by a desire for public recognition, like Amazon's badge for a "top 1,000 reviewer," or for the admiration of peers: Wikipedia articles carry no authorship credit, yet authors earn the respect of other contributors.

Altruism

Why would a person write a glowing online review of a restaurant – when it may become harder to get a table if others act on the opinion? Some people want to help local diners or reward superb restaurant owners. Others simply want the truth to be heard.

Cost Advantage

What does Wikipedia pay the authors and editors of its articles? What does Facebook or MySpace pay those who painstakingly fill in and update the personal profiles that make the site so valuable? Nothing. These sites enjoy free "raw materials," as users perform gratis work that companies typically have to pay for. People contribute for various reasons, some of them self-serving but all of them sufficient to make formal payment unnecessary.

Scalability Advantage

Craigslist's free classified advertising sites feature more than 30 million new offerings every month, and eBay's virtual shelves feature 120 million items, many times more than any other store on the planet can offer. Such scale doesn't require broad or deep contribution: Only a small percentage of users may contribute (about one user in 1,000 for Wikipedia) and active contributions may require little effort (as with Flickr, the photo-sharing site).

Competitive Advantage

Some contribution systems give companies a structural advantage over rivals because of network effects. That is, the more people who contribute to the system, the more useful it becomes, creating an upward spiral in which increasingly more people choose to use and contribute to it. Network effectsonce drove the winner-take-all market-share gains of Microsoft's Windows; today, they propel the success of sites like Wikipedia and Facebook.

Contribution systems won't displace most traditional products or businesses: I'm not expecting Wiki-Milk to displace real milk or the dairy industry. Still, given the power of user contributions, too many business leaders are failing to look for opportunities to leverage these systems in their industries. I think that's partly because of the novelty of the phenomenon, but it's also because of beliefs rooted in the past. All too often, executives mistakenly view user contribution as:

THREAT TO PROFIT BUSINESSES

But consider Schibsted, a 170-year-old Norwegian newspaper publisher that, instead of ignoring the online threat savaging much of the newspaper industry, started reinventing itself in the mid-1990s by embracing user contribution and becoming a leading European provider of online classified advertising.

Only for Tech Companies

But consider the Canadian grocery store chain Loblaws, which solicits online customer reviews and incorporates them in the marketing of new products.

Unreliable and Error-ridden

But consider the study in Nature that found volunteer-written Wikipedia to be, in general, about as accurate as expert-written articles in Encyclopaedia Britannica's online edition.

Lacking a Strong Business Case or Profit

But consider LinkedIn, whose social networking site for businesspeople now profits from numerous revenue streams: traditional ones, such as site advertising, upgrades to premium membership with more features, and paid job postings, along with more novel ones, such as tools that corporate HR departments can use to screen job candidates.

CONTRIBUTION

Even without knowing your business, I'd be willing to bet that contribution systems can address one or more of the business challenges you face better than the methods you currently use. To spur your thinking, let's look at some of the different ways that traditional companies are employing user contribution systems in a wide variety of business activities and functions.

Customer Service

Company-hosted online support forums, in which product users answer questions from other users free of charge, are commonplace among software and personal computer companies. I admit my initial surprise when I experienced firsthand how a user community can answer tough questions that even the manufacturer cannot. Now non-computer firms, such as AT&T, are beginning to follow this practice.

Troubleshooting is just one way to harness user contributions for service. Hyatt Hotels and Resorts has launched an online concierge service called Yatt'it that aggregates and lets users rate travel tips posted by Hyatt's customers and concierges. The aim is both to reduce the burden on concierges and to give travelers tailored, extensive city information in advance of their trip – and, if they've already arrived, without their having to wait in line.

Companies also use contribution systems to serve customers in ways that create a brand-new business. Westlaw, the legal research service, created a B2B contribution system that helps its customer base of law firms address important strategic issues. West PeerMonitor automatically aggregates anonymized financial and operating information from participating law firms.

The firms access the database to see how their performance compares with that of peers and how other markets compare with their own – data that may help a firm decide, for example, whether to expand geographically or whether a key practice area is operating efficiently. This customer service is valued so much that Westlaw charges handsomely for it.

Marketing

The power of contribution systems is now being tapped by traditional marketing powerhouses, including two of the giants: Procter & Gamble and Unilever.

Procter & Gamble has created a website, BeingGirl, aimed at teen and preteen girls – a difficult group to reach in the marketing of its feminine-hygiene products because young girls are often uncomfortable viewing TV ads on the topic in the company of friends or family. The site originally consisted solely of information from experts.

But in 2005, P&G borrowed the contribution concept from tech websites, adding forums where girls could interact with one another. Now users can share their questions and personal experiences and get support and advice from other girls. This creation of a community around an important topic promotes engagement with the site – and with the Always and Tampax brands that it discreetly promotes. P&G says that as a marketing tool BeingGirl is now four times as effective as comparably priced television advertising.

The website In the Motherhood, cosponsored by Sprint and by Unilever's Suave line of personal-care products, also offers a community forum where users can share stories and offer tips – in this case on the subject of being a mom. In addition, mothers can submit stories (3,000 of them so far) that serve as potential plotlines for an online comedy series.

The community votes on the submissions, and those selected by the users are produced by professional directors and actors and subsequently posted to the site. (Several dozen have been produced so far, and cumulative views have passed the 20 million mark — it has been picked up for television by ABC.) Unilever research finds that the site increases users' intent to purchase a Suave product and engenders a feeling in customers that the makers of Suave really understand their lives.

Employee Support

Most company intranet sites are oneway streets, with management broadcasting the "company line" to employees. Best Buy, the U.S. retail chain, uses the opposite approach in a contribution system dubbed BlueShirt Nation. BlueShirt Nation allows employees to share and discuss their ideas and experiences: what works and what doesn't in carrying out a particular task or in interacting with customers, for example. The site, launched two years ago by two junior employees with no corporate IT support or funding, today has more than 20,000 registered employee users.

Best Buy has discovered that unfiltered information from colleagues can be more effective than memos from HR. For example, Blue Shirt Nation ran a contest in which employees submitted videos they had conceived and produced, with no company oversight, to spur employee adoption of 401(k) plans. The result of the buzz generated by the contest? A 30% increase in plan enrollment.

Capital Resources

Build a global telecommunications system with almost no capital equipment? Make free, high quality video calls anywhere in the world? Both once were unfathomable. But that's what Skype has done, thanks to a contribution system.

Founded by Swedes and engineered in Estonia, Skype is the marquee example of how a company can reduce the cost of capital equipment to almost nothing by having users contribute the capital goods.

Skype's free software utilizes idle computing power on users' PCs to manage the calls – as many as 12 million simultaneously – for its 300 million customers. Its costs are so low that the company, which was acquired by eBay in 2006, can deliver high-quality voice and video computer-to-computer calls between subscribers at no charge. And it's profitable: revenue comes from calls made by Skype users to mobile phones and landlines, as well as from services such as voice mail.

Traditional companies, too, get customers to contribute needed capital. In Japan, Honda captures real-time traffic data from GPS systems that Honda owners buy from the company. Speed and location reports from each vehicle contribute to a data stream that Honda aggregates with other traffic data to provide information on traffic jams and other conditions to Honda drivers who subscribe to the company's InterNavi service. Users benefit from enhanced traffic updates; the company can offer a superior subscription service without having to pay for the capital infrastructure. And there's more: Honda drivers also contribute reviews of local businesses and points of interest that other drivers can read from their InterNavi-equipped Hondas – an automotive version of a Zagat guide. Honda's system thus combines three user contributions – capital equipment, data about user location and vehicle speed, and reviews.

Design and Development

User contribution can tackle creative challenges from the technical to the artistic. The emblematic example of contribution in R&D is open source software, such as the Linux operating system and the Mozilla Foundation'sFirefox web browser, which is created and regularly upgraded by communities of unpaid volunteer developers. (This low-cost model makes Mozilla one of the rare nonprofits that is highly "profitable.")

In the creative arts, Thread less, a company that manufactures T-shirts, relies on a community of volunteer designers and artists to submit designs and a community of customers to select those that will go into production. Both of the user groups, as well as the company, benefit. The designers get free exposure for their work and a chance at monetary compensation: They receive $2,500 plus a percentage of sales if their design is chosen by Threadless customers.

Note that the Threadless user contribution system is subtly different from customer innovation approaches likecrowdsourcing, which are used with success by Dell, Starbucks, and other companies. Crowdsourcing is not a user contribution system in the pure sense, because the company stands between the input and the output. For example, it sifts through people's ideas for new products and services, selects ones to pursue, and then invests the time and expense needed to develop them.

Production

In some cases, organizations can "delegate" some or all of the production process to users. Wikipedia delegates all of it. The producers of Fox Television's American Idol delegate part of the process.

The show relies on users (through their votes for performers) to make decisions traditionally reserved for television producers; it relies on amateur performers to offer entertainment usually provided by high-priced stars. The contributing singers benefit from a shot at stardom. Viewers, who contribute their opinions, benefit from compelling entertainment (if the show's high ratings are any indication) and a strong sense of engagement because their votes determine the show's content. Fox and its producers benefit from lower costs and fromadvertising revenue driven by the show's tremendous popularity – which results, in part, from the drama generated by the show's user-contributed surprises.

INTUIT AND USER CONTRIBUTION SYSTEMS

As a member of the boards of eBay and Amazon in the late 1990s, I was exposed to user contribution through the work of Jeff Bezos, Pierre Omidyar, and Meg Whitman. But the concept seemed rare and specialized, so I missed seeing its broader application and value. (I once told Jeff Bezos I thought his plan to supplement professional book reviews on Amazon with reviews written by anyone who felt like it was crazy:

Early success

At our annual off-site in 2005, I put this question to the company's top 300 executives: How might we leverage user contribution at Intuit, both to enhance existing businesses and to create new ones? Two executives in our Plano, Texas, division began to think about how to solve a common problem faced by professional tax preparers – getting answers to obscure questions.

The result was a quickly cobbled-together wiki/forum site where tax preparers could contribute both questions and answers for the benefit of other tax preparers. Just 33 days after the executive off-site, TaxAlmanac was launched. Today, it has 170,000 pages, drawing on the collective expertise of thousands of tax professionals, and is used by 400,000 unique visitors – about equal to the number of tax preparers in the country. Tax preparers benefit from expertise that's free. Intuit benefits when visitors then buy our tax prep software – customer acquisition at almost zero cost.

However, despite my evangelizing, the idea of contribution systems wasn't taking off elsewhere within the organization. TaxAlmanac was a small island in a sea of indifference.

A Major Setback

I then resurrected an idea that had been proposed several years before by an Intuit engineer: a website with user-generated reviews of local businesses to help folks find a good plumber, car dealer, or restaurant, linked to our Quicken financial software products. It seemed like a sure bet, so we put a big team on it, we launched Zipingo. But the site failed to attract a critical mass of users, and we shuttered it in August 2007.

What went wrong? We made mistakes that stemmed from the difference between traditional products and contribution systems. User contribution is first of all about the users and their content. We failed to nurture and encourage early contributors, and we got distracted creating our own content – ancillary information like business addresses for the listings.

Zipingo's failure hurt. I stopped pushing big team efforts to develop new contribution systems at Intuit. But even as I pulled back, small contribution-system projects started sprouting up

Gaining Traction

One of our engineering leaders conceived the idea of embedding a Q&A community into a product itself – that is, creating a user forum on every page of TurboTax, with questions and answers relevant to the topic of the particular page. Many were wary of the idea, and some were even hostile. I encouraged the group's efforts, but in an echo of my own skepticism about Amazon's user reviews years earlier, I wondered silently whether people striving to finish their own taxes would stop to answer some stranger's questions.

Working with the support of his division manager, the engineer's team of three built the system and tested it in the least popular version of TurboTax Online in January 2007. Just five weeks into the initial test, one-third of the questions posed already had answers. Crucially, our internal tax experts were pleased by the quality of the answers, which seemed to be self-correcting as other users refined them. TurboTax Live Community, as it's called, was the kind of clear success I'd been seeking. Live Community systems have spread to our other divisions and are inspiring more contribution experiments.

Yet wariness persists. This year, when the TurboTax marketing team decided to solicit and post all user reviews, unedited, on a prominent link from the product's home page, I blanched and took a deep breath. Again a surprise: The vast bulk of reviews are so positive that it looks as if we've posted only the good ones (which, I hasten to add, is not the case). Once again, we're learning from that most reliable of sources – our customers.

COMPANY WITH UCS

User contribution seems messy and scary; giving customers a public podium to comment freely about your products and company seems to violate the management canon "Don't hold me accountable for what I don't control."

Naturally, adopting these methods is easier when competitors have beaten you to the punch and shown you where user contribution works in your industry. But what if you want to lead your rivals? Here's my advice for senior managers trying to create contribution systems in their companies.

Use Personal Experience to Move Mind-set

I've found that heads and hearts don't change until people participate in contribution systems themselves. To overcome wariness in inexperienced executives, ask enthusiasts to share stories of their personal experience with user contribution systems. To build awareness, have people count the user contribution systems found on an Amazon page and classify them by type. (If you look hard, you'll find 23 separate systems on a single Amazon product page.) Ask inexperienced executives to find and use contribution systems of personal interest to them – that helps develop a visceral feeling for how they work. Get sub-teams of leaders to brainstorm about contribution systems that might solve customer or employee problems and then ask them to sketch out prototypes they can present to a larger group.

Nurture Small Experiments

Encourage unofficial and "guerrilla" experiments. Challenge employees to create contribution systems that they are passionate about, without requiring them to get clearance from management. Experiment with small batches of employees or customers. (At Intuit, we tried one experiment on the TurboTax version that has the smallest sales volume, accounting for less than 1% of customers for that product.) Most of the experiments will fail; tell the organization in advance that this is OK. Communicate the value of the lessons learned from those failed experiments so that other teams benefit.

Ideas and Leadership

Expect ideas for contribution systems to emerge from those who use them the most. Often, these will be your youngest employees. Seek them out. Make them your mentors. Ask them to take the lead in creating ways for your company and customers to benefit from user contributions. Have them develop prototypes and show them directly to you; then help them act on some of the ideas that emerge.

Set Boundaries

I'm not advocating that you blow up your current business and completely reinvent it around a contribution system. Experiment at the edges of your business. Give experimenters a defined sandbox – spacious, perhaps, but defined – rather than an endless expanse of beach. Within those limits, though, make sure they aren't distracted by experts and that their experiments aren't smothered by larger initiatives with broader mandates.

Protect Experiments

Ceding some control of business processes to outsiders, even in a sandbox, will be scary for your organization. Leaders in certain functional areas – marketers and lawyers, for example – will feel especially anxious. (I can identify, having had to swallow hard a few times over things we were about to try at Intuit.)

To counter the instinct to preserve control and the status quo, name a godfather or godmother with big-time clout to protect experiments and break through barriers when initiatives meet organizational resistance. (Three people, two division general managers and I, played this role in our early experiments at Intuit.)

Customer Base

Some new contribution systems face a chicken-or-egg problem – that is, they're empty and useless until folks begin contributing to them, but few visitors will be attracted to something that is empty and useless. Your company probably has advantages that start-ups can only dream of: existing customers, traffic to your website, accumulated behavioral data, and, sometimes, media that will find your experiments newsworthy.

Let users "vote," Early and Often

Customers are better than executives at picking winners in this arena, so get experiments into the hands of real customers as quickly as possible. Minimize or eliminate time lost to market research, lengthy analysis, PowerPoint presentations, or frequent reviews by management.(We've borrowed an idea from Google by creating a public webpage – intuitlabs.com – that displays our current experiments and gives experimenters a fast, direct path to customers, bypassing normal product-launch procedures.)

Seek Organizational

The guerrilla experiments are designed to get around organizational resistance. Ultimately, you want innovation in user contribution to become embedded in the organization's normal processes, but you'll most likely struggle to shift mindset until you can point to a successful experiment or two.

The meeting earlier this year of Intuit's top executives to spur action on user contribution systems would have been a wasted effort two years ago. Then, we had only begun to experiment. But with several successful initiatives now in operation, Intuit's newly promoted CEO, Brad Smith, and I felt the time was right to move the idea into the mainstream and talk about why user contribution is a focus of our evolving company strategy. I can't say everyone at that meeting bought into the concept. Some undoubtedly saw it as a distraction from their day jobs.

Still, there was real energy in the room that day. In the middle of the meeting, I stopped to ask whether folks had questions. Rather than answer them myself, I wrote the questions on the board and asked the entire group to tackle them.

As I watched, people provided answers, better than the ones I would have given. (In fact, some of them became content for this article.) As we moved to take a break, I reminded our executives that we all had just experienced user contribution in action.

BREAK EVEN ANALYSIS

INTRODUCTION

Break-even analysis is a technique widely used by production management and management accountants. It is based on categorising production costs between those which are "variable" (costs that change when the production output changes) and those that are "fixed" (costs not directly related to the volume of production).

Total variable and fixed costs are compared with sales revenue in order to determine the level of sales volume, sales value or production at which the business makes neither a profit nor a loss (the "break-even point").

THE BREAK-EVEN CHART

In its simplest form, the break-even chart is a graphical representation of costs at various levels of activity shown on the same chart as the variation of income (or sales, revenue) with the same variation in activity. The point at which neither profit nor loss is made is known as the "break-even point" and is represented on the chart below by the intersection of the two lines:

In the diagram above, the line OA represents the variation of income at varying levels of production activity ("output"). OB represents the total fixed costs in the business. As output increases, variable costs are incurred, meaning that total costs (fixed + variable) also increase. At low levels of output, Costs are greater than Income. At the point of intersection, P, costs are exactly equal to income, and hence neither profit nor loss is made.

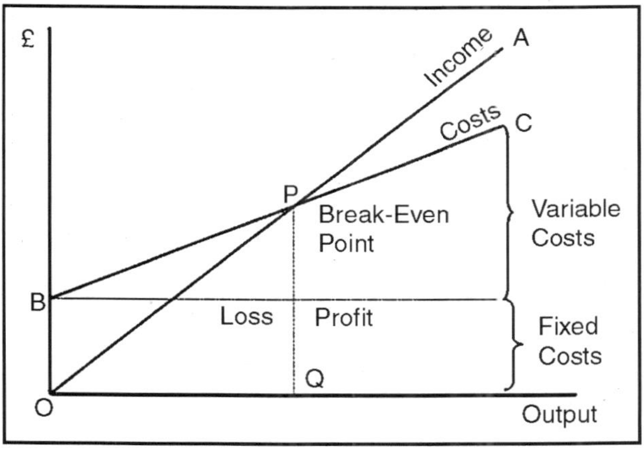

FIXED COSTS

Fixed costs are those business costs that are not directly related to the level of production or output. In other words, even if the business has a zero output or high output, the level of fixed costs will remain broadly the same. In the long term fixed costs can alter - perhaps as a result of investment in production capacity (e.g. adding a new factory unit) or through the growth in overheads required to support a larger, more complex business.

Examples of fixed costs

- Rent and rates
- Depreciation
- Research and development
- Marketing costs (non- revenue related)
- Administration costs

Variable Costs

Variable costs are those costs which vary directly with the level of output.

They represent payment output-related inputs such as raw materials, direct labour, fuel and revenue-related costs such as commission.

A distinction is often made between "Direct" variable costs and "Indirect" variable costs. Direct variable costs are those which can be directly attributable to the production of a particular product or service and allocated to a particular cost centre. Raw materials and the wages those working on the production line are good examples.

Indirect variable costs cannot be directly attributable to production but they do vary with output. These include depreciation (where it is calculated related to output - e.g. machine hours), maintenance and certain labour costs.

SEMI-VARIABLE COSTS

Whilst the distinction between fixed and variable costs is a convenient way of categorising business costs, in reality there are some costs which are fixed in nature but which increase when output reaches certain levels. These are largely related to the overall "scale" and/or complexity of the business. For example, when a business has relatively low levels of output or sales, it may not require costs associated with functions such as human resource management or a fully-resourced finance department. However, as the scale of the business grows (e.g. output, number people employed, number and complexity of transactions) then more resources are required. If production rises suddenly then some short-term increase in warehousing and/or transport may be required. In these circumstances, we say that part of the cost is variable and part fixed.

TYPES OF DECISION-MAKING

IRREVERSIBLE

This are those type of decisions, which, if made once cannot be unmade. Whatever is decided would than have its repercussions for a long time to come. It commits one irrevocably when there is no other satisfactory option to the chosen course. A manager should never use it as an all-or-nothing instant escape from general indecision.

REVERSIBLE

This are the decisions that can be changed completely, either before, during or after the agreed action begins. Such types of decisions allows one to acknowledge a mistake early in the process rather than perpetuate it. It can be effectively used for changing circumstances where reversal is necessary.

EXPERIMENTAL

This types of decisions are not final until the first results appear and prove themselves to be satisfactory. It requires positive feedback before one can decide on a course of action. It is useful and effective when correct move is unclear but there is a clearity regarding general direction of action.

TRIAL AND ERROR

In this type of decisions, knowledge is derived out of past mistakes. A certain course of action is selected and is tried out, if the results are positive, the action is carried further, if the results appear negative, another course is adopted and so on and so forth a trial is made and an error is occurred. Till the night combination this continues. It allows the manager to adopt and adjust plans continuously before the full and final commitment. It uses both, the positive and negative feedback before selecting one particular course of action.

MADE IN STAGES

Here the decisions are made in steps until the whole action is completed. It allows close monitoring of risks as one accumulates the evidence of outcomes and obstacles at every stage. It permits feedback and further discussion before the next stage of the decision is made.

CAUTIOUS

It allows time for contingencies and problems that may crop up later at the time of implementation. The decision-makers hedge their best of efforts to adopt the night course. It helps to limit the risks that are inherent to decision-making. Although this may also limit the final gains. It allows one to scale down those projects which look too risky in the first instance.

CONDITIONAL

Such types of decisions can be altered if certain foreseen circumstances arise. It is an 'either/or' kind of decision with all options kept open. It prepares one to react if the competition makes a new move or if the game plan changes radically. It enables one to react quickly to the ever changing circumstances of competitive markets.

DELAYED

Such decisions are put on hold till the decision–makers feel that the time is right. A go-ahead is given only when required elements are in place. It prevents one from making a decision at the wrong time or before all the facts are known. It may, at times result into forgoing of opportunities in the market that needs fast action.

BEING DECISIVE

The ability to take timely, clear and firm decisions is an essential quality of leadership, but the type of decision needed varies according to the circumstances. Learning to recognize the implications of taking each type of different decisions leads to error minimisation.

BEING POSITIVE

Taking decisive action does not mean making decisions on the spur of the moment. Although, it may be necessary in emergencies and also occasionally desirable for other reasons. A true leader approaches the decisions confidently, being aware of what must be taken into account and fully in command of the decision–making process.

MAKING FAST DECISIONS

It is important to be able to assess whether a decision needs to be made quickly or it can wait. Good decision-makers often do make instant decisions – but they then assess the long-term implications.

IDENTIFYING ISSUES

It is crucial to diagnose problems correctly. Before any decision is made identifying and defining the issue removes the criticality. This also means deciding who else needs to be involved in the issue, and analyzing what their involvement means.

PRIORITIZING FACTORS

While making a decision, a manager needs to prioritize on important factors. Some factors in a process are more important than others. The use of Pareto's rule of Vital few and trivial many helps in setting up of the priorities. Giving every factor affecting a decision equal weight makes sense only if every factor is equally important, the Pareto rule concentrates on the significant 20 per cent and gives the less important 80 per cent lower priority.

USING ADVISERS

It is advisable to involve as many people as are needed in making a decision. In making collective decisions, specific expertise as well as experience of a person both can be used simultaneously. The decision-maker, having weighed the advice of experts and experienced hands, must then use authority to ensure that the final decision is seen through.

VETTING DECISIONS

If one does not have the full autonomy to proceed, it is advisable to consult the relevant authority – not just for the final go, but also for the input. It is always in the interest of the subordinate to have the plans vetted by a senior colleague whose judgment is trusted and is experienced. Even if there is no need to get the decision sanctioned, the top people are likely to lend their cooperation well if they have been kept fully informed all the way along the decision path.

SINGLE-PRODUCT PRICING

DEFINITION

Present a robust optimization approach to the problem of pricing a capacitated product over a finite time horizon in the presence of demand uncertainty. This technique does not require the knowledge of the underlying probability distributions, which in practice are difficult to estimate accurately, and instead models random variables as uncertain parameters belonging to a polyhedral uncertainty set. A novelty of the proposed approach is that, instead of imposing an upper bound on the number of uncertain parameters that can reach their worst-case value, which is known as a budget-of-uncertainty constraint and has received much attention in the robust optimization literature, we introduce a budget of resource consumption by the uncertainty.

This budget limits the amount of the resource that can be used by the random part of the cumulative demand, and allows us to derive key insights on the structure of the optimal solution for a broad class of nominal demand functions. We establish the existence of a reference price for the product and show that this new parameter plays a crucial role in understanding the impact of uncertainty on the optimal prices.

In particular, it is not always optimal to decrease prices when demand is uncertain. Whether it is optimal or not will instead depend on whether the price at a given time period is above or below the reference price, and whether the maximal amount of uncertainty at that time exceeds a threshold. We compare the optimal solution in the cases of additive and multiplicative uncertainty and analyse the problem with linear nominal demand in detail. Numerical results are encouraging.

MULTI PRODUCT PRICING

INVESTIGATION

This dissertation investigates a number of related topics in dynamic multiproduct pricing arising in a competitive setting in markets with memory-sensitive consumers.

The first problem is concerned with simultaneous pricing of a line of several products, both complementary products and substitutes, with a number of distinct price differentiation classes for each product.

A game-theoretic problem extension where the product line demand is sensitive to prices of outside competitors' products is also considered.

The second problem features a number of firms simultaneously competing in price and inventory level decisions, and considers the effect of excess demand, where the firm faces part of the demand its competitors could not satisfy because of stockout.

An iterative relaxation algorithm is proposed to solve the problems stated, and sufficient conditions for convergence of the algorithm are proven. Extensive computational examples and a case study are included to illustrate solutions' practical applications.

The third problem is concerned with profit-maximizing product innovation and pricing for firms that produce and sell short life-cycle products in a competitive environment. We incorporate the effects reference innovation level and reference price have on profits, and model consumers in the market with two attributes: their sensitivity to product innovation levels and their sensitivity to product prices.

We characterize both open-loop and closed-loop Nash equilibria for competition among firms that execute different types of product innovation and pricing strategies. The fourth problem deals with a firm's decision on the product introduction timing and pricing for successive product generations in the presence of consumer memory.

We analyse the case where a firm introduces multiple generations of a product, for which demand is impacted by the reference price formed by consumers' shopping experience. We characterize the product introduction timing and pricing strategies explicitly for two successive product generations, and propose a quasi-analytic solution method, based on the structure of the memory-dependent problem, for an arbitrary number of generations.

We also extend our analysis to a duopoly environment. Our results help firms manage development and sales of their multiple product generations. Finally, we also include the summary of our recent results on the application of vehicular traffic theory to blood rheology, a collaborative effort with the Department of Cardiology

The theory of multiproduct pricing is well developed in stylized models, although a unified theory has yet to be developed. As such, empirical analyses are rarely guided by strong theoretical hypotheses and are therefore scarce. This paper analyses the interactions of ticket, parking, and concession prices in Major League Baseball for the period 1991-2003 using a principal components methodology. The approach allows inferences to be formed about the factors underlying intertemporal price variation in the absence of information about costs and demand. The most important factor influencing prices in baseball is a general increase in the demand for baseball, but general demand shifts explain less than half of all price variation.

The second most important factor is pricing interactions between tickets and concessions that are consistent with theories of nonlinear multiproduct pricing. Secondary empirical analysis confirms these economic interpretations.

The results show that the principal components methodology is an effective way to draw inferences about the economic forces underpinning pricing in a multiproduct context using data on prices alone. Utilization of a simple multiproduct price competition model revealed the presence of a complete strategy equilibrium. The equilibrium becomes efficient when overall social surplus is maximized. Moreover, an equilibrium outcome is obtained when the willingness to pay function of the consumer is convex. This signifies weak competition and the surplus is being taken by the firms. On the other hand, a concave willingness to pay function reveals that the equilibrium price of a product also marginally accounts for the total willingness to pay.

DIFFERENTIAL AND INCREMENTAL COSTING

DIFFERENTIAL COSTING

Decisions involve choosing between alternatives. In business, each alternative will have certain costs and benefits that must be compared to the costs and benefits of the other available alternatives.

A difference in cost between any two alternatives is known as differential cost. A difference in revenue between any two alternatives is known as differential revenues. Differential cost includes both cost increase (incremental cost) and cost decrease (decremental cost).

In general the difference (cost and revenue) between alternatives are relevant indecision making. Those items that are the same under all alternatives can be ignored. The accountant's differential cost concept can be compared to the economist's*marginal cost* concept. In speaking of changes in cost and revenue, the economists employ the term *marginal cost and marginal revenue.*

The revenue that can be obtained from selling one more unit of product is called marginal revenue, and the cost involved in producing one more unit of a product is called marginal cost. The economists marginal cost is basically the same as the accountant's differential concept applied to a single unit of out put.

Example: Differential cost can be either variable or fixed. To illustrate assume that a company is thinking about changing its marketing method from distribution through retailers to distribution by door to door direct sale. Present cost and revenues are compared to projected costs and revenues in the following table.

Description	Retailer Distribution (Present)	Direct SaleDistribution (Proposed)	Differential Costs and Revenues
Revenue (variable)	$700,000	$800,000	$100,000
	---------	---------	---------
Cost of goods sold (V)	350,000	400,000	50,000
Advertising (V)	80,000	45,000	(35000)
Commissions (F)	-0-	40,000	40,000
Warehouse depreciation (V)	50,000	80,000	30,000
Other Expenses (F)	60,000	60,000	-0-
	----------	----------	----------
Total	540,000	625,000	85,000
	----------	----------	----------
Net Operating Income	$160,000	$175,000	$15,000
	=======	=======	=======
F = Fixed V = Variable			

According to the above analysis, the differential revenue is $100,000 and the differential cost is $85,000,leaving a positive differential net operating income of $15,000 under the proposed marketing plan. The net operating income under the present distribution is $160,000, whereas the net operating income under door to door direct selling is estimated to be $175,000. Therefore the door to door direct distribution method is preferred, since it would result in $15,000 higher net operating income.

Note that we would have arrive at exactly the same conclusion by simply focusing on the differential revenue, differential cost, and differential net operating income, which also shows a net operating advantage of $15,000 for the direct selling method. The company can ignore other expenses of $60,000. Because it has no effect on the decision. If it were removed from the calculation, the door to door selling method would still be preferred by $15,000. This is an extremely important principle in management accounting.

Using Those Empty Seats

Many corporate jets fly with only one or two executives on board. Priscilla Blumwondered why some of the empty seats could not be used to fly cancer patients who specialized treatment outside their home area. Flying on a regular commercial airline can be an expensive and grueling experience for cancer patients. Taking the initiative, she helped found the Corporate Angle Network, an organization that arranges free flights on some 1,500 jets from over 500 companies. Since the jets fly anyway, filling a seat with cancer patient does not involve any significant incremental cost for the companies that donate the service. Since its founding in 1981, the Corporate Angel Network has arranged over 14,000 free flights.

OPPORTUNITY COST

Definition

Opportunity cost is the potential benefit that is given up when one alternative is selected over another. To illustrate this important concept, consider the following examples:

Example 1: Vicki has a part-time job that pays her $200 per week while attending college. She would like to spend a week at the beach during spring break, and her employer has agreed to give her the time off, but without pay. The $200 in lost wages would be an opportunity cost of taking week off to be at the beach.

Example 2: Suppose that Neiman Marcus is considering investing a large sum of money in land that may be a site for future store. Rather than invest the funds in land, the company could invest the funds in high-grade securities. If the land is acquired, the opportunity cost will be the investment income that could have been realized if the securities had been purchased instead.

Example 3: You are employed in a company that pays you $30,000 per year. You are thinking about leaving the company and returning to school. Since returning to school would require that you give up $30,000 salary. The forgone salary would be anopportunity cost of seeking further education.

Opportunity cost is not usually entered in the accounting records of an organization, but it is a cost that must be explicitly considered in every decision a manager makes. Virtually every alternative has some opportunity cost attached to it.

SUNK COST

Definition

A sunk cost is a cost that has already been incurred and that cannot be changed by any decision made now or in future.

Example: Sunk costs cannot be changed by any decision. These are not differential costsand should be ignored in decision making. To illustrate a *sunk cost,* assume that a company paid $50,000 several years ago for a special purpose machine. The machine was used to make a product that is now obsolete and is no longer being sold.

Even though in hindsight the purchase of the machine may have been unwise, no amount of regret can undo that decision. And it would be folly to continue making the obsolete product to recover the original cost of the machine. In short, the $50,000 originally paid for the machine has already been incurred and cannot be differential cost in any future decision. For this reason, such costs are said to be sunk costs and should be ignored in decision making.

4

Accounting and Integrity

INDEPENDENCE

Independence may be defined in a professional context as a state in which one is self-reliant and not easily influenced by others. Professionals rely upon their own expertise and judgment rather than opinions, biases, or emotions of other persons. Independence, as an ethical concept, is prominent in the accounting profession. Indeed, all professionals should be independent in that they should not subordinate their judgment to make a client happy.

Using some of the ethical concepts we have considered earlier, we may say that the professional should give no utilitarian weight to the happiness of the client. Some professionals, including accounting professionals, may succumb to this temptation. However, in the realm of public accounting, any consideration of the client's interests must be subordinated to a greater duty—the duty owed to third parties and to the public.

Let us consider the medical profession as an example of how utilitarian weight may be given to the well-being of the client as opposed to the happiness of the client. Suppose a patient comes to his doctor complaining of pain and requests a strong prescription painkiller by name. In the doctor's judgment the pain is illusory.

Moreover, she knows that the painkiller requested by the patient is potentially addictive. In her judgment the risks of prescribing such a medication far outweigh any benefits to the patient. She therefore ought to refuse to grant the request even if she knows that this will displease the patient and that he may choose another doctor.

The sort of independence illustrated by this case means independence from the expressed will of the client. Because a key tenet of the whole notion of professionalism is that the professional has greater experience, ability, or familiarity with a certain area than a client, the professional should not subordinate professional judgment to client desire as a matter of ethical principle.

As in all professions, this aspect of independence is a wellestablished ethical norm in public accounting. In every engagement, including engagements of tax services and consulting, the CPA must refuse to subordinate her professional judgment to the judgment of the client. Like the doctor/patient relationship, a primary concern here is that the client will receive the best professional advice and service the professional CPA can provide.

A danger does exist in emphasizing independence. The danger is creeping paternalism. In medicine the fear is that the doctor will not hear the real story since she, as a professional, already has the "answer." The same danger can and does exist with respect to the CPA and her client. Ultimately some degree of mutual respect must exist between professional and client.

INDEPENDENCE AND PUBLIC ACCOUNTING

Independence is a more fundamental and pervasive concept in accounting than in the other professions. Indeed, former Chief Justice Burger stated that independence is a critical concept that sets CPAs apart from other professions. This is true because the core mission of the CPA is as auditor, one who certifies the public reports that describe a corporation's financial status. This is the only exclusive function that the CPA performs for society.

In rendering an opinion the independent auditor assumes a public duty. Moreover, this public duty must transcend any employment relationship or other duty toward the client. The CPA has what Burger calls a "public watchdog" function that demands that the auditor subordinate responsibility toward the client in order to maintain complete fidelity to the public trust.

So important and ingrained is independence in the public accounting profession that it may be regarded as a cornerstone upon which much of the ethics peculiar to the profession is built. Note the radical change in focus when the accounting profession speaks of independence. The perceived peril in lack of independence is not to the client but to an outside third party. This third party may be any person who reads and relies upon the financial statements upon which the auditor has rendered an opinion.

We find that to serve the third party the auditor must take an unbiased viewpoint when he performs audit tests, evaluates the results of those tests, and then issues an audit report and opinion with respect to the financial statements. Traditionally accountants have viewed independence on three ethical planes. First, in order to take an unbiased viewpoint, an auditor must possess the virtues of honesty, objectivity, and responsibility. In other words, on this plane we are concerned with the character of the auditor. We may regard this as the highest form of independence.

At the second level independence refers to the relationship of the CPA and the client. Here independence means avoiding any relationship that would likely, even subconsciously, tend to impair the CPA's ability to take the unbiased viewpoint. The public accountant must avoid personal and business relationships with clients that could cause even the most well-meaning person to slip or compromise in professional judgment.

On the final level, independence means the CPA should avoid any relationship that might suggest to a reasonable observer that a conflict of interest exists. Even when the professional is completely satisfied that no relationship impairs her judgment as a professional, she has not gone far enough. She must concern herself with the jaundiced eye of the beholder. So, even is she is completely satisfied that she can render an impartial judgment or opinion for a client with whom she has a particular business relationship, the standards of the profession still might prohibit her from acting as independent auditor. In this respect we can compare the accounting profession with the legal profession, which demands of the judiciary that no appearance of impropriety exists.

We thus see that on two levels independence is a condition of the mind and character of the professional. On the third level the issue is not about the professional herself but the way others view her. The common expressions used in professional circles to describe these phenomena are independence in fact and independence in appearance.

INDEPENDENCE IN FACT

Independence in fact is one of the most elusive aspects of ethics in the accounting profession. Most public accountants are ready to assert that for the most part independence in fact is the norm in daily professional life. Yet they are at a loss to provide evidence for this assertion or even to explain why they believe it is true.

After all, it is difficult to discern the virtues necessary for independence in fact. Moreover, we have little basis to doubt the existence of independence in fact in a particular circumstance until the most dramatic of events, the audit failure, comes to light. An audit failure is said to occur when a CPA opines to third parties that a client's financial statements are fairly presented in accordance with generally accepted accounting principles when in fact they are not. Often the root of the audit failure is found to be a lack of independence in fact.

Some frequently cited examples of a lack of independence in fact include lacking objectivity and skepticism, accepting the work of management for something that normally requires independent verification, agreeing to a significant client-imposed restriction on the scope of the audit, or knowingly neglecting the critical evaluation of a significant client transaction. Failure to test the accounts receivable by independent confirmation would be a concrete example. Some people also believe incompetence is a manifestation of a lack of independence in fact. In each of these cases, the virtues required to render an unbiased opinion are missing. Independence is thus violated on its highest plane.

Another dimension of independence in fact originates in relationships with clients. The Securities and Exchange Commission, in Accounting Series

Release 234, has tightened the restrictions here. "The application of an independent viewpoint is particularly important with respect to judgements exercised in the determination of appropriate principles and methods applied to the recording, classification and presentation of financial data. By their nature such judgements cannot subsequently be evaluated on an impartial and objective basis by the same accountant who made them." In other words, the CPA cannot serve two masters: he cannot hold himself out to the public in a traditional auditor-client mode while at the same time serving that client as a controller, treasurer, or internal auditor. Neither can the CPA hold a direct financial or a material indirect financial interest in a client about whom he is rendering an opinion.

INDEPENDENCE IN APPEARANCE

Independence in fact exists when an auditor is actually able to maintain an unbiased attitude in the conduct of the audit. By contrast, independence in appearance refers to the interpretation or perception of others about the auditor's independence. Most of the value of the audit report stems from the independent status of the auditor. Therefore, if auditors are independent in fact, but readers of the financial statements or members of the public at large believe them to be advocates for the client, most of the value of the audit function would be lost. These users of financial information can have faith in an auditor's representations only when they are confident that the auditor has acted as an impartial judge.

The entire reason for a profession of public accounting rests upon the foundation of independence in appearance. Otherwise the audit function could be performed by internal auditors who work for the company. These men and women are honorable people who possess requisite virtue for performing audits. Moreover, organizational systems could be devised to protect them from management retaliation. It is therefore at least possible that they could be independent in fact.

Nevertheless, users would almost always have a lingering doubt about the statements' impartiality and freedom from bias. Readers might suspect that the auditors were really serving the best interests of the company for which they worked. In other words, the internal auditor would not appear independent.

Hence her representations would not have value to the user. An analogous phenomenon may be found in our government, where an independent prosecutor is appointed when a federal official, especially one in the Justice Department, is accused of a crime.

Concern about lack of independence in fact not only lowers the value of a particular audit report but also can have an adverse effect on the profession. Certified public accounts are given special status in society—the status of "professional"—because of the perceived role that they play in that society.

The role of the auditor is to give an unbiased opinion on reported financial information based upon professional judgment. If CPAs on the whole are not viewed as independent, the validity of the auditors' role in society is threatened.

The very credibility of the profession, public accounting, depends ultimately upon society's perception about independence rather than the fact of independence.

AREAS OF CONCERN

Four areas in particular are significant with respect to independence in appearance:

- The competition that now exists among audit firms;
- The increasing role of management advisory services offered by auditors;
- The large and growing size of audit firms; and
- The length of time an audit firm has been filling the audit needs of a given client. Each of these areas has the potential of weakening public perception about certified public accountants' independence.

The competition we observe today among auditors was brought about because of action of the Federal Trade Commission and a Supreme Court decision. Before these events CPAs kept themselves above the fray, so to speak. They seemed content with their existing client base and were constrained by the then existing code of ethics from doing much to change that base. This way of doing business, despite being declared illegal, at least gave the illusion of being "professional."

Today auditors conduct business in a more capitalistic fashion utilizing advertising, personal selling, and other advanced marketing techniques to capture as much of the audit market as they can. It is all perfectly legal and legitimate business activity, but somehow it does not seem as "professional." The lingering question in the mind of the outside observer is whether a professional might not be willing to sacrifice independence in order to gain business advantage in an unrestrained competitive environment. Notice that the primary problem here is the appearance rather than the fact of independence.

The role of CPAs as business consultants through their management advisory services creates a similar problem. This role of the auditor is admittedly an old one. Yet today it is increasingly important to the practice of public accounting because competition for audit clients has made audit service less profitable. Moreover, the profitability of these services has been followed by increased publicity concerning the activities of CPAs in the consulting area. This is compounded by the fact that CPA firms have expanded into more and more diverse areas of consulting. The problem once again is how the public perceives all of this. Can a person play this increasingly important role as an advisor to clients on how to conduct their businesses and at the same time give an unbiased opinion about the reported financial information? The profession strongly defends the position that by keeping auditing and consulting activities separate, independence is in fact maintained. Perhaps this is true. Yet the very fact that the question is raised means that independence in appearance is threatened.

A third problem with respect to independence in appearance arises due to the sheer size of the firms in which many certified public accountants practice. Increasingly the profession is being dominated by huge, multinational firms known as the Big Six. Ethically, there is nothing wrong here. But to the public these large firms are beginning to look more and more like big business. Therefore, these firms must be especially careful to guard against perceptions of a lack of independence.

A final factor that can erode independence in appearance is the length of time a particular client is served by a single auditor. In many cases an auditor-client relationship has stretched across decades. As time passes the client and the firm are increasingly identified with one another in the public eye. Again, the danger here is in appearance. The organizations may seem to be too close in the eye of the beholder even if the strictest measure of independence in fact is maintained.

Problems of credibility in each of the above cases almost always arise outside the profession. Therefore accountants must be constantly aware of the perception issue, which can have an adverse impact upon auditing firms and the direct and indirect users of their services. The issue is rarely concerned with the validity of negative perceptions, but rather the *belief* that users and society hold with respect to objectivity and freedom from bias.

THE CODE OF ETHICS

Concern about the issues of both independence in fact and independence in appearance is clearly reflected in the current Code of Professional Conduct of the American Institute of Certified Public Accountants (AICPA). Currently this code of ethics consists of two sections—

- The principles and
- The rules. The principles are designed to provide a framework for the rules. In turn the rules are designed to govern the performance of professional services by members of the AICPA.

We first encounter the concept of independence as a principle. Article IV, Objectivity and Independence, states: "A member should maintain objectivity and be free of conflicts of interest in discharging professional responsibilities. A member in practice should be independent in fact and appearance where providing auditing and other attestation services." Note that by making independence a principle, the AICPA formally raises independence to the level of a deontological construct of the profession.

Independence resembles a deontological principle rooted in one of Ross's prima facie duties: fidelity. By holding herself out as a certified public accountant, the auditor is making a faithful promise to the public when she signs an opinion on the client's financial statements. She is promising that her opinion is based upon her best professional judgment and is free from bias. In order to keep this promise she must maintain independence in fact.

With respect to its membership, the AICPA imposes stricter standards upon those who practice as public accountants. Those members must hold to the principle of independence in fact and to the principle of independence in appearance. Members who are not in public practice are required only to adhere to independence in fact. This recognizes that maintaining independence in appearance with one's employer is impossible.

The AICPA closely links independence with the auditor's ability to render an objective opinion based upon professional judgment. "Objectivity is a state of mind, a quality that lends value to a member's services. It is a distinguishing feature of the profession. The principle of objectivity imposes the obligation to be impartial, intellectually honest, and free from conflicts of interest. Independence precludes relationships that may appear to impair a member's objectivity in rendering attestation services.'' The AICPA rule on independence is a rather straightforward statement that a member in public practice shall be independent.

The AICPA believes the appearance of independence is so important that it gives a rather lengthy interpretation of the rule on independence: Independence shall be considered to be impaired if, for example, a member had any of the following transactions, interests, or relationships: During the period of a professional engagement or at the time of expressing an opinion, a member or a member's firmHad or was committed to acquire any direct or material indirect financial interest in the enterprise.

Was a trustee of any trust or executor or administrator of any estate if such trust or estate had or was committed to acquire any direct or material indirect financial interest of the enterprise.

Had any joint, closely held business investment with the enterprise or with any officer, director, or principal stockholders thereof that was material in relation to the member's net worth or the net worth of the member's firm.

Had any loan to or from the enterprise or any officer, director, or principal stockholder of the enterprise. This proscription does not apply to the following loans from a financial institution when made under normal lending procedures, terms, and requirements:

Loans obtained by a member or a member's firm that are not material in relation to the net worth of such borrower.

Home mortgages: Other secured loans, except loans guaranteed by a member's firm which are otherwise unsecured. During the period covered by the financial statements, during the period of the professional engagement, or at the time of expressing an opinion, a member or a member's firm Was connected with the enterprise as a promoter, underwriter or voting trustee, as a director or officer, or in any capacity equivalent to that of a member of management or of an employee. Was a trustee for any pension or profit-sharing trust of the enterprise. The above examples are not intended to be all-inclusive.

Financial Interest

Note the distinction made between direct and indirect financial interest. Direct financial interest refers to the ownership of stock in a client and applies to the CPA and members of his immediate family. Indirect financial interest occurs in two ways. One is where there is an intervening institution, such as when a CPA has interest in a mutual fund that in turn owns stock of the CPA's client. The other is when the ownership is by someone related to the CPA, but not in his immediate family, such as a grandparent.

The standard of materiality is applied only to indirect financial interest. Materiality, like beauty, exists in the eye of the beholder. This is quite appropriate for independence in appearance. Here materiality refers to the wealth of the CPA and to the amount of ownership. If a large portion of a CPA's personal wealth were invested in a mutual fund that in turn owned a large portion of that CPA's client, independence would be violated under the rules.

In the realm of financial interest, the AICPA holds that the rule on independence applies to all partners and shareholders for all clients of a particular CPA firm, not just the partner on the audit engagement. Non-partner CPAs who work for large auditing firms are not affected by the rule as long as they are not in the office doing the audit or involved in the audit in any other way. However, many of the large CPA firms hold their staff to a higher standard and do not permit anyone on the professional staff to own stock in any client of the firm.

Further Interpretations of the Rules

CPAs are prohibited from serving on the board of directors of a company, primarily because of independence in appearance considerations. The concern is that in these capacities the CPA is working too closely with the managers who make the decisions in a company. This proximity to the decision-making process could at least create the illusion that independence did not exist in the conduct of the audit. Exceptions to this rule are generally made when the partner of a CPA firm serves as an honorary member of a board of a charitable institution that the firm audits, so long as that partner does not participate in any management decisions.

Independence is generally considered lost when litigation arises between the CPA firm and the client. It does not seem reasonable to expect the professional to maintain objectivity in circumstances where she is either suing or being sued by the client. In cases where the CPA and the client are both being sued by a third party, independence is usually not deemed to have been impaired.

Sometimes a CPA is asked to perform bookkeeping services for the client. Is independence maintained if the same CPA conducts the audit? This role is allowed under strict guidelines where it is clear that the client assumes responsibility for the financial statements, that the CPA is not a client's employee or agent, and that generally accepted auditing standards are adhered to with respect to the sets of books that the CPA has maintained.

INDEPENDENCE AND MANAGEMENT ADVISOR

Concern about the potential conflict between a public accounting firm's role as auditor and business consultant to the same client is an old one. Almost twenty-five years. ago J. L. Carey and W. O. Doherty, in their book on ethics published by the AICPA, used two primary arguments to support the CPA's dual role. The first was that consulting fees were minor when compared with audit fees. Thus the CPA would be careful not to place the latter at risk. The second was a rejection of the notion that we should have two kinds of accountants-auditors and consultants.

Today both arguments hold no validity. The fees collected for management advisory services (MAS) work are now more profitable for many firms than fees for audit services. At the same time, because of the complexity of the MAS work done by large public accounting firms, the functions of audit and MAS are clearly segregated in most instances. With these developments in the profession, the controversy about the propriety of the same firm doing MAS work and issuing an opinion on financial reports is again on the front burner.

The distinction between independence in fact and independence in appearance must be kept in mind. Some theoretical research conducted by A. Goldman and B. Barlev yielded some rather surprising conclusions with respect to independence in fact. These researchers argued that the greater amount of power a party in a relationship has, the greater that party's actual independence. Furthermore, they concluded that the higher the proportion of non-routine problems dealt with by a professional, the more power he wields vis-à-vis the client. Moreover, the higher the proportion of services the professional renders directly to the paying client, the more important are these services to the client. Hence, the power of the professional is greater and the professional's degree of independence is enhanced.

The conclusions of these researchers fly in the face of both conventional wisdom about independence and the problem of independence in appearance. The former chief accountant of the Securities and Exchange Commission, John C. (Sandy) Burton, tends to verify these conclusions from his own experience.

Burton notes that supposed conflicts between MAS work and audit services are seldom buttressed by empirical data of either a systematic or anecdotal nature. In fact, Burton's experience indicates that too little involvement by auditors in the affairs of clients creates more problems than too much involvement.

We are left, then, with the independence in appearance problem facing the auditor. Here the perception in the eye of the beholder is the primary problem. Burton notes that it is critical to consider who the beholder is:

The basic question to be resolved in dealing with an appearance criterion is whether appearance should be examined on the basis of that which would be perceived by an informed person with knowledge of the facts or by a person with no understanding of the audit process or the relationships that conventionally exist. Most reported surveys of the perceptions of independence indicated that the greater the degree of knowledge about the profession and auditing, the less concern there is about threats to independence emerging from the scope of services performed. On the other hand, those without information or background of this sort are inclined to perceive a problem.

Thus we see that by its very nature independence creates a tension between fact and appearance. More MAS work may increase the CPAs independence in fact. Those with a high degree of understanding about auditing apparently appreciate this and are not concerned about conflicts of this sort. Yet, independence in appearance is a construct designed for the lay public, those who do not have a high degree of understanding about the audit process and independence in fact. It is for these people that the concept of independence in appearance was designed. Therefore the profession must take care to maintain the fact and the appearance of independence.

CURRENT ISSUES

One of the most troubling questions that may be asked about independence is whether a CPA may truly maintain independence in fact and appearance while accepting a fee from the client. Some critics have suggested that the solution to this dilemma is to have the government or some other public agency pay the auditor's fee.

Such suggestions have not met with great favour within the profession as a whole. Opinion shopping is another troublesome area. It is sometimes alleged that when a company is displeased with the professional judgment of the independent auditor, management has the option of finding an auditor whose professional judgment is more to management's liking. This allegation, if true, would obviously tempt the independence of the first auditor in the event of a difference of opinion. Moreover, the independence of the second audit firm can also be impaired if they accept an engagement based upon an opinion they discussed and once involved in the engagement they find the facts and circumstances to be different than originally represented by management. The AICPA has taken steps in its official auditing standards to attempt to protect auditors from a loss of independence in these circumstances.

One movement that has enhanced the independence of the auditing firm is the formation of audit committees made up of members of the corporation's board of directors. Ideally, these board members are outside directors who are not part of the company's management. The duties and powers of audit committees vary from company to company, but their objective is primarily to protect the independence of the outside auditor.

Audit committees are a requirement for listing on the major stock exchanges and over-the-counter markets. In addition, the Securities and Exchange Commission strongly encourages them. Some concern has been expressed that audit committees might create an anti-competitive effect in public accounting, but recent research has failed to support this allegation.

5

Strategic Cost Management

KNOWING CUSTOMERS' EXPECTATIONS

Providing a product or service that customers perceive as excellent requires a company to know what its customers expect. This is the most critical component of delivering excellent customer service. Virtually every company thinks it knows what its customers want. However, if a company is only slightly inaccurate about its assumptions, it could lose its customers' business to another company that has more accurately filled their needs. Being only "slightly" inaccurate can lead an organization to spend money, time, and effort on things that are not important to customers. And in a worst-case scenario, it can mean not surviving in an intensely competitive environment.

EXPECTATION GAP

At times a gap occurs between what customers expect and what management presumes they expect. This often happens because companies overlook or do not fully understand customers' perceptions and expectations. In spite of a strong commitment and sincere desire to provide quality service, many companies fall dramatically short of the mark, usually because they have an internally directed rather than externally directed focus. An internally directed focus assumes that the company knows what customers should want and delivers or produces that. This orientation often leads to providing products and services that do not match customers' expectations- important features and benefits may be left out and levels of performance may be inadequate. In looking at several different types of organizations, common elements contribute to the gap between customer expectations and the product or service offered.

The common elements are:

- Inadequate "bilateral" communication between front-line personnel and management.
- An absence of regular interaction between management and customers.
- An absence of a strong market research programme.
- An absence of customer service accountability.

COMMUNICATING WITH FRONT-LINE EMPLOYEES

Front-line employees are in regular contact with customers. As a result, they know a great deal about customers' perceptions and expectations. This information must be regularly passed on to management. When channels of communication are closed or inadequate, managers cannot know about problems occurring in product and service delivery as well as critical information about changing customer expectations.

Communication between front-line employees and management can be enhanced in a number of ways:

- Formal types of communication (*e.g.*, memos, suggestion cards, and open meetings).
- Informal communication (*e.g.*, discussions over coffee, walking around the facility, going out into the field).

It is essential to assess customers' perceptions and expectations regularly, but it is also very important to assess whether managers understand the needs and expectations of front-line employees. Managers who communicate with front-line people not only build morale but also learn a tremendous amount about their customers, thereby reducing the expectation gap.

Some questions to ask concerning the communication between management and front-line employees in an organization are:

- How often do managers have direct contact with front-line employees?
- Do managers encourage suggestions from front-line employees concerning the quality of products or services?
- Are there too many levels of management, causing managers to be cut off from direct contact with and feedback from front-line employees?
- Are there formal or informal opportunities for front-line employees to communicate with management on a regular basis?
- Has management adequately determined and monitored the expectations of front-line employees?
- Do front-line employees feel strongly supported?

INTERACTION BETWEEN MANAGEMENT AND CUSTOMERS

The larger a company is, the more difficult it is for managers to deal directly with customers. Consequently, managers have less information about customers' perceptions and expectations. However, in smaller companies, managers can receive more direct information concerning their customers.

Even when they are regularly given reports, managers readily lose the customer perspective if they do not have the opportunity for direct customer contact. Theoretical knowledge is a poor substitute for a face-to-face encounter. To truly understand and appreciate customers' needs and expectations, managers should experience firsthand what really happens in the field—in stores or on the customer- service line—by answering the service line themselves or dealing with customers face to face. Managers can better empathize with employees if they have experienced some of what employees deal with on a regular basis.

Here are some questions to consider concerning regular interaction between management and customers:

- Does the company have a programme in which managers rotate to different service positions within the organization?
- Does top management make it a priority to get out in the field and see customers?
- Do managers randomly interact with customers (*e.g.*, those waiting in line, browsing in the store, or calling the service desk)?

NEED FOR A STRONG MARKET RESEARCH PROGRAMME

Because marketing research is an important tool in assessing customers' perceptions and expectations, a company that fails to regularly collect such information may be more likely to have a significant customer expectation gap. To effectively deal with expectation versus performance issues, marketing research measurements should focus on product or service quality issues.

These might include:

- Which features and benefits are most important to customers?
- How much do customers expect, at what price and in what time frame?
- What do customers think the company should do if problems occur in product or service delivery?

  Determining what customers expect is essential to providing superior quality. Regardless of a company's size and resources, there are ways to obtain this kind of information.

Questions to consider concerning a company's marketing research efforts include:

- Are research findings shared throughout the company when appropriate?
- Are the research findings integral to the company's strategic planning?
- Can research findings be readily understood and used by managers?
- Does research focus on quality of service provided?
- Is research conducted on a regular basis to generate high-quality, reliable information about what customers want and expect?

CUSTOMER-SERVICE ACCOUNT ABILITY

Policies and procedures are important, but when they impede a firm's ability to meet customer needs, they are counterproductive.With many companies experiencing an increase in policies and procedures over the last several years, initiative has been stifled and employees are less willing to get involved.

For companies to compete effectively in an increasingly competitive marketplace, employees must be enabled to identify problems, resolve them, and share suggestions with management. They should not be allowed to withdraw into a bureaucratic environment and assume that someone else will take care of problems. All the while, customers may be migrating elsewhere.

The following list provides questions to ask regarding customer service accountability:

- Are employees encouraged to "take ownership" of a problem, and are they supported in their efforts?
- Is the business unduly bureaucratic, and does it encourage an attitude of "someone else will take care of it"?
- Does the business empower its employees to find ways in which customers can be better served?

Any organization, regardless of size, can reduce customer expectation gaps if it improves communication between managers and front-line employees, increases interaction between management and customers, develops a strong market research programme, and insists on accountability for customer service.

KEEPING CUSTOMERS

Customer retention is one of the most important strategic issues companies have faced in recent years. Retention is critical for increasing profits and remaining competitive. Studies show that a 5 per cent change in the rate of customer retention can shift profits from 25 per cent to 100 per cent in either direction. In manufacturing, measuring the number of defects is an important index of quality. In measuring service, the number of defections (customers going elsewhere) is important. Many companies underestimate the cost of customer defections. Few companies track defections (otherwise known as migration) or invest in reducing them. Companies should measure customer migration, and their goal should be customer retention. They must regularly evaluate and modify training programmes, information systems, organizational structure, complaint handling procedures, hiring objectives, incentives, and even the company culture. Providing superior customer service is an effective strategy for increasing customer retention, which can lead to an increase in profits, because customers will beat a path to the company that provides superior customer service.

HIGH COST OF MIGRATION

Failure to realise the high cost of losing customers stems in part from aggressive selling and marketing. In many companies, the work involved in keeping customers is seen as dull and tedious. Selling is what is truly exciting. Many companies view unhappy customers as chronic complainers who are not worth the effort required to satisfy them. It is true that some customers are habitual complainers, but too often companies apply this label to every customer who complains. If this attitude permeates a company, dissatisfied customers will probably receive poor treatment and their problems will remain unaddressed. Prospective and first-time customers usually are treated well during the selling courtship. Many companies aggressively pursue new customers, but these customers go right out the door if service is poor. They come in with great expectations but leave with disappointment, frustration, and possibly resentment.

MARKETING: A TWO-PART PROCESS

The marketing function should be viewed as a two part process:

1. Getting customers.
2. Retaining customers.

The first part of the marketing process rarely has inadequate resources and seldom suffers from a lack of attention. Sales budgets, advertising campaigns, and promotional efforts usually take a significant percentage of a company's operating budget. However, retention marketing often has little or no budget at all.Research shows that, depending on the specific industry, it costs between five and seven times as much to get a new customer as it does to keep an existing one. Most companies have little difficulty defending the significant costs of acquiring new customers. But what if the new customers are only replacements for dissatisfied customers?

Such companies find themselves barely holding on to customers, or worse, they experience a net loss of customers. Companies that do strive to retain customers have return policies, customer complaint departments, and occasional customer mailings. But few companies engage in aggressive, well-constructed strategies of retentionoriented marketing that keep customers happy and mend relations with dissatisfied customers.

MOMENT OF TRUTH

Every point of contact a customer has with a company (whether by phone, in person, or by mail) is a point at which service is delivered—or not delivered. It is a point at which the customer forms one more impression and makes one more judgment about the company. Some call it the "moment of truth." Nordstrom's, a department store, operates by the following maxim: "Listen to the customer; the customer is always right. Do anything to satisfy the customer." Every time a company fails to live up to a promise to its customers, it loses some credibility.

Advertising, public relations, architectural design, and other high-profile efforts may create favourable impressions. But the critical difference in customer retention usually occurs in less glamorous areas. For example, customers may be impressed by the behaviour and appearance of employees, the way phones are answered, the clarity and accuracy of billings, or the overall promptness and reliability in handling complaints. "Little things" are important, and companies must be vigilant and consistent in their attention to detail. Such vigilance may require redefining the role of marketing, rearranging priorities, and reallocating budgets.

OBSTACLES TO SUPERIOR CUSTOMER SERVICE

There are several obstacles to customer service that at one time or another affect most businesses.

Attitude that Custmor are Replaceable

The days of monopolistic enterprises and taking customers for granted have long since passed away. Customers should be considered valuable assets that are obtained only through hard work and at considerable expense. Although employees are often relieved when disgruntled customers leave, this is an unfortunate attitude for any employee or business to have.

Insensitive Managers

The old expression that "no two people are alike" applies to both employees and customers. Problems develop when managers become insensitive to the characteristics or behaviour of their employees and customers. Managing the human element is a considerable challenge in providing superior customer service. Managers must continuously respond to changing situations. They must be able to make instantaneous decisions in an environment in which education, experience, skills, perceptions, values, and prejudices have a direct impact on transactions with employees and customers. Other concerns-such as divorce, financial trouble, or sick children-also affect employee-customer transactions. Given these human idiosyncrasies, companies must monitor, train, motivate, evaluate, and periodically retrain employees so that they are empowered to be of assistance to customers.

Budgetary Problems

Some companies do not properly fund efforts to improve customer service. As a result, they end up with inconsistent customer-service strategies and poor implementation of programmes to improve customer service. In a highly competitive economy, budgetary constraints can drive away frustrated customers who may be told, for example, that there are not enough qualified people, or that there simply are not enough people to catch up on back orders. In many companies, the financial resources required to meet customer needs exist, but they are allocated elsewhere. Insufficient funding inherently devalues the importance of customer service in the minds of frontline employees.

Lake of Strong Commitment

In many cases, management lacks a strong commitment to superior customer service. Managers may claim to have a strong commitment, but in reality they pay only lip service to customer service. Unless management undertakes a full-scale effort and requires an intense commitment to superior customer service throughout the organization, the prospects of achieving superior customer service are seriously diminished.

Inconsistecy

Customers usually measure a product or service by the satisfaction they expect and subsequently receive. If a customer is sold a product or service that fails to live up to its promises, dissatisfaction is the result. Customers who are oversold or promised undeliverable levels of satisfaction usually forget the salesperson and concentrate instead on the product or service involved and the company behind it. Thus, companies must strive for consistency in the delivery of products and services, in representations made about product and service characteristics, and in the professionalism of all employees who deal with customers.

Lack of Listening

Managers are typically concerned with the big picture, so they seldom have the time to get out and really listen to what customers need and think. Many managers are comfortable believing that if customers are not complaining, things must be going all right. But this can be a dangerous assumption. Managers must be available to both employees and customers. They must observe and listen purposefully and systematically. Most important, they must be open to discussion: They should not be defensive, closed-minded, or apprehensive about being proved incorrect.

Inertia

Computer systems, policy guides, and procedures often take on a life of their own in many companies. Customers usually feel frustrated when they are told, "I'm sorry, but our policy is...," or "There is nothing I can do about it." In some companies, the computer systems are often handy excuses for mistakes. Although computer systems, policies, and procedures are important, they can stifle a company's primary mission—to sell and serve customers—if they are not kept in check. Companies that excel in providing superior customer service focus on the customer and strive diligently not to allow "the system" to interfere with what is best for the customer.

Different Frames of Reference

Words frequently used to describe customer service include "prompt," "reliable," "satisfaction," "courtesy," "professional," "timely," and "quality," along with such phrases as "quick response to customer complaints," "accuracy in billing,""prompt repairs,"and "satisfaction guaranteed."For these words and phrases to have relevance, specific definitions, measurements, or other explicitly stated standards have to exist. For example, "quick response to customer complaints" might be defined to mean "within 24 hours,"whereas "accuracy in billing" might mean that if errors are identified within seven days of receipt, a correction will be made.When definitions are clearly understood from the start, a company and its customers will have a common denominator for measuring the quality of service.

Lack of Perspective

Providing high-quality customer service is not a programme that can be bought and paid for in a short time. High-quality customer service cannot be effectively implemented and sustained through memos, short-lived promotional efforts, or advertising campaigns designed to boost sales.

Management must view high-quality customer service as an ongoing process. The "tyranny of the urgent" often prevents managers from taking steps that will keep customers the company worked so hard to get.

HOW TO INCREASE CUSTOMER RETENTION

Just as there are frequently encountered obstacles to superior customer service, there are also several suggested ways to help a company successfully retain as many of your customers as possible.

Reliability

Customers want consistent performance most of all.

To be reliable, a company should strive for the following:

- Do what you say you are going to do.
- Do it when you say you will.
- Do it right the first time.

Credibility

Customers will go back to businesses that want to help them and have their best interests in mind. Customers do not want hidden agendas, fine print, hardsell tactics, or extra charges. They want the products or services they buy to be free of danger, risk, and doubt.

Responsiveness

We live in a time of instant gratification. When customers want service, they usually want it immediately. Being responsive requires being available, accessible, and willing to help customers whenever they have a problem.

Empathy

Being empathetic means putting oneself in the position of a customer. Management must ask itself whether it would do business with the company. Every customer is unique and wants to be treated uniquely. To accomplish this, companies must ask the right questions, listen intently, and then design products or services to meet stated needs.

Select Front-Line Employees Carefully

Companies oriented towards customer service should have customer-friendly people in front-line positions. Such positions are not for everybody. Great care should be exercised in selecting prospective employees based on their personality traits and other skills.

A psychological consulting firm has singled out the following attributes as especially helpful for employees in front-line positions:

- An ability to make sound judgments in a stressful setting.
- A problem-solving orientation.
- A desire to be liked.
- A naturally optimistic outlook.

Provide Sufficient Employee Training

Customers want to be served by knowledgeable employees. Thus, employees should be well trained before interacting with customers. Employee training should not be viewed as a one-time entrance requirement. Regular training sessions are needed to keep employees updated on new policies and procedures, new product features and benefits, competition, customer needs, new programmes, developments in other parts of the company, and core corporate goals.

Create a Sense of Belonging

Employees also need a sense of their company's mission and their role within the company. They need to receive encouragement to enhance their roles while also receiving recognition for contributions made. Regardless of the methods used by different companies, employee recognition is an important motivator and a fundamental tool for nurturing an environment committed to customer service.

Avoid Premature Release of Products, Concepts, or Policies

Taking a new product or service to market before it is ready, changing policies rapidly, or introducing a new computer system before all the bugs are worked out erode customer satisfaction levels. Companies must take great care not to sacrifice customers while trying to achieve progress. Customers want consistency and stability.

Make Things Easy for the Customer

Making things easy for the customer requires careful planning, coordination, and diligence. When companies do not work at these fundamentals, customer service *can* suffer.

Following are ways to make things easier for customers:

- Install a toll-free number.
- Provide adequate incoming phone lines.
- Hire enough employees to answer phones quickly.
- Use business-reply mail (postage-paid).
- Implement easy refund and exchange procedures.
- Provide prompt and accurate information.
- Do not assume that the customers have extensive knowledge about a product or service.
- Speak and write in plain English. Do not use highly technical terms or company jargon.
- Debrief customers who leave the company for competitors.

If a Customer Leaves, Ask Why

Whenever the company loses a customer, find out why. Few customers are more honest or candid than a dissatisfied customer.

INVESTING RESOURCES IN THE RIGHT PLACES

It is important that companies regularly assess their competitive positions. Such an assessment can help identify strengths and weaknesses vis-a-vis the competition, thereby enabling companies to focus on their strengths and eliminate weaknesses. Few companies can effectively compete against all competitors on all fronts simultaneously. It is important, therefore, to identify key strategic points of difference so that a company can allocate its finite resources optimally.

The key areas to evaluate include:

- Markets
- Customers and the products or services offered to them
- Personnel
- Operations, facilities, and technology
- Finances

To be valuable in the marketplace, companies must maximize the return on available and invested capital. They must regularly evaluate their allocation of resources to different areas.

MARKETS

Many companies make decisions about critical components of their operations as if they were in a vacuum: They show little sensitivity to, or awareness of, what other companies are doing in the market.

To be effective, they should be asking questions such as:

- What are the trends in the market?
- In which direction is the market headed?
- What do the customers want (versus what they need)?
- Is the company aware of the difference?
- What is the size of other competitors in the market?

To have strategic significance, terms or units of measure should be used that enable companies to compare themselves to competitors. Statistics regarding the number of employees or customers a competitor has may have a marketing impact. Other information- such as the amount of capital invested, asset base, profits, inventory levels, the number of inventory turns, the number of support personnel, and the number of sales representatives-can help a company determine the investment required to compete effectively and identify areas that may not be well served.

CUSTOMERS AND PRODUCTS OR SERVICES OFFERED

Why does a company offer the products or services it offers? Is there a rational process in place by which new products or services are added or deleted from a company's portfolio? Is there a threshold of revenue generation below which a product or service will no longer be carried or offered?

Too often companies offer products or services that management feels should be offered, or they continue to offer the products or services that they have historically offered, as opposed to what the market dictates.however, companies should periodically assess their offerings and determine whether customers and potential customers are aware of all the products or services in their portfolios. Not long ago, a large, well-known law firm disclosed in a meeting that it had budgeted a significant sum towards practice development. Before launching the development campaign, the firm performed an assessment on existing clients to determine their awareness of the services offered.

Much to the chagrin of the firm's partners, almost two-thirds of the clients used more than one law firm for their legal work. Further analysis revealed that none of those clients used other law firms because of dissatisfaction but, rather, because they did not realise all the other services available from the firm. Thus, the law firm realised that one of its biggest challenges was to increase the awareness of existing clients before spending significant funds on pursuing new clients.

In another case, a company offered 12 different kinds of services to its customers. Upon careful objective analysis of customer input, the company determined that the customers really had a viable interest in only 7 of the 12 services.

At that point, the company had a choice to make: to pursue additional customers that may have an interest in the other services or drop the other services and the costs associated with offering them.

The key point in these examples is that by getting objective information from customers, both organizations could make decisions that enabled them to allocate re- sources where they could generate the greatest return.without this information, both organizations would have continued operating in a manner that presumed business as usual and thus consumed resources inefficiently. A well-designed customer questionnaire can prove helpful in determining the awareness, utilization, and interest levels of customers.

OPERATIONS, FACILITIES, AND TECHNOLOGY

Companies should periodically assess competitive

OPERATIONS, FACILITIES, AND TECHNOLOGY

Companies should periodically assess competitive strategies utilized in terms of operations, facilities, and technology. Information concerning competitors in these key areas can provide important insight regarding their strategic direction.

It is particularly helpful to consider how competitors compare in the following areas:

- Locations of branch offices, field offices, and the types of buildings used.
- Creative channels of distribution used.
- Databases, communication networks, and computers employed.
- Technology used downstream with customers, branch offices, field offices, and sales representatives.
- Facility management, overall appearance, and the integration of other offices or facilities.

Because many companies must increasingly compete based on how they allocate scarce capital, a company's ability to profitably compete will increasingly depend on the proper deployment and utilization of operational capabilities, facilities management, and technology. Customer input is a critically important tool in assessing these areas.

FINANCIAL ALLOCATION DECISIONS

Customer satisfaction information is helpful in allocating the financing and operating responsibilities needed to manage a company. Financing responsibilities pertain to how a company obtains the capital needed to provide for assets. Operating responsibilities relate to how a company uses those assets once they have been obtained.

Return on Total Assets

One tool that is helpful in making financial allocation decisions is a calculation of the return on total assets. The formula for return on total assets can be used in assessing a product or service, overall financial performance, or the re- turn on an individual customer. It is a measure of how well assets are utilized—that is, a measure of operating performance.

Cost-Benefit Analysis

Another financial measurement, cost-benefit analysis, can prove helpful in allocating a company's financial resources. By carefully measuring specific levels of customer satisfaction on a product-by-product or service-by-service basis, a company can analyse how each element is faring from a customer's perspective.

Break-Even Analysis

Break-even analysis is a tool that helps a company assess whether it should continue providing a particular product or service. Simply defined, the break-even point occurs when total sales revenue equals total expenses. Break-even analysis helps a company determine whether to go forward in launching a new product or service or to continue offering an existing product or service. The calculated break-even point, determines how many units (*e.g.*, Products, services, engagements, memberships, patients, or clients) must be successfully engaged for a company at least to cover its costs.while reviewing the numbers derived from a break-even analysis to assess the reasonableness or probability of attaining a particular profit level, a company can factor in valuable customer-based information gleaned from an assessment of awareness, utilization, and interest to aid in the process of determining whether such levels are also realistic in light of customer satisfaction.

PLANNING FOR THE FUTURE

Planning for the future requires a thorough and realistic understanding of existing products, services, markets, margins, profits, return on allocated capital, and availability and skills of employees. When contemplating a company's specific mission, management must have a clear understanding of how well the company is doing today. As has been demonstrated, customer input and assessment of satisfaction can play an enormously important role in setting objectives.

PRUDENT PLANNING

Prudent planning helps a company, regardless of its size, focus on where it wants to be three to five years in the future. Too often, managers are focused only on short-term needs and prospects, largely because of their immediacy. As a result, long-term problems and opportunities are deferred or given only slight attention. Management must distinguish between current operating challenges and longer-term goals and plans. Some executives search for ways to increase the size, efficiency, and profitability of their company's operations. But if the forecasted performance of existing operations fails to produce expectations of profitable growth, many of them build on the operations that presently exist and accept the status quo.

STRATEGIC PLANNING

Some executives are not satisfied with nominal growth rates into the future. Empowered with well-founded, customer-based information (*e.g.*, measures of customer satisfaction; information about awareness and utilization of products and services; customer wants, needs, expectations; perceived strengths and weaknesses; and suggestions for improvement), they stretch the forecasts and establish new and challenging standards of performance for the future. Increasingly, companies realise the importance of strategic planning. Several large companies go to the extreme of considering a range of plans that cover simultaneous possibilities across a wide set of assumptions.

However, this involved approach usually requires a highly structured strategic planning process and a large planning staff. Although this type of intensive approach has considerable benefits, few companies can afford such a commitment. Smaller companies or larger companies without extensive strategic planning resources can use a simplified approach more effectively. The underlying assumption with this approach is that a person or group can only commit parttime efforts to the strategic planning process.

CALL TO ACTION

A management consultant recently wrote, "Future historians may well describe the 1980s and possibly the 1990s as the era of customer sovereignty. Perhaps 'customer rebellion' is more accurate."1 To a large extent, which organizations will prosper in today's economy will depend on which organizations recognize the "customer rebellion" and make the preparations necessary to provide superior customer service. Every organization must vigorously assess the status and quality of its relationships with both external customers (existing, potential, and past) and internal customers (employees).Where do we stand? What do we need to improve? How can we improve?

In doing so, remember the following points:

- Customers, potential customers, and former customers perceive value in their own terms. If an organization wants to meet their needs, it must always look at products and services from their perspective.
- Customers, potential customers, and former customers think that an organization's reason for being in business is to meet their needs.
- If an organization sincerely desires to deal successfully with dissatisfied customers, employees must be empowered to focus on saving the customer, not the sale.
- An organization must strive to provide dissatisfied customers with a positive reason for dealing with the organization again.
- In all likelihood, an organization's employees will not treat customers or potential customers any better than they themselves are treated by the organization.
- Input from customers, potential customers, or past customers is

invaluable. An organization should actively seek, appreciate, and review this input.

- The entire process by which an organization creates and delivers its products and services should exhibit superior customer service and support the creation of high levels of customer satisfaction.

Regardless of the size of an organization, it is increasingly difficult to compete primarily on the basis of price or product. In many cases, product differentiation is imperceptible. Thus, in the burgeoning battle for the customer, the key is usually not product superiority (or at least not for long) but service. The quality of service provided has rapidly become the standard by which organizations are judged. Thus, customer satisfaction— and continual improvement in customer satisfaction—has become a primary indication of sustainability.

In a world of increasing complexity and automation, the successful organization must find the means by which it can operate efficiently and profitably while maintaining a commitment to manage with integrity, compassion, intelligence, competitiveness, and an unwavering commitment to providing superior customer service and generating high levels of customer satisfaction. Although not on the balance sheet, customers are the greatest asset that any organization has. They need to be treated as treasured, longterm investments that, if properly nurtured and cultivated, will provide significant dividends.

How does a company know how it is doing with its customers, its prospective customers, and its employees? Are they satisfied? Do they perceive that the company has a strong commitment to providing superior service? The only way to know for certain is to ask—candidly, objectively, and following a good methodology. As Yogi Berra said so well, "The only way to begin is to begin." Regardless of the type or size of an organization, management can seize the competitive advantage, provide superior customer service, and build high levels of customer satisfaction.

6

Total Cost Management

INTRODUCTION

To sustain long-term profitability, corporate managers must consider environmental policy as an essential component of corporate strategy for achieving and maintaining competitive superiority. In response to increasing public concern for environmental issues, recent court decisions and more aggressive legislation and regulatory policies have greatly expanded corporations' potential liability.

Thus, corporations need to reconsider their environmental efforts and to proactively manage, rather than react to, environmental problems. Total cost management (TCM) is a business paradigm for managing all company resources and the activities that consume those resources with a focus on stimulating and managing changes. Under the TCM paradigm, companies can consider the entire environmental impact of their products by looking for substitutes for inputs that are hazardous and for processes that can reduce the generation of waste.

TCM offers a systematic approach to continuously improve operations and reduce waste generation throughout the product life cycle. Firms will find such integration desirable to reduce costs, reduce liability, and minimize adverse community concerns over their operations.

BACKGROUND

The extant literature indicates that cost management systems of world-class manufacturers play a unique role. The focal point of such systems is to provide needed support for company-wide strategic planning and revitalization. Advanced manufacturers must adopt an integrated cost planning approach with their market-based strategic product development. World-class manufacturers perform extensive cost planning to manage costs through cost reduction at the product design and development stage.

The fact that most cost decisions are made prior to production in the engineering design, prototype and vendor sourcing stages is the basis for this emphasis. This is the stage where many decisions are made that will eventually determine environmental costs. Cost planning activities generally involve value engineering and target costing analyses. Value engineering examines the functions that products are to perform and then evaluates those functions with respect to customer demands and function costs. Value engineering goes beyond the analysis of production costs and includes the analysis of a product's entire life-cycle to determine the cost implications of design and product development decisions in a particular product.

In addition, target cost analysis is often used to gather information and to foster commitment from all departments involved. Each new product, or major revision of an existing product, will be developed based on cross-functional input from sales and marketing, engineering design, engineering production, and cost management. The formal target cost is jointly determined by all functions involved which is set between the allowable cost based on customers' expectation and the potential cost based on the current technology and production methods.

As a result, the purposes of designating target costs are to encourage cost reduction and control and to achieve the corporation's strategic goals. In addition, target costing supports activity-based costing to develop the cost of quality data that promote quality being designed into products. To meet the challenge of environmental conservation and waste management, world class manufacturers must include environment policies into their strategically oriented, integrated systems. Studies of technologically intensive companies have shown that the key to achieving a sustainable competitive advantage is sound management of technological innovation. Technological innovation programmes should be an element of a company's overall business strategy and unite activities in all functional areas including R&D, product design, process design, manufacturing, marketing and environmental preservation.

TCM creates the environment for cross-disciplinary cooperation and manages the process towards innovation and environmental preservation. In addition, TCM provides tools to incorporate changes in the views of business ethics and social responsibility.

TOTAL COST MANAGEMENT APPROACH TO SUSTAINABILITY

TCM does not accept costs as "given" but instead as a point of reference upon which to constantly improve. The tools of environmental economics continue to remain useful, but they must be viewed as guides for improvement. Environmental economics is justifiably concerned with the externalities created by the divergence in private costs and social costs. TCM is more normative in viewing more of these costs as part of private costs.

At the firm level, economic analysis focuses on the adjustment towards equality between the marginal private cost of control and the marginal cost (damage) to the firm. TCM is focused on learning to become more efficient in preventing pollution instead of correcting pollution, thereby shifting the marginal cost of control downward. TCM is also focused on recognizing that more cost "should" and will be borne by the firm, thus shifting the marginal damage upward.

Combining these two directional shifts will continually move the firm towards (but not necessary to) zero pollution. Based on the target costing process outlined by Cooper and Slagmulder (1997), TCM offers the following features that promote the development of innovative environmentally friendly products. Establish.

MARKET-BASED PRICING

It has always been a risky and challenging task to develop profitable new products as companies face ever-increasing competition. The development of innovative, environmentally friendly products would pose even more uncertainties because their market prospects are largely unknown. Target costing is driven by market price and desired profits and thus, creates the critical alignment between the innovative products with the marketplace.

TCM demands a highly disciplined process based on thorough market analysis of what customers want and what price they are willing to pay. In support of launching an innovative product its target price cannot be established in a vacuum but needs to be determined by external market factors, in particular, the strength of the new product compared to competitive offerings and market prices for comparable products. For the innovative environmentally friendly products, customers can be expected to pay more for them because these products offer more perceived value than their existing peers do.

Research has shown that thirty per cent of customers will pay up to 20 per cent extra for the environmentally friendly products and many products (*e.g.*, Green Vista, Eco-sport, Green Tag, green electricity) have commanded such price premiums. TCM helps firms to better understand the availability of competitive products and their perceived values and to ensure the most realistic possible selling prices of the environmentally friendly products.

B2B E-COMMERCE

The recent development of Internet and e-commerce open up many new opportunities for more free flow of information between suppliers of innovative products and their potential customers. The Internet enables the seamless flow of information through a web-based platform that links customers, suppliers, and contents for the benefits of all the partners participate in the supply chain. It provides the registered users the opportunities of conducting market analysis by interacting with those operators, technicians, engineers, and business executives who are active or have an interest in improving operations involving solid-waste handling and disposal.

The Solid Waste site also offers B2B features such as "Request for Quote" (RFQ) that allow a firm to create responses online, track and manage responses and requests (invitations to quote, submit quotes, acceptances, rejections, etc.), and correspond online with potential buyers. Industry-based independent web sites offer competitive products' market price information. Online business-to-business e-commerce platforms and makes it easier for a firm to determine the customer perceived value and, thus, help them to determine the new product's target price.

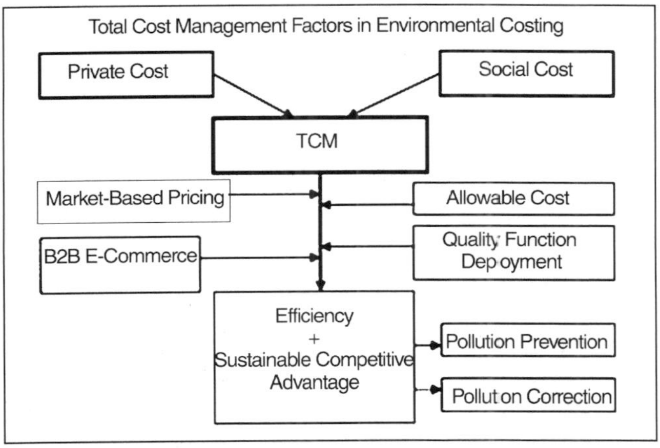

Fig. Total cost Management Factor in Envvironment Costing

DETERMINE THE ALLOWABLE COSTS

The market-based target prices of the new products determined above become the driving force of new product design because:

Allowable cost = Target price – Target profit margin

The target margin is established to ensure achievement of the company's long-term profitability. Since the allowable cost is derived from external conditions, the risk is that the allowable cost will not be achievable with the existing product design and production facilities. In order to achieve allowable cost, an interactive process using the cost tables and quality function deployment (QFD) will be used and continuously updated to reflect the current and alternative materials and engineering methods. The cost tables contain detailed estimates of the costs of various parts or activities depending on the materials, manufacturing methods and functions involved.

Quality function deployment is typically used for systematically analyzing the product features, component functions and customer preferences in a matrix format. Both cost tables and QFD are used to formulate a value index to direct the new product's value engineering activities to achieve the target costs. An example of constructing high-density textile particle boards for furniture application from recycled textile waste is used to demonstrate how QFD can direct value engineering activities to reduce the total product costs. In the example the QFD matrix also is used to aid in the evaluation of the original target market.

QFD OF HIGH-DENSITY TEXTILE PARTICLE BOARD FOR FURNITURE APPLICATION FROM RECYCLED TEXTILE WASTE

The idea of evaluating the possibility of manufacturing high-density particleboard from recycled textile waste had two drivers. On the one side the manufacture of particleboard from wood chips requires the use of adhesives that contain toxins. On the other side the textile industry has long tried to recycle its waste material. In most cases it makes economic sense, but in some cases it is not possible and alternative uses have to be found. When alternative uses are not found, the waste material typically ends up on landfills, and synthetic materials do not decompose for a very long time.

Within the scope of TCM, the waste cost to the textile industry includes the cost of the wasted raw material including all processing cost up to the manufacturing step where the waste is generated and the disposal cost of land-filling the waste materials. The potential costs to wooden particleboard manufacturers for health hazards due to the release of formaldehyde is harder to determine. The case study concentrates on target costing concepts that are used in the product development steps for synthetic particleboard.

While a marketable product has not yet been produced, the results of the target costing analysis lead to implications in the manufacturing process as well as the marketing of the boards. Following the process of target costing as described by the Consortium for Advanced Manufacturing International, a target price was established through market research and competitive analysis of wooden particleboard. The specific market niche was determined as outdoor construction panels because of the superior water resistance of synthetic materials. Tests had shown that the synthetic samples absorbed extremely low amounts of water, and therefore no deterioration of the product was to be expected.

Customer requirements were determined through testing standards and discussions with building contractors. The price range for the particleboard in the market at the time of the study ranged from $11.59 to $16.05 for a 4 by 8 feet panel (5/8-inch thickness). 4-Layer plywood (stronger and better aesthetics, just as to the contractors) sold for $17.47 to $18.74. The Quality Function Deployment matrix (QFD matrix) links the customer requirements systematically with product components or functions. At the same time the customer requirements are ranked by relevance or importance, and the own product can be compared with competitor rankings as to how well the requirements are being fulfilled.

The customer requirement rankings for the requirements that were discussed with the potential users of the synthetic particleboard. The Relative

Rankings show how much each of the requirements contributes to the overall requirements a potential customer has for the product.

These rankings serve as a guide in product development, showing which needs ought to be addressed with how much effort. The competitive ranking is based on some discussions with building contractors and to a large extent on the testing results that were performed on manufactured synthetic samples and on purchased wooden samples. The results are somewhat theoretical because the man ufactured samples were small lab samples rather than full size 4 by 8 feet sheets. As they would be revealed through market research, and how important these requirements are to the customer on a 1 to 5 scale.

These rankings are then set in proportion under relative rankings and can be compared with actual ratings of the products in the customers' minds. In this case one can see some distinct problems of the synthetic particleboard at this stage of the development. The comparison with the wooden competitor clearly shows areas of the product that require further improvement or at the very least they show the necessity to make new tools to replace nailing and screwing more appealing. From a marketing point of view the table also shows that the areas with competitive advantage are not ranked as very important in the contractor market. As a result of this analysis, the target market should be redefined with a focus on areas that require water resistance, shaping, and less dependence on traditional nailing or screwing.

Table Custmor Rankingof Particleboard Requirements

Customer Ranking	Customer Ranking	Relative Ranking	Competitive		Requirment
			Wooden Particle board	Synthetic Practice board	
Strength	5	14.3%	4	4	
Screw Withdrawal	5	14.3%	4	3	
Nail Withdrawal	5	14.3%	4	4	
Ease of Nailing*	4	11.4%	5	2	
Ease of Screwing*	3	8.6%	4	1	
Weight/Ease of Handling	3	8.6%	4	4	
Water Resistance	4	11.4%	2	5	
Ability to Shape**	2	5.7%	1	4	
Ability to Tool***	4	11.4%	5	4	

* Ease of Nailing and Screwing refers to the ability to use traditional nails and screws without special tools.

** Ability to Shape refers to the ability to mould the material, e.i. by heating and shaping it.

*** Ability to Tool refers to the ability to sand and saw the product.

Compatitive Ranking: Wood Practiceboard refers to how wooden practiceboard ranks for this requirment.

Competitive Ranking: Synthetic Practiceboard refers to how synthetic practiceboard ranks for this.

The QFD matrix for the synthetic particleboard. It shows a correlation matrix that links customer needs with manufacturing steps in the production of synthetic particleboard. Typically this matrix shows a correlation of requirements with product components, but in this case manufacturing steps influence the features of the product. The degree of correlation between each customer requirement and each manufacturing step is determined by engineers in product development and manufacturing. For this example the researchers determined the correlations based on various testing results.

Table QFD Matrix for Synthetic Particalboard- Correlation Matrix for the Influence of Manufacturing Steps on Customer Requirment

Manufacturing Step / Requirment	Web Formation	Temperature	Pressure	Surface Treatment
Strength	■■■	■■■	■■■	
Screw Withdrawel Resistance	■■	■■■	■■■	■
Nail WithdrawalResistance	■■	■■■	■■■	
Ease of Nailing		■■	■	■■■
Ease of Screwing		■■	■	■■■
Weight/Ease of Handling	■	■	■■■	
Water Resistance		■■	■■	■
Ability to Shape		■■■	■	■
Ability to Tool		■	■■	■■■

■■■ = Strong Correlation
■■ = Moderate Correlation
■ = Weak Correlation

When linking the relative ranking of the customer requirements from table with the degree of correlation of the requirement with the different manufacturing steps in table, it is possible to deduct how important specific manufacturing steps are to satisfying customer requirements overall. This step constitutes a functional cost analysis of the manufacturing steps, and the results are shown in the summary table. The higher values indicate a higher importance in achieving customer satisfaction, and these steps should then be allowed a higher portion of the manufacturing cost.

Table. Result of the Functional Cost Analysis of Manufactureing Steps

Manufacturing Steps	**Web Formation**	**Temperature**	**Pressure**	**Surface Treatment**	**Relative Ranking**
Componant Value	13.1%	33.2%	32.9%	20.8%	100%

In this case the table shows the significance of temperature and pressure during the manufacture of synthetic particleboard from an engineering perspective and the impact they will have on customer requirements. A subsequent step compares the perceived value the components (or manufacturing steps) contribute to the product with the actual cost of these steps. The relative value of each manufacturing step and the actual cost of this step. The cost is expressed as a percentage of the total cost (respectively the total value). The actual cost is based on a subjective estimation, as some of the equipment needed for full-scale production of the synthetic particleboard does not exist yet. By dividing the relative value by the actual cost one finds a value index. Close to 1, the value index shows that the cost reflects the value of this step to the customer. If the value index is below 1 (cost higher than component's value), the cost of this manufacturing step needs to be reduced.

If the value index is higher than 1 (cost less than component's value), the component or manufacturing step needs to be enhanced. The purpose of the value index is not to reduce overall cost but to distribute the cost portions just as to the perceived value for the customer.

Table. Value Index for Synthetic Practiceboard

Manufacturing Step	Actual Cost(%)	Relative Value	Value Index
Web Formation	35.0%	13.1%	0.37
Temperature	25.0%	33.1%	1.32
Pressure	28.0%	32.8%	1.17
Surface Treatment	12.0%	20.0%	1.73

In this case the value index shows that the cost of the manufacturing step "Web Formation" clearly exceeds the value the customers obtain from it, while the surface treatment could be enhanced. It also indicates that the temperature step could be enhanced in order to meet the customer requirements better. The case study shows how target-costing concepts can be used not only for traditional product components, but also to analyse different manufacturing steps.

The results of the QFD matrix alsc aid in assessing the original target market. In the illustrated case it will be necessary to focus on a different segment where traditional tools are less important, and water resistance and the ability to shape the material are more important.

CONCLUSION

Total cost management is a feasible approach of integrating environmental preservation activities over the entire product life cycle into corporate long-term strategies. Environmental conscious manufacturing is made possible through TCM because it seeks to reduce overall product life cycle costs and conserve resources. The case presented in the study explores the possibility of transforming a specific textile waste product into a useful product.

Although the evaluated example has not been commercialized, this research shows how target cost management can be used to promote the development of commercially viable and environmentally friendly products in an effort to recycle textile wastes. This case demonstrates that TCM offers a dynamic modeling approach that will adjust to technological innovation.

TCM helps build a corporate culture that stimulates creativity and proactively manages technological innovations that are beneficial to the environment.

Total cost management is a feasible approach of integrating environmental preservation activities over the entire product life cycle into corporate long-term strategies. Environmental conscious manufacturing is made possible through TCM because it seeks to reduce overall product life cycle costs and conserve resources. The case presented in the study explores the possibility of transforming a specific textile waste product into a useful product.

Although the evaluated example has not been commercialized, this research shows how target cost management can be used to promote the development of commercially viable and environmentally friendly products in an effort to recycle textile wastes. This case demonstrates that TCM offers a dynamic modeling approach that will adjust to technological innovation. TCM helps build a corporate culture that stimulates creativity and proactively manages technological innovations that are beneficial to the environment.

7

Cost Control Techniques

INTRODUCTION

The cost control definition suggests that a company should investigate good procedures for finding out the reason why the costs of the company are not as per the pre-decided or budgeted costs. Thus, cost control can help a company determine, if it is really spending more than it should actually spend. Though it is not essential to be a finance expert to understand the definition of cost control, planning and actually implementing the cost control techniques can be quite a big challenge.

It is essential for the senior level managers to have a good understanding of the cost control software which is a part of effective cost control techniques. The next few paragraphs will give you more information about the cost control management and the cost control techniques.

TECHNIQUES AND WAYS FOR CONTROLLING COSTS

The first step in the cost control management is to find out the cost centers and arrive at a conclusion in how much percentage they differ or vary from the standards of the industry. It is also important to study how the close competitors of your company manage to control their costs and in turn, maximize their profits. Before discussing about the cost control methods or the cost control techniques, it is very important to carry out a very proper cost analysis. The costs incurred by all the departments of the company should be considered so that, you can chalk out some smart cost control strategies to overcome these financial problems.

It is very important to find out the exact and relevant reasons for why the costs of the company are more than the standards adhered to by the industry. The most important of all the cost control techniques is to appoint a small team of highly qualified and experienced people well versed in the financial management team to manage the daily finances of the company in a very professional and systematic manner. The finance team should take correct decisions in favour of the company and opt for less expensive materials and resources for the company without compromising on their quality. You should be very clear about the number of employees you require for a particular project. There are many companies who find it difficult to earn decent profits as their employee count is way beyond the necessity. You can also consider the idea of recruiting employees on contract basis to cut down your costs. While deciding how much salary to pay to a particular employee, you need to be very careful. You should decide the salary strictly on the basis of overall performance. Instead of giving awards to the employees in the form of frequent salary hikes, you should give out bonuses to eligible employees. Following practices recommended in cost method of accounting may benefit your company. The cost control software can be helpful in doing the work in comparatively less time and with more accuracy. In the times of recession, many firms resort to cost control techniques such as reducing the extra facilities to the employees such as the recreational facilities. The cost control techniques might also include cutting down the expenditure incurred on traveling by air and luxury hotel accommodations in order to harness the cash flow. As a part of the cost cutting measure, few firms may postpone or cancel their plans of acquiring new companies, investing in new businesses and buying new machinery or systems. The cost control techniques should be utilized to save cash and bring back the financial strength of the company.

The cost control techniques used by different organizations are different and are largely dependent on their business model and strength of their balance sheet. The better the implementation of these techniques, the better would be the future of the concerned organizations.

BUDGET

- A budget is generally a list of all planned expenses and revenues. It is a plan for saving and spending. A budget is an important concept in microeconomics, which uses a budget line to illustrate the trade-offs between two or more goods. In other terms, a budget is an organizational plan stated in monetary terms.
- *Business start-up budget:* The process of calculating the costs of starting a small business begins with a list of all necessary purchases including tangible assets and services, working capital, sources and collateral. The budget should contain a narrative explaining how you decided on the amount of this reserve and a description of the expected financial results of business activities. The assets should be valued with each and every cost. All other expenses are like labour factory overhead all freshmen expenses are also included into business budgeting
- *Corporate budget:* The budget of a company is often compiled annually, but may not be. A finished budget, usually requiring considerable effort, is a plan for the short-term future, typically one year. While traditionally the Finance department compiles the company's budget, modern software allows hundreds or even

thousands of people in various departments to list their expected revenues and expenses in the final budget. If the actual figures delivered through the budget period come close to the budget, this suggests that the managers understand their business and have been successfully driving it in the intended direction. On the other hand, if the figures diverge wildly from the budget, this sends an 'out of control' signal, and the share price could suffer as a result.

- *Event management budget:* A budget is a fundamental tool for an event director to predict with reasonable accuracy whether the event will result in a profit, a loss or will break-even. A budget can also be used as a pricing tool.
- *Budget types:*
  - *Sales budget:* The sales budget is an estimate of future sales, often broken down into both units and dollars. It is used to create company sales goals.
  - *Production budget:* Product oriented companies create a production budget which estimates the number of units that must be manufactured to meet the sales goals. The production budget also estimates the various costs involved with manufacturing those units, including labour and material.
  - *Cash Flow/Cash budget:* The cash flow budget is a prediction of future cash receipts and expenditures for a particular time period. It usually covers a period in the short term future. The cash flow budget helps the business determine when income will be sufficient to cover expenses and when the company will need to seek outside financing.
  - *Marketing budget:* The marketing budget is an estimate of the funds needed for promotion, advertising, and public relations in order to market the product or service.
  - *Project budget:* The project budget is a prediction of the costs associated with a particular company project. These costs include labour, materials, and other related expenses. The project budget is often broken down into specific tasks, with task budgets assigned to each.
  - *Revenue budget:* The Revenue Budget consists of revenue receipts of government and the expenditure met from these revenues. Tax revenues are made up of taxes and other duties that the government levies.
  - *Expenditure budget:* A budget type which include of spending data items..

BUDGET PREPARATION

A critical aspect of intervention planning is preparing a budget of income and expenses. The budget must include funding for materials and supplies for the intervention activities, but also for staff, facilities, and promotion. Keep in mind that each intervention requires different resources, and organizations have unique capacities to conduct interventions with existing resources. The following are typical budget categories.

CATEGORIES FOR AN INTERVENTION BUDGET

- *Personnel and benefits expense:* Personnel includes all individuals who will have responsibilities in the intervention. Others who may be hired to help with the project, such as consultants or contractors, are not budgeted in Personnel, rather are included in the Purchased, Consultant or Contractual Services. Fringe benefits are typically budgeted at a per cent of the personnel salary, and are dependent upon the benefits paid by the employer.
- *Things to consider:* Do you have enough people to implement the intervention? Will you need to hire additional part-time or full-time staff to help you? What benefits will be paid and to whom? Will your staffing needs change over the duration of your intervention from year to year?
- *General Office Expenses:* Includes office supplies needed to support the intervention.
- *Things to consider:* What basic materials or supplies are needed to support the intervention? You should be able to budget more for office supplies the first year of the project and less in subsequent years.
- *Intervention Supplies and Materials:* Intervention materials are the actual materials you will need to implement your intervention.
- *Things to consider:* How many participants you are anticipating? Can you prepare the materials yourself or do you need to hire someone to prepare them for you? Do you need to conduct research or a needs assessment before designing your materials?
- *Meeting and Activity Expenses:* Space outside your organization's office may be needed for meetings or intervention activities. Some places may charge a rental fee as well as for use of audio visual equipment, such as projectors or TVs. Food and drinks provided at the meeting may be included in this category or in Intervention Supplies, depending on the organization's preference.
- *Things to consider:* Does your current office space accommodate everything you will need for the intervention? Do you have room to conduct meetings with other partners or internal staff? Do you have appropriate space to conduct your intervention activities or will you need to use other spaces? Will any of your partners donate space for meetings or intervention activities? Will you need to rent

facilities to conduct your intervention? Will you need to travel to your intervention's participants or partners, if so where will you meet with them?

- *Transportation/Travel Expenses:* Transportation can involve providing a means for participants to travel to your intervention activities in order to increase participation or providing transportation for you and your staff to travel to other locations to conduct intervention activities. This may also include fees or stipends to attend professional meetings or perform interviews and surveys out-of-town.
- *Things to consider:* Do your participants have access to public or personal transportation or will you need to provide it? Do your staff members need to travel to participants' homes or communities to conduct intervention activities? Will your staff need to travel to conferences or to make presentations outside of your city?
- *Purchased, Consultant or Contractual Service Expenses:* These expenses are payments to individuals or companies for a specific service, usually occurring temporarily during the project, that are not completed by the regular project staff.
- *Things to consider:* What specific expertise and services will you need in planning, implementing and evaluating your intervention?
- *Indirect Costs:* Indirect costs are the expenses incurred by the organization to keep the organization operating. Indirect cost are typically calculated by multiplying an agreed upon percentage by the total direct costs, or by the total of personnel and benefit costs. These costs are sometimes also referred to as administrative costs.
- *Things to consider:* Will your organization obtain sufficient indirect costs from your intervention income? Are there partners who are willing to cover some indirect costs?
- An "in-kind" donation is a contribution of time, service or goods made by a donor to help support the operations or services provided by your organization. It isn't cash. Therefore the donor does retain a degree of control over the donation that doesn't occur when the donor gives you a cash donation. Because of this "relationship" your organization should keep the donor well informed on how their donation is being used.

As you prepare your budget it is critical you account for anticipated in-kind donations. If you don't track these donations, you aren't truly acknowledging the total capacity of your organization. Also tracking these donations will help you better acknowledge the donors for their contribution.

BUDGET PREPARATION WORKSHEET

When creating your intervention budget, take into consideration that your budget and allocation of funds may vary from year to year. For example, in Year 1, many of your funds may go into buying supplies or investing money in materials for start-up. In Year 2 and beyond, you may be spending most of your budget disseminating your intervention materials or on evaluation efforts. It is important to create your yearly intervention budget to reflect these changes.

Personnel

Personnel refers to all staff members who will be involved in the various intervention activities. Others helping with the intervention, such as consultants or technical assistance, are not considered Personnel, but are rather included in the Purchased Services Total. Remember: When creating Year 2 and beyond budgets, it is important to adjust for Personnel salaries based on increases in cost of living.

When calculating Personnel salaries for Year 2 and beyond, multiply personnel by the expected increase of cost of living for each year.

Calculating Personnel:

- *Base Salary:* For each personnel position, state the base salary for the position.
- *% of Time:* For each personnel position, determine the per cent of that person's total time that will be used to work on the intervention project.
- *Project Salary:* For each personnel position, determine the project salary by multiplying base salary by% of time.
- *Fringe Benefit%:* Fringe benefits include all taxes, as well as health insurance, paid time off, retirement, and other benefits provided. Fringe benefits may or may not be offered to all employees. Fringe benefit%s are at the discretion of the organization based on amount of funding and what it offers its employees in terms of benefits. Fringe benefit for a graduate research assistant may be a little as 3% perhaps providing worker's compensation only, as opposed to 20- 40% for senior full time employee of the project receiving full benefits.
- *Fringe Amount:* To determine fringe amount, multiple the fringe benefit percentage rate by the project salary amount. (Remember: {Base Salary} X {% of Time} = {Project Salary})
- *Total:* To determine the total cost of each personnel position, add the project salary + the fringe amount.
- *Principal Investigator:* Includes project time associated with such positions as project direct, principal investigator, or any co-principal investigators that provide the main leadership to the project.
- *Project Staff:* Includes salary costs of the project staff such as project manager, project coordinator, or senior staff, who directly work on

the project. Project staff can also include nurses, statisticians, researchers, graduate assistants, epidemiologist or any other staff with roles directly related to aspects of the project.

- *Administrative Staff:* Includes any staff providing administrative support, such as secretaries, administrative assistant, bookkeeper, data entry staff or any staff used for this type of work.
- *Other Staff:* Any other staff not included in the other personnel categories, such as a stipend or salary for interns
- *Other Direct Costs:* These are direct non-personnel cost of any materials and resources that are necessary for completing the research or intervention.
- *General Office Supplies and materials:* Includes any of the fixed costs of having your organization remain in operation. Office operations and equipment are included in this category. These categories encompass computers, software, office supplies/materials, telephones, copy machines, office furniture, postage, etc. You may spend more on office supplies and materials in your first year of the intervention than in subsequent years.
- *Intervention Materials:* Intervention materials are those that are needed to implement your programme that are not already included general office supplies and materials. Intervention materials include any money spent on incentives or promotions for intervention participants. This can also include the costs for materials such as pre/post surveys and copies, other intervention materials such as brochures, posters, or any other materials created to promote the intervention, including distribution costs of intervention materials. Intervention material costs may vary from year to year.
- *Meeting and Intervention Activity Space:* Includes cost for the use of meeting or intervention activity space. If these types of activities occur outside the office, you may need to rent a meeting room. Some places may also charge a fee for use of audio visual equipment, such as projectors or TVs. Food and drinks provided at the meeting should also be included in this category.
- *Transportation/Travel:* Refers to travel and transportation costs for project staff or consultants to perform intervention duties. This may include fees or stipends to attend professional meetings or perform interviews or surveys out-of-town. Transportation/Travel costs can also include those incurred by providing a means for participants to get to your intervention activities in order to increase participation.
- *Other:* Refers to any other costs not covered in the other direct costs. This might include workshop fees, data purchases, and subscriptions to journals or any other miscellaneous programme costs.

Purchased Services

This refers to fees paid to individuals or companies for a specific service, usually occurring temporarily during the intervention that is not completed by the regular project staff. Purchased services may vary from project year to project year.

- *Consultants:* Includes individuals providing expert or professional advice for an agreed per diem rate. Consultants could provide services such as proposal review, speaking engagements, or services for an advisory board/committee. Consultants are usually hired on an hourly or daily rate. When calculating consultant fees, include the hourly rate and how many hours you expect them to be needed for that project year.
- *Contracts:* Includes agreements entered into with individuals or companies, to provide a specific service to the project. Contracts could include hiring a company to survey participants by phone or to design intervention materials. Contracts are usually negotiated for a set amount for the provided service.
- *Technical Assistance:* Includes any fees for professional technical services, such as; setting up or maintaining computer systems, providing training on software programmes, or providing repairs for office technology. Technical assistance can vary from company to company and by service, some may charge an hourly rate or charge a set amount for maintenance.

Iidirect Costs

This is a percentage that includes costs incurred by the organization as a result of the intervention, but that is not easily identifiable with any specific component of the intervention. Indirect costs are sometimes also referred to as facilities and administrative costs. Indirect costs include building maintenance costs, utilities, property insurance, accounting, or legal expenses. If your intervention is being housed in university space, your indirect cost may be upwards of 30-60%, however if your space is in a community organization's building, it may be much lower, for instance, 10-15%. Remember: Indirect Cost is a percentage that is multiplied by the total direct cost to determine your total project cost

Grand Total

Project budget total (Personnel Total + Other Direct Cost Total + Indirect Cost Total) for Year 1. Remember that you are calculating your project budget by year or cycle, and that your expenses may fluctuate from year to year. You will need to take into consideration how your budget will change from year to year and what categories may need more or less money during the course of the intervention. It is also important to remember increases in cost of living for personnel salaries.

BUDGET CONTROL SYSTEM

The State University of New York Fiscal and Accounting Procedures for Mandatory Student Activity Fee Programmes require the custodial and disbursing agent to establish and maintain budgetary accounts. The basic structure for recording and monitoring revenues and expenditures is the Annual Operating Budget.

As part of its accounting system, Sub-Board I provides a Budgetary Control System modeled after those commonly used by governments and other not-for-profit entities which satisfies the fiscal guidelines, policies and procedures of the Board of Trustees and the State University of New York. All student governments and clients for whom Sub-Board I acts as Fiscal Agent must use the Budgetary Control System.

UNDERSTANDING THE BUDGET

A budget is your management's plan or blueprint, in structured form, which projects or anticipates the desired outcome of financial activity for a specific set of resources, for a fixed period, usually one year. For our purposes, the Annual Operating Budget is divided into two separate components: Estimated Revenues - What are the anticipated sources of revenue and how much can management realistically expect to receive? Estimated Expenditures - How much does management expect to spend, and for what purposes are resources to be spent?

IMPORTANCE OF BUDGET

A budget acts as the formal process that establishes the authority on how funds are to be collected and spent. Management's objective is to provide a logical, detailed and realistic spending plan.

Once a plan has been decided upon and is formally adopted by the student government/client governing body, the budget acts as an effective management tool by providing a means of identifying and allocating limited resources and monitoring their use.

The budget also is used to help prevent the student government/client from overspending. Budget reports provide management with information on operations, allowing the organization to monitor and control spending and revenue collection while they are in progress. Hence, budgets alone are meaningless unless they are used to motivate responsible action and to direct operations towards accomplishing objectives that have been established by management as desirable.

The budget is the single most important source of financial information. Almost all financial transactions are recorded in the budget. The budget is used to track all cash receipts, encumbrances and cash disbursements, and provides a means of tracking these transactions back to original source documents.

STRUCTURE OF BUDGET

In determining the basic elements of Estimated Revenues and Estimated Expenditures, a logical structure must be developed to codify and arrange the elements into units or sections that reflect the nature and structure of the operations themselves. The basic structural tool is the budgetary account. A budgetary account identifies a specific source of revenue or a particular type of expenditure by using a budgetary account number.

Sub-Board's Budgetary Control System uses the following budgetary account number format:

- *Fund:* The first three digits of the account number identify the student government/client and the overall purpose of the funds accounted for in a particular budget, *e.g.* operating funds, capital funds, etc.
- *Department:* The next four digits of the account number identify the department, division, activity center, etc. within the internal operations of the student government/client.
- *Line Item:* The next four digits of the account number identify the specific source of revenue or the type of expenditure for a particular department, *e.g.* Advertising Revenue, or Telephone Expense.
- *Project:* In certain situations, the account number may be extended by an additional four digits to further identify a particular project.

HOW DOES THE BUDGETARY PROCESS BEGIN?

The first step in the budgetary process is for the student government/client to review its operations. What is working well and what needs to be changed? What are the goals and objectives for the coming budget year? What projects does the student government/client wish to support? Which recognized clubs and organizations has management agreed to fund? What are the primary sources of revenue? Clubs, organizations, project managers and department heads may be required to submit budget requests to whoever is responsible for preparing the initial or "proposed" budget.

These requests can then be reviewed and modified before being incorporated into the proposed budget. It may also be helpful for whoever is preparing the proposed budget to review past budgets – historical information can be very helpful in determining how the student government/client has operated in the past and can help identify areas that management would like to continue, eliminate or change. All student governments/clients must prepare their budgets just as to the fiscal year.

The fiscal year begins on August 1 and ends on July 31 of the following year. Once the proposed budget has been prepared, it must be formally approved or adopted in accordance with the student government/client constitution, by-laws or governing rules. During this process, the budget may be discussed, modified, or challenged before being formally adopted. For student governments/clients that maintain more that one fund in addition to the operating budget, a separate budget for each Fund must be adopted.

AFTER THE BUDGET IS ADOPTED, WHAT IS THE NEXT STEP?

For all student governments/clients subject to administrative review and certification, approved budgets must be submitted using the Required Budget Format to the Administrative Designee no later than June 1 prior to the start of the fiscal year. A copy of the approved budget must also be submitted to the SBI Accounting Office by the same date, June 1. For independent clients whose budgets are not subject to administrative review and certification, approved budgets must be submitted to the SBI Accounting Office no later than June 1 prior to the start of the Fiscal Year.

Budgets must be accompanied by a completed Certification of Budget Form signed by at least two officers or authorized representatives of the student government/client, attesting that adoption and approval procedures were correctly followed. For student governments/clients that maintain more than one budget, a separate Certification of Budget Form must be submitted with each budget.

In order to continue operating without an interruption in accounting services, budgets must be submitted by the due date of June 1.

WHAT HAPPENS AFTER THE BUDGET IS SUBMITTED AND CERTIFIED?

Upon receiving the adopted budget, Sub-Board I will review the budget for accuracy and conformity to fiscal guidelines. Budgets must be balanced; *i.e.* Total Estimated Revenue must equal or exceed Total Estimated Expenditures. Unbalanced budgets will be returned to the student government/client unprocessed. Estimated Revenues and Estimated Expenditures must be based on realistic projections. Assuming that budgets have been submitted by the required deadline, in the required format, and with the proper officer certification, and the administrative designee, where applicable, has approved the budgets, Sub- Board I will enter the adopted budgets into the accounting system. On August 1, the adopted budgets will go into effect. All student governments/clients will receive initial budget reports as of August 1, before any activity begins, as verification that Sub-Board I has accurately entered the budgets. The student government/client should closely review these initial budget reports and report any problems or errors immediately to the SBI Accounting Office for correction.

WILL ANY ACTIVITY FROM THE PRIOR YEAR BUDGET HAVE AN EFFECT ON THE CURRENT BUDGET?

Since there may be financial activity in process between the end of one fiscal year and the beginning of the next, the budget will be affected in several ways.

- On the revenue side, the Fund's cash balance as of July 31 will be added to Estimated Revenues and Annual Revenue Receipts in the new budget on the first day of the new fiscal year, August 1. This cash balance, if sufficient, can be used as a reserve to accommodate outstanding encumbrances and accrued payroll expenses. Any remaining cash balance not reserved for other purposes may be re-appropriated in the new budget. This adjustment will take place as soon as all cash activity has been recorded and reconciled for July, usually sometime in early August.

- On the expenditure side, any encumbrances outstanding at the end of the fiscal year will be added to budgeted expenditures in the next fiscal year's budget. The date that this adjustment actually takes place depends on the final accounting of year-end activity, preparation of year-end financial statements, the progress of the annual independent audit, etc., and usually takes place sometime after October 15. Until this final accounting for outstanding encumbrances is completed and the prior year budget is "closed", the accounting system will automatically account for encumbrances from the prior fiscal year that are paid in the new fiscal year. This is done so that budgetary expenditures for the new fiscal year are not depleted by payments for which encumbrances existed in the prior fiscal year's budget.
- Accrued payroll expenses, if any, as of July 31 will be added to Estimated Expenditures in the next fiscal year when the new budget goes into effect on August 1. You must provide a sufficient reserve in your budget to accommodate this additional appropriation and to maintain a balanced budget. This adjustment to the budget will take place after all payroll activity has been received and recorded, usually sometime in September.

WHAT IF THE BUDGET NEEDS TO BE MODIFIED OR ADJUSTED DURING THE COURSE OF THE FISCAL YEAR?

It is not realistic to prepare a budget at the beginning of the fiscal year and then leave it as a rigid plan of action. Important unforeseen changes in internal or external conditions may require budget revisions during the fiscal year. It is essential that management receive timely information on its actual results in comparison with the plan. A comparison of actual operating results with the original budget plan would show management what the organization did in comparison with what it initially planned to do.

It may not reveal, however, how well the organization did with regard to how it should have performed under the conditions which actually existed. Therefore, Sub-Board I will provide periodic budget reports to assess performance of actual results with the original plan and the adjusted budget plan. Whenever an adjustment or revision to the original budget is necessary, the student government/client must notify Sub-Board I of the adjustment(s) to be made by entering a Budget Adjustment into the on-line KVS Accounting System. Budget Adjustments require the approval of two officers.

In addition, student governments and independent clients who are subject to administrative review must have all budget adjustments or changes to the budget reviewed and certified by the administrative designee. All approvals can be done on-line. Sub-Board I will update the budget adjustments only after all approvals have been obtained.

ZERO-BASED BUDGETING

Zero-based budgeting is a technique of planning and decision-making which reverses the working process of traditional budgeting. In traditional incremental budgeting, departmental managers justify only increases over the previous year budget and what has been already spent is automatically sanctioned. No reference is made to the previous level of expenditure. By contrast, in zero-based budgeting, every department function is reviewed comprehensively and all expenditures must be approved, rather than only increases. Zero-based budgeting requires the budget request be justified in complete detail by each division manager starting from the zero-base. The zero-base is indifferent to whether the total budget is increasing or decreasing. The term "zero-based budgeting" is sometimes used in personal finance to describe the practice of budgeting every dollar of income received, and then adjusting some part of the budget downward for every other part that needs to be adjusted upward. It is more technically correct to refer to this practice as "zero-sum budgeting". Zero based budgeting also refers to the identification of a task or tasks and then funding resources to complete the task independent of current resourcing.

Advantages:

- Detects inflated budgets.
- Drives managers to find cost effective ways to improve operations.
- Efficient allocation of resources, as it is based on needs and benefits.
- Forces cost centers to identify their mission and their relationship to overall goals.
  Identifies and eliminates wasteful and obsolete operations.
- Identifies opportunities for outsourcing.
- Increases communication and coordination within the organization.
- Increases staff motivation by providing greater initiative and responsibility in decision-making.
- Useful for service departments where the output is difficult to identify.

Disadvantages:

- Difficult to define decision units and decision packages, as it is time-consuming and exhaustive.

- Forced to justify every detail related to expenditure. The R&D department is threatened whereas the production department benefits.
- Honesty of the managers must be reliable and uniform. Any manager that exaggerates skews the results.
- In a large organization, the volume of forms may be so large that no one person could read it all. Compressing the information down to a usable size might remove critically important details.
- Necessary to train managers. Zero-based budgeting must be clearly understood by managers at various levels to be successfully implemented. Difficult to administer and communicate the budgeting because more managers are involved in the process.

INCREMENTAL BUDGETING

Incremental Budgeting uses a budget prepared using a previous period's budget or actual performance as a base, with incremental amounts added for the new budget period. The allocation of resources is based upon allocations from the previous period. This approach is not recommended as it fails to take into account changing circumstances. Moreover, it encourages "spending up to the budget" to ensure a reasonable allocation in the next period. It leads to a "spend it or lose it" mentality.

Advantages:

- Conflicts are avoided when departments appear to be treated similarly.
- Co-ordination between budgets is easier to achieve.
- Managers can operate their departments on a consistent basis.
- The budget is stable and change is gradual.
- The impact of change can be seen quickly.
- The system is relatively simple to operate and easy to understand.

Disadvantages:

- Assumes activities and methods of working will continue in the same way.
- Encourages spending up to the budget so that the budget is maintained next year.
- No incentive for developing new ideas.
- No incentive to reduce costs.
- The budget may become out-of-date and no longer relate to the level of activity or type of work being carried out.
- The priority for resources may have changed since the budgets were originally set.
- There may be budgetary slack built into the budget, which is never reviewed. Managers might have overestimated their requirements in the past in order to obtain a budget which is easier to work within, and which will allow them to achieve favourable results.

STANDARD COSTING

Standard costing is an important subtopic of cost accounting. Standard costs are usually associated with a manufacturing company's costs of direct material, direct labour, and manufacturing overhead. Rather than assigning the actual costs of direct material, direct labour, and manufacturing overhead to a product, many manufacturers assign the expected or standard cost.

This means that a manufacturer's inventories and cost of goods sold will begin with amounts reflecting the standard costs, not the actual costs, of a product. Manufacturers, of course, still have to pay the actual costs. As a result there are almost always differences between the actual costs and the standard costs, and those differences are known as variances. Standard costing and the related variances is a valuable management tool.

If a variance arises, management becomes aware that manufacturing costs have differed from the standard costs. If actual costs are greater than standard costs the variance is unfavourable. An unfavourable variance tells management that if everything else stays constant the company's actual profit will be less than planned. If actual costs are less than standard costs the variance is favourable. A favourable variance tells management that if everything else stays constant the actual profit will likely exceed the planned profit.

The sooner that the accounting system reports a variance, the sooner that management can direct its attention to the difference from the planned amounts. If we assume that a company uses the perpetual inventory system and that it carries all of its inventory accounts at standard cost then the standard cost of a finished product is the sum of the standard costs of the inputs:

- Direct material
- Direct labour
- Manufacturing overhead
  - Variable manufacturing overhead
  - Fixed manufacturing overhead

VARIANCE ANALYSIS

Variance analysis is usually associated with explaining the difference (or variance) between actual costs and the standard costs allowed for the good output. For example, the difference in materials costs can be divided into a materials price variance and a materials usage variance. The difference between the actual direct labour costs and the standard direct labour costs can be divided into a rate variance and an efficiency variance.

The difference in manufacturing overhead can be divided into spending, efficiency, and volume variances. Mix and yield variances can also be calculated. Variance analysis helps management to understand the present costs and then to control future costs. Variance analysis is also used to explain the difference between the actual sales dollars and the budgeted sales dollars. Examples include sales price variance, sales quantity variance, and sales mix variance. A difference in the relative proportion of sales can account for some of the difference in a company's profits.

RESPONSIBILITY ACCOUNTING

Responsibility accounting is an underlying concept of accounting performance measurement systems. The basic idea is that large diversified organizations are difficult, if not impossible to manage as a single segment, thus they must be decentralized or separated into manageable parts.

These parts, or segments are referred to as responsibility centers that include:

- Revenue centers,
- Cost centers,
- Profit centers and
- Investment centers.

This approach allows responsibility to be assigned to the segment managers that have the greatest amount of influence over the key elements to be managed. These elements include revenue for a revenue center costs for a cost center a measure of profitability for a profit center and return on investment for an investment center.

CONTROLLABILITY CONCEPT

An underlying concept of responsibility accounting is referred to as controllability. Conceptually, a manager should only be held responsible for those aspects of performance that he or she can control. In my view, this concept is rarely, if ever, applied successfully in practice because of the system variation present in all systems. Attempts to apply the controllability concept produce responsibility reports where each layer of management is held responsible for all subordinate management layers.

ADVANTAGES AND DISADVANTAGES

Responsibility accounting has been an accepted part of traditional accounting control systems for many years because it provides an organization with a number of advantages. Perhaps the most compelling argument for the responsibility accounting approach is that it provides a way to manage an organization that would otherwise be unmanageable.

In addition, assigning responsibility to lower level managers allows higher level managers to pursue other activities such as long term planning and policy making. It also provides a way to motivate lower level managers and workers. Managers and workers in an individualistic system tend to be motivated by measurements that emphasize their individual performances. However, this emphasis on the performance of individuals and individual segments creates what some critics refer to as the "stovepipe organization."

Others have used the term "functional silos" to describe the same idea. Information flows vertically, rather than horizontally. Individuals in the various segments and functional areas are separated and tend to ignore the interdependencies within the organization. Segment managers and individual workers within segments tend to compete to optimize their own performance measurements rather than working together to optimize the performance of the system.

An implicit assumption of responsibility accounting is that separating a company into responsibility centers that are controlled in a top down manner is the way to optimize the system. However, this separation inevitably fails to consider many of the interdependencies within the organization. Ignoring the interdependencies prevents teamwork and creates the need for buffers such as additional inventory, workers, managers and capacity. Of course, a system that prevents teamwork and creates excess is inconsistent with the lean enterprise concepts of just-in-time and the theory of constraints.

For this reason, critics of traditional accounting control systems advocate managing the system as a whole to eliminate the need for buffers and excess. They also argue that companies need to develop process oriented learning support systems, not financial results, fear oriented control systems. The information system needs to reveal the company's problems and constraints in a timely manner and at a disaggregated level so that empowered users can identify how to correct problems, remove constraints and improve the process. These critics, accounting control information does not qualify in any of these categories because it is not timely, disaggregated, or user friendly. This harsh criticism of accounting control information leads us to a very important controversial question. Can a company successfully implement just-in-time and other continuous improvement concepts while retaining a traditional responsibility accounting control system?

Although the jury is still out on this question, a number of field research studies indicate that accounting based controls are playing a decreasing role in companies that adopt the lean enterprise concepts. In a recent study involving nine companies, each company answered this controversial question in a different way by using a different mix of process oriented versus results oriented learning and control information. Since each company is different, a generalized answer to this question for all firms in all situations cannot be provided.

8

Financial Intermediation

MANAGERIAL AND REGULATORY ISSUES

The financial landscape is undergoing a substantial transformation, with growing cross-border capital movements, ongoing consolidation in the banking and financial services industry, and new functions and methods in financial interme-diation. Many factors are contributing to this transformation: the dismantling of certain government restrictions, the acceleràtion of competition, new customer needs or behavio-urs, innovations in financial products and staggering advances in information technology.

This has two main objectives:

- To identify, and reflect on, the key challenges encountered by decision makers at the helm of financial intermediaries (banks, securities firms and insurance firms), financial market platforms or channels, and technical infrastructures; and
- To review important regulatory issues. In particular it addresses selected aspects of competition and innovation, corporate strategies, risk management, mutations in financial markets, public intervention and financial stabilisation.

COMPETITION AND INNOVATION

The actors in the financial services industry are becoming increasingly diverse. On the supply side, the so-called traditional banks (notably the deposit-taking institutions) are faced by an array of competitors from various backgrounds: newly established financial firms, industrial enterprises that have developed financial functions to cater for third-party needs, information technology and software companies, consumer product distributors and so on. These newcomers have been drawn in by the attractive opportunities in the financial sector and their entry has been facilitated by tumbling entry barriers.

Barriers to competition consist of multiple factors whose relative importance varies considerably between markets and over time for individual financial products or services. These barriers arise inter alia from scarce talents and skills, expensive technology and infrastructure, differences in culture or business practices, legal-regulatory controls, monopolistic constraints and fiscal charges. Strategically positioned financial intermediaries can thus impose barriers in the form of onerous conditions governing the transaction of financial operations, and constraints on the flow of know-how or data. A number of factors contribute to a financial space's comparative attractiveness in terms of competition, notably for investors, creditors and users of funds. The principal factors are as follows:

- A wide choice of financial products and services.
- A broad and diverse customer base.
- Market liquidity.
- Innovativeness.
- Proper use of risk management and control techniques.
- Truthfulness and transparency of key data on accounts and operations.
- Efficient and strong intermediaries.
- Safety nets.
- Lively competition.
- The availability of high-quality managerial-technical talents and skills.
- A sound and effective legal-regulatory system.
- Macroeconomic and financial stability.

Several of the foregoing characterise developed market economies, such as those of the US, Western Europe and Japan. Traditionally the principal function of banking has been to transform depositors' funds (callable on demand or at short notice and at their face value) into longer maturity loans. The management's expectation is that the longer the maturity of a loan, the higher the interest margin obtainable, other things remaining equal. The banker of the past was therefore essentially a deposit taker and a credit originator, keeping loans until their maturity. Banks have increasingly enlarged the range of their products and services in response to the more diverse and complex needs of the modern economy, and to defend their markets vis-à-vis other enterprises with financial intermediation activities, such as mutual funds, pension funds, insurance companies, brokers/dealers, and department stores or supermarkets that offer financial products. Among the diverse functions that banks currently have, six are very likely to remain important:

- Accepting savings in the form of deposits.
- Originating credit or guarantees.
- Providing payment services and transferring assets between economic agents.
- Providing liquidity to holders of sight deposits and beneficiaries of standby lines of credit.
- Identifying, separating, packaging, retaining and selling the

components of risk (the latter is generally defined as the uncertainty associated with an event or an outcome).

- Providing information, advice and certification on the quality of assets or projects.

Innovations in financial products and progress in information and communication technology have promoted business expansion, heightened competition and reduced costs. In the field of financial innovation, derivatives have enjoyed spectacular growth.

The value of these financial products is derived from or determined by an underlying asset (stocks, bonds or commodities), a reference rate (interest rates, exchange rates) or an index (reflecting the collective value of various financial products or commodities). Standardised derivatives are usually traded through organised exchanges, while custom-made derivatives are privately negotiated and transacted outside the exchanges or over the counter (OTC).

Among the recent promising developments are credit derivatives. The latter involve swap and option contracts whose function is to transfer all or a portion of the credit exposure of a financial asset over its lifetime (or a shorter period), while the institution buying the protection retains the title of the asset, thereby maintaining the existing relationship of lender-borrower. A standard 'master agreement' has been issued by the Inter-national Swaps and Derivatives Association (ISDA) to facilitate OTC or exchange-traded transactions.

One example is 'credit default swap', in which the buyer of total protection receives the face value of a debt upon default by the borrower, or the so-called 'credit event'. The buyer of the protection is insured against the credit event (default) by paying a premium (a lump sum or fixed periodic payments) of the loan's face value to the seller of the protection.

When appropriately used as coverage instruments, derivatives allow economic agents, including banks, to neutralise or at least moderate their risk of exposure. Some institutions or individuals use them as instruments for speculation. They may multiply the effects of the reward (or loss) through debt financing (the leverage factor). Naturally the market will penalise unreasonable behaviour by any party.

Recent developments in financial derivatives have been useful in improving the negotiability of financial assets, and in raising the liquidity and depth of financial markets.

The liquidity provided by derivatives has, however, proven to be procyclical, in that these instruments are readily available during boom periods but in short supply during periods of crisis. Accordingly their utility in offering protection in the management of risk disappears in times of crisis, when the few financial intermediaries that control the market are loath to issue such instruments.

CORPORATE STRATEGIES

The process of globalisation has enlarged economic actors' choices and opportunities. This applies particularly to financial firms, whose ability to diversify their portfolios has improved considerably. Some have even strengthened their ascendancy over specific markets, frequently by means of alliances, joint-venture strategies, acquisitions or mergers. Indeed, with the liberalisation of financial markets, financial intermediaries have been able to extend the spectrum and reach of their activities. Business strategies can rationally be founded on any of the following considerations: risk diversification, economies of scale or scope, utilisation of human and other resources, maximisation of opportunities and optimally servicing customers.

Guided by the ultimate interests and objectives of their dominant stakeholders (notably capital providers, key promoters or top management), financial firms may choose either of the following strategies or hybrids thereof:

- A strategy of core or niche businesses, focusing on one central activity or a few related activities at which they are best;
- A strategy of 'multidimensional expansion', aimed at building a sizeable financial institution that offers a wide array of products and services to a large number of markets and a variety of customers. To avoid duplication, the global financial firm tends to centralise the design of its basic financial products, leaving it to the management of its business units to adapt these products to local market needs and regulations in the most efficient and judicious manner.

Traditionally interest margins (the spread between interests on loans and deposits) have been the major source of income for banks. Depositors and borrowers are increasingly finding attractive opportunities in capital markets, a phenomenon referred to as bank 'disintermediation'. This has prompted banks to develop various fee-bearing activities, posted off their balance sheet. Strategies of a financial firm: conglomerative and extensive versus selective

- Geographical span: one market versus several markets, regions or countries.
- Range of customers targeted: branches of economic activity, small or big institutions, high-net-worth persons, wholesale operations, retail customers, government agencies and so on.
- Array of products or services provided: deposit and fiduciary accounts, credit, corporate finance, project finance, cash management, foreign exchange, underwriting and trading in securities, derivatives, guarantees, trust and investment funds, asset management, insurance, brokerage, M&A, LBO, IPO, equity participation in non-financial firms, custody, counselling, e-commerce and so on.

The optimal strategy for a particular firm is that which enables its management to have the 'right' mix of lines of business and countries in order to produce superior risk-adjusted results. The latter are often judged by reference to profitability, stable earnings, growth of turnover, significant market share and staying power. Benchmarks for the foregoing are usually set according to four yardsticks: targets pre-established by management, recent performance of the firm, the financial sector's mean results, and the leading competitors' results.

Improved performance is management's declared reason for the adoption of a particular strategy. In the case of a strategy of merger and acquisition (M&A), the expected benefits are one or more of the following: the creation of new business opportunities, complementarity of existing activities, economies of scale and scope, technological and operational efficiency, sharing information on customers, career opportunities for staff, joint research and ultimately higher earnings.

Compared with expansion from within, an acquisition is generally deemed a more rapid means of growth, assuming the acquiring firm has a sufficiently strong capital base. If a firm has a relatively high market capitalisation, however, this might dampen the desire of an interested acquirer to bid for that firm.

Empirical studies have shown that management has often sought larger size for reasons of market power or egotism. A strategy of merger or takeovers presents a number of challenges, notably in the areas of integrating information technology, corporate culture and organisational streamlining. The success of a merger will heavily depend on a shared vision by the business leaders concerned, and on analysing very carefully, objectively and in sufficient detail the foregoing issues.

Moreover mutual understanding and trust among the top executives of the merging firms, their management style, their abilities and their commitment to work together to complete the process of integration are fundamental to outperforming competitors.

Duplication or overlap of functions, bureaucracy, poor coordination, management infighting and the demoralisation of personnel are sources of reduced efficiency. Such problems can open the way for the poaching of top staff by competitors and can undermine the strength of the new combined enterprise. Ultimately, difficulty in integrating the parties concerned can prevent the consummation of an intended merger or acquisition. The foundering in April 2000 of the proposed Deutsche-Dresdner Bank deal is one illustration of a botched merger.

Shareholders and investors can have reservations about a policy of outright diversification if it leads to an overextension of scarce managerial talent and yields a lower return than a more focused approach. The management of a firm generally strives to ensure that the remuneration paid to its shareholders is at least in line with that received by the shareholders of similar-risk firms. If a bank has a risky profile, this will discourage the providers of funds unless they are enticed by commensurately higher remuneration. Well-managed small and medium-sized financial firms, by applying their expertise to selected activities, can achieve high levels of cost effectiveness and performance.

The main interests of a financial firm's stakeholders. The latter comprise the board of directors and senior management, share holders (big and small), creditors (including depositors), employees, customers, suppliers, subcontractors and public authorities. Good corporate governance in a bank sets guidelines for rules and relationships among the stakeholders of the firm, aimed at optimising wealth creation.

They cover various areas: strategy, efficient assignment of responsibilities, proper incentives, control systems, avoidance of conflicts of interest, adequate transparency and protection of depositors' interests. The board of directors-ideally comprising competent and independent persons-normally has the crucial task of supervising senior management with a view to protecting the prosperity and ensuring the survival of the firm. The evaluation of the performance of a bank cannot be restricted to the sole criterion of risk-adjusted financial reward to shareholders.

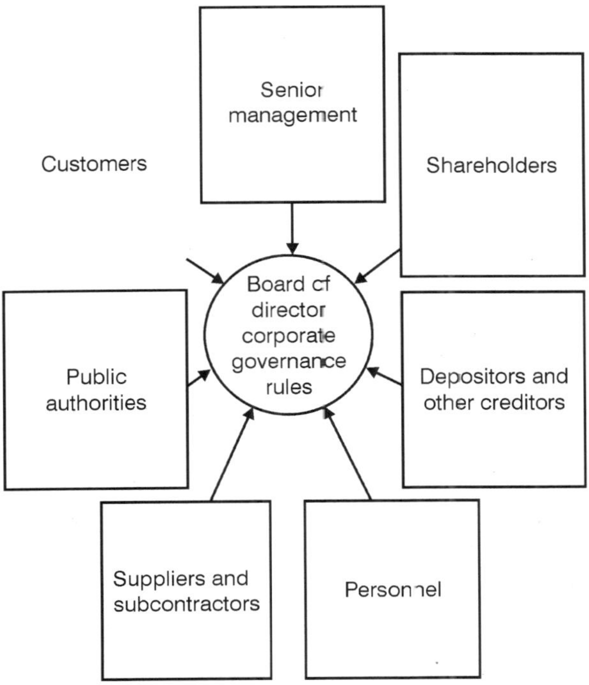

Fig. Major Stakeholders Affecting Corporate Governance in a Financial Firm

A comprehensive evaluation from the standpoint of all stakeholders is needed, based on the following principal groups of factors:

- Financial solidity, which comprises the bank's earning capacity, capital adequacy, asset quality, liquidity and operational efficiency, measured over the long-term.

- The quality of the management, evaluated by reference to vision, a clear and coherent strategy, innovativeness, control of risks and judicious judgement.
- Social responsibility and ethical conduct of business.
- Respect of the physical environment with regard to the bank's own activities and those of customers using the bank's resources.

Researchers have identified two major corporate governance models: the Anglo-American model, in which shareholders' interests are paramount; and the traditional German-Japanese model, in which not only the owners' interests but also those of employees, customers, partners and the community have a significant effect on corporate decision making. The general current trend in corporate governance privileges two areas: raising shareholder value; and enhancing managerial resources (finding, developing, rewarding and retaining executive talent). The management's drive to create shareholder value needs to have a longer-term perspective, insofar as short-term profit pressures can inhibit investment in the development of new products or entry into new markets.

The external environment of a financial firm influences its strategic choices, and eventually its results. The external factors are diverse and can be classed into two broad (but interrelated) categories: market conditions, and governmental frameworks.

Governmental frameworks cover regulatory-supervisory standards, safety nets and macroeconomic policies. Market conditions comprise customers needs, competitiveness by the providers of financial services, diversity of products and services, business facilities and expertise, demography and socioeconomic structure, economic growth and cycles, authenticity and transparency of accounts, and sociopolitical stability. Both categories vary among countries or over time.

RISK MANAGEMENT

Banks' credit relationship (originating, holding and monitoring loans until their ultimate recuperation) is changing. Loans and their risk elements are increasingly tradable. This trend has helped to enhance the liquidity of financial markets-with one adverse consequence: potentially higher volatility. Financial crises or turmoils have heightened the interest of financial firms in risk management, especially with respect to:

- Improving risk diversification.
- Optimising the funding or the liquidity of the firm.
- Holding selected risks that the firm is capable of managing profitably (involving a positive risk-reward analysis) and transferring the other risks.

- Setting equity capital at a level that maximises the firm's market value.

RISK DYNAMICS

In a dynamic world characterised by unending and unexpected change, the management of risk is a continuous process. It starts with the identification and measurement of risk elements, and with ascertaining their linkages. Accurate measurement is crucial to the appropriate pricing of risk elements. Other functions of risk management include forecasting the behaviour of risk factors over a given time horizon, speedy reporting and monitoring, internal control and audit, internal and external rating of exposure positions, independent evaluation and eventual adjustments for risk mitigation.

Since the risk profile of a financial firm changes rapidly, the risk manager has to be forward looking when assessing the impact of past and current decisions and practices, and when giving advice on the potential risks/rewards of future strategies and decisions. This responsibility entails continuous vigilance: in identifying areas of risk, and in improving measurement tools under the supervision of top management. The latter's primary concern is to choose those risks it can manage profitably and to transfer the others.

The array of risks encountered by the management of a financial firm is varied. Five major categories of risk-credit risks (debtors or counterparties), portfolio concentrations, market volatility and liquidity risks, legal risks and operational risks-and extraneous problems, including governmental mismanagement. A firm's chief risk officer has to grapple with various risk elements using a holistic approach. This enterprise-wide risk management acknowledges

- The fact that risks are interconnected, and
- The need to gauge risk exposures more accurately in order to quantify the economic capital needed.

Some risk elements are very difficult to measure, for example those linked to payment systems and reputation. The important elements in the pricing of a financial product to a single loan transaction. Banks use different debt rating models, which vary with respect to methodology and the choice of key qualitative and quantitative factors to assess the probability of default by a borrower and to estimate the average loss on a homogeneous portfolio of borrowers. Statistical techniques are applied to historical data to identify, measure and price the risk factors.

These techniques are also used to assess the risk impact (reduction, increase or neutral) of adding another product, for example a new loan to a particular credit portfolio. Credit scoring is one method of estimating the relative creditworthiness of a customer within a given category of borrowers. Such a method is, however, retrospective in that it focuses on how parties have handled their loans in the past, while current loans are extended against future income. Therefore credit scoring has to be supplemented by other, forward-looking evaluations.

Helped by their long experience, diverse exposure and sophisticated expertise, large global banks are developing reliable analytical and predictive tools to assess the riskiness of customers, counterparties, products and facilities

RISK MITIGATION

Banks and other firms use various risk-management techniques. The techniques used to mitigate credit risk include:

- The syndication of large loans or exposures among several financial firms.
- The sale by a firm of a given category of loans (such as accounts receivable or promissory notes) to a specialised financial institution known as a 'factor'; the latter usually buys the financial assets in question on a non-recourse basis and at a discount that reflects the interest charge and the risk of default by the debtors.
- Asset-backed securitisation, that is, the sale of a given portfolio of a firm's standardised loan assets to specially created, separate legal entity or special-purpose vehicle whose securities are issued for placement with private or institutional investors.

The total or partial transfer of credit risk to underwriters or insurers.

The use of flexible interest rates on loans to allow for repricing or the transfer of changes to a bank's funding costs (for example interest on deposits) to the loans, thereby maintaining stable interest margins for the bank concerned.

Hedging market and credit risks through the use of derivative instruments such as futures and options traded on regulated exchanges, and OTC swaps, options and forwards;

Selective approval at origination of credits and other exposures to optimise concentrations.

An increasingly greater number of the risks encountered by a financial firm or its clients can now be mitigated. This can be done inter alia for computer breakdown and for political risks. The former can be transferred for a fee to an IT services vendor, who assumes responsibility for computer maintenance and back-up. Political risk insurance is provided by private underwriters (for example Lloyd s and Zurich-American), national agencies (in the case of the richer trading nations of the OECD) and multilateral agencies.

Multilateral political insurance agencies are affiliated to intergovernmental development institutions such as the World Bank, the Inter-American Development Bank and other regional development banks. The function of the Multilateral Investment Guarantee Agency (MIGA) of the World Bank is to encourage the flow of funds for productive purposes to its 127 developing member countries, mainly through the issuance of investment guarantees against political risk. This international insurance market has grown considerably in coverage capacity, with increased cooperation among insurers to share risks (by reinsurance or coinsurance) and to draw on each other's special capabilities.

VALUE-AT-RISK

Several models have been developed to measure and control risk. None, however, has proven foolproof. Notable among these models is the value-at-risk (VaR) model, which purports to show the maximum loss (say x) a financial firm might incur on an asset or a portfolio of exposures.

It assumes:

- Immediate liquidation of the portfolio,
- A given probability or confidence level (for example 99 per cent),
- A given time horizon or holding period (for example 10 working days);
- Sufficient data on the firm's recent experience.

This means that, on average, in 99 holding periods out of 100 the loss on the portfolio under consideration will not exceed x. Put differently, in one 10-day spell out of 100, the portfolio will, on average, sustain a loss greater than x. However the VaR does not provide information on the timing or the size of the loss in excess of x.

For financial firms, in principle it is possible to design market-risk VaR models for the trading book (trading portfolio) and credit-risk VaR models for the banking book (loan portfolios). The existence of a large volume of empirical data on securities prices and the availability of this data on a daily basis have enabled financial firms to develop VaR trading-book models and to evaluate their reliability. Similar information is not readily available for VaR banking-book models, so researchers use bond data as a substitute for loan performance. Although most VaR models integrate the effects of diversification and hedging, the prudent manager should not overlook a detailed risk analysis of significant individual positions within the portfolio under scrutiny. The limitations of these models arise, inter alia, from the following:

- Price changes are distributed normally, thereby understating the probability of large price declines (and consequently the probability of large losses).
- Too small a number of correlations between price changes are used.
- The historical data used may understate risk, especially illiquidity risk during periods of crisis.
- The composition of the portfolio is assumed to be fixed during any one day.
- The probabilities of price changes used as certainties are in fact statistical estimates.

The future will not, however, replicate the past, upon which the VaR models are based, so risk analysts complement their evaluation with the scenario approach, which predicts how the firm might be affected by a complex chain of events, including a worst case scenario. However few analysts are able to imagine the full range of nightmare scenarios. This was the case with the UBS, whose post-tax loss reached CHF 659 million in 1997 and CHF 987 million in 1998 (over $1. 1 billion in these two years). The loss in 1997 was attributed to problems with its global equity derivatives business, the main elements of which were risks resulting from the use of an inappropriate model on its 'worst of dual asset call spread options' (CHF 120 million), loss on its Japanese convertible bonds (CHF 275 million), an 'adverse' change in the UK's fiscal legislation (CHF 80 million) and high volatility in the international shares market (CHF 150 million). The UBS's loss in 1998 resulted from participation in a large hedge fund, the Long Term Capital Management (LTCM), and a non-hedged credit to the LTCM.

The LTCM, founded in 1994, had on 31 August 1998 $125 billion in assets on a capital of $4. 8 billion at the beginning of that year-that is, a 25:1 leverage ratio. Fourteen of the large banks and securities firms who were creditors of the LTCM in 1998 failed to enforce their own credit risk management standards. Although large and sophisticated, the UBS did not have documentation on the execution and supervision of its transactions with the LTCM, and failed to identify or properly to evaluate major risks. The lax behaviour of senior bankers can be partly explained by the following factors:

- The 'halo' bestowed on the LTCM by virtue of the fact that three of its principals had outstanding credentials: a former vice chairman of the Federal Reserve Board and two Nobel laureates.
- The attractive past performance of the LTCM and other hedge funds created an infatuation with these funds, even on the part of sophisticated financial firms, and there was a degree of herd-like behaviour.
- The generally favourable economic conditions in 1995-97 prompted over optimism by bankers

It was established that the analytical tools used by banks and by securities and futures firms to assess the LTCM's risks were flawed: they did not question the fact that the LTCM's strategy across markets was uniform, that is, it lacked appropriate differentiation. Furthermore they underestimated the size of potential shocks in world markets, and the constraints on the rapid liquidation of the LTCM's positions.

THE ROLE OF JUDGEMENT

Risk models, no matter how sophisticated, cannot encompass all risks and their linkages. Furthermore, they are subject to human error. Hence they should be looked upon as aids to-not substitutes to-the making of judgements.

Independent expert control of risks should exist within the firm on a continuous basis to assist top management to assess the risks taken by its managerial staff, including traders. Chief financial market traders can receive bonuses of 10-15 per cent of their group's profits, and consequently are motivated to scout around for financial firms that are willing to take risks in order to make outsize gains.

One such trader personally earned some $15 million over four months while operating in the investment banking unit of the Credit Suisse Group. Other financial firms have chosen to reduce the level of risk their trading officers can take. The remuneration package of the latter does not incite them to focus solely on short-term gains, thereby neglecting longer-term positive results for the bank. The Swiss Federal Banking Commission has found that bonuses can reach several times the annual salary of a trader, and that these are linked to short-term gains, even though they are only partially realised. Usually banks bear the losses alone, some of which arise in the medium or longer term.

For banks that have invested heavily in information technology, data on exposure can be obtained in real time. In the management of risks, better informed senior executives can thus make their decisions on sounder bases and exercise control without costly delay. Several private rating agencies are in the business of judging the capacity of companies or countries to honour their financial obligations. Their ratings are usually made at the demand of borrowers, who pay the agencies for their services.

In recent years, major rating agencies have started to publish 'unsolicited ratings', reportedly to counter the tendency of debt issuers to shop around for the lowest fees among the agencies and/or for better ratings. Credit-rating agencies have occasionally failed to identify looming risks and to warn investors about the increased vulnerability of borrowers, for example in the case of the Asian crisis in 1997-8. Certain risks cannot be reasonably measured or anticipated, particularly systemic risk (the risk of failure of the financial system). This refers to the domino-like transmission of disruption of default risk (of a firm, a market segment, a payment and settlement system, and so on) to other institutions and/or countries.

Contagion spreads to institutions or countries that are perceived by investors or creditors to have similar problems or to be economically vulnerable to the collapse of the first victim. The impact of the Asian crisis, which broke out in Thailand in the second half of 1997, was estimated by the IMF to have halved world economic growth in 1998 and 1999 from a projected 4 per cent to 2 per cent.

The management of systemic risk and other macroeconomic risks is the responsibility of the public authorities, and individual banks need not hold capital against the possibility of an overall financial breakdown. Nevertheless the more capital a bank has, the higher the losses it can absorb, including those that arise from systemic risk. The central bank, in its responsibility as lender of last resort, normally protects sound and solvent banks against a liquidity crisis in the event of massive transfers or cash withdrawals by panicky depositors. Otherwise a forced liquidation of assets could lead banks-hitherto sound and safe-into insolvency and default. Such default can also affect debtors, whose credit lines are cut, and cascade-like breakdowns can become systemic, with a chain reaction of financing problems affecting many economic agents and disrupting payments, savings and credit distribution channels.

MUTATIONS IN FINANCIAL MARKETS

Over the past few decades, large business enterprises in developed market economies, led by US firms, have been successfully tapping the securities markets for lower-cost funding than that obtainable from banks. Begining in the 1980s various firms, including banks, started to unload selected portfolios of standardised credits through securitisation. The latter enables the bank to shift the credit risk and the funding of these portfolios to investors, enticed by the attractive terms of asset-backed securities. Banks that securitise portfolios of loans seek to generate fee income upon performing certain functions: originating and distributing credit, risk assessment, monitoring borrowers, collecting interest and capital reimbursements, and various accounting and administrative services.

In more recent years, smaller enterprises have been able to turn to financial markets to satisfy some of their funding needs. Even development capital and start-up equity can be partially raised through various specialised stock exchanges or trading platforms. The opportunity to issue stocks and other securities has been enhanced by the willingness of individual and institutional savers to channel a significant portion of their wealth into tradable financial instruments.

EXCHANGES

Exchanges are organised markets that have traditionally focused on the trading of equity shares and commodities. In more recent years derivatives and fixed-income securities (such as corporate bonds and commercial papers) have become tradable on exchanges, mostly electronically: in early 2000 the Swiss Exchange, for example, traded some 40 per cent of the Eurobond retail volume, valued at euro 541. 12 billion (the wholesale market was over 10 times larger). In 2000 the largest electronic trading system for European government bonds, Euro MTS, accounted for over 30 per cent of all trading volumes (14 billion euros worth of transactions a day) in these securities.

Venture capitalists and high-growth companies are increasingly able to raise capital through exchanges geared to their needs, at conditions more favourable than bank financing. With the globalisation of financial markets gathering momentum, competition has been building up among exchanges at the national and international levels to raise fresh capital for all kinds of business enterprises and for trading in various financial instruments. Exchanges have been competing for the custom of users by enhancing the utility of their services through a variety of novel approaches.

NASDAQ is one example of an exchange based on an electronic communication system, whereby market makers display the prices at which they are willing to buy or sell stocks for their own account or for their customers. It has pioneered the provision of capital access to budding high-technology and/or high-growth companies, such as those in information technology. In contrast the New York Stock Exchange (NYSE) is based on the traditional auction system.

It has stricter listing requirements for firms with respect to size, equity, shareholding and performance, including those seeking an initial public offering (IPO). Furthermore it has erected protective barriers, for example it denies other exchanges the right to trade in the stocks it lists. A few exchanges have also limited the flow of data and routing orders, thereby constraining the growth of electronic systems.

Under the aegis of governmental regulatory entities, most exchanges are authorised by the jurisdictions in which they operate to be self-regulated. This covers the control of market manipulations and the supervision of broker/dealer conduct. Besides operational efficiency, the challenge for interconnected exchanges and the Internet is to agree generally accepted regulatory rules to protect the markets from false information.

The opening of new exchanges in competition with established ones has yielded significant advantages in terms of improved service and lower charges. Emulating NASDAQ, several new exchanges have helped young start-up and high-growth companies (mostly in the high-tech field) to raise finance by overcoming the stringent listing of traditional exchanges. For IPOs the latter normally require an operating history, and set minimum conditions in respect of profitability or sales over recent periods, as well as minimum levels of capital and assets, and a minimum number of founding shareholders with lock-up periods (that is, with the obligation of keeping their shares over pre-agreed minimum periods). In 2000 the European exchanges for innovative companies comprised the Brussels-based Easdaq, the Alternative Investment Market (AIM) in London and the Euro NM alliance of five continental European exchanges. The latter enables investors in these five exchanges to transact shares listed in any of the partner exchanges, using the same trading and settlement system.

The proliferation of independent exchanges has, however, the potential to fragment liquidity pools. Such fragmentation could be overcome by alliances or mergers of exchanges aimed at creating common platforms with shared rules for the cross-border listing, margining, transaction, clearing and settlement of trade. Alliances or mergers might be prompted by a number of expected benefits: extension of the distribution network and client base, improved division of labour, economies of size (for example through joint research or shared investment in new technologies), cross-trading arrangements and an improved competitive position for the cooperating parties vis-à-vis rivals.

In the field of derivatives, one example of a successful international alliance is Eurex, a common electronic trading system set up by the Frankfurt and Zurich exchanges. Eurex has also entered into an alliance with the Chicago Board of Trade, the Helsinki Exchange and others with the objective of connecting international derivatives markets. Its major competitor in the derivatives sector is the Globex Alliance, which links the Paris Bourse, the Chicago Mercantile Exchange and the Singapore International Monetary Exchange, joined later by the Montreal and Brazilian exchanges.

Other examples include the merger (with their respective ownerships) of the French (60 per cent), Dutch (32 per cent) and Belgium (8 per cent) stock exchanges in early 2000, driven by pressure to reduce costs. The Paris, Amsterdam and Brussels exchanges thus became a single exchange called Euronext, with one membership, one rule book (including listing) and one clearing-netting and settlement system. Euronext handles equities, options, derivatives and commodities. The London Stock Exchange and the Deutsche Börse followed suit in May 2000 to form the biggest European co-owned exchange. The latter intended to become a global trading platform through alliances-notably with NASDAQ to be effected through cross-shareholding. However, the deal collapsed later that year.

Technological advances can be illustrated by reference to electronic trading systems, which are replacing the floor-based, open outcry method. The latter (also known as pit trading) consists of a public auction at a centralised exchange, where financial instruments are traded by authorised floor participants who make bids and offers to each other verbally or through hand signals. In contrast electronic trading systems, commonly referred to as electronic communications networks (ECNs), are screen-based: they allow authorised investors (institutions and persons) to use computer terminals-regardless of geographical location-anonymously to enter bids and offers into a host computer, which matches orders and executes operations. These operations cover order-routing, clearing and settlement, and allow investors to trade after hours at the major traditional exchanges.

ECNs have several advantages: they reduce the market impact of transactions; they eliminate bid/offer spreads or dealer-broker commission; and they are neutral. Some ECNs, such as Island, anonymously display all limit orders (those in which investors specify the purchase or sale price at which they are willing to transact) in a format available on the Internet at no charge. ECNs are also important to NASDAQ's trade, accounting for about

30 per cent. By trading on ECNs, institutional and private traders reduce their reliance on market makers.

Some stock exchanges have also combined their equity and fixed income operations with ECNs (Market XT and Archipelago respectively). Investors and traders thus receive multiple benefits: extended trading hours, access to information and stocks from several exchanges, regulator oversight, high-speed electronic trading and access to more opportunities. Other exchanges have announced similar plans. Greater market transparency can be achieved by requiring the full range of investor limit orders received by competing exchanges, electronic systems and stand-alone dealers to be displayed. This would permit all market participants to ascertain the extent of supply and demand for any stock, and it would enhance the liquidity of financial markets.

E-TRADING

On-line business via the Internet-by means of personal computers and mobile devices-has proliferated and enjoyed spectacular growth. By easing access to markets, cutting trading costs and broadening the range of investment opportunities, on-line brokers have attracted millions of investors. Some brokers are independent while others are affiliated to diversified financial firms. A few on-line brokers may not be guided by professional practices and ethics, notably the rules of 'suitability' and 'know your customer' observed by traditional firms that offer judicious advice aimed at protecting investors from inappropriate financial risks. Beyond distributional advantages, investment bankers-thanks to their research capabilities-can offer large institutional investors quality advice.

Electronic commerce (often referred to as e-commerce) is bound to expand with customer adaptation to change, ready access to technology, transparency of costs and prices, and assurances about the protection of privacy. Relationship-based financial transactions are increasingly being replaced by automated operations. 'Over the counter' instruments (equity, debt, derivatives, indices and so on)-hitherto with prices quoted privately-will thus become increasingly available on-line, not only for institutions but also for savvy individuals. Investors all over the world can now directly access actively traded instruments in the secondary market and newly launched securities such as IPOs in the primary market at negligible marginal cost. Investors are likely to reap certain advantages by trading with electronic brokers via the Internet, rather than with traditional dealer/broker firms. The following advantages can be realised, subject to the judicious choice of an efficient and neutral broker (that is, without its own portfolio to compete with its customers):

- Lower cost structure and lower fees and commissions (for transaction, clearing, settlement and so on).
- Direct electronic access to major stock exchanges, and global reach.

- Instantaneous trade execution, with speedy settlement and clearance.
- Extended trading hours (24-hour access to brokers).
- Greater transparency through real-time prices, up-to-date news, performance measurement and charting.
- Better prices (except after normal trading hours, when the bid-ask spreads are larger, the choice of stocks is smaller, the information is less complete, volumes are smaller and prices are more volatile).

The trading-hour constraint is rapidly disappearing with the creation of alliances among stock exchanges in different time zones, notably the exchanges in America, Asia and Europe. Investors thus have 24-hour platforms of active trading. Furthermore competition has prompted on-line stockbrokers to expand their range of activities.

One rapid means of expansion is by takeover, as was done in early 2000 by E Trade (buying Telebank Financial, the Internet banking group) and Charles Schwab (buying US Trust, a financial firm in investment management, private banking, estate planning and fiduciary services). One of the world's largest electronic brokerages-Reuters' Instinet-caters for institutional investors and equity brokers. In 2000 it expanded its offering to include fixed-income securities and retail business. Through a single brokerage vehicle, Instinet offers its customers access to the major market-economy exchanges, thereby providing them with a large pool of liquidity, global opportunities and lower transaction costs. In addition to its brokerage business, it offers trading research and analytics to its institutional customers.

Its participation interests span over other independent electronic trading platforms, such as Tradepoint in the UK and Archipelago in the US.

A continuous stream of current data and the ability to trade on a real-time basis are increasingly available not only to financial firms and their traders, but also to private investors.

Sophisticated, high-speed order routing and execution systems enable investors and traders to be linked directly (that is, without an intermediate firm being involved in routing orders) to other traders and to market makers in various stock markets. Transactions are executed within seconds of traders placing their orders, against the payment of fees for computer and electronic services. On-line traders and investors do not, however, have the benefit of the advice normally provided by a full-service broker/dealer on the suitability of a particular trade.

BANKING AND IT DEVELOPMENTS

Notwithsanding the spectacular growth in financial markets instruments, bank credit remains important for two categories of borrower: individuals and small enterprises that are unable to access the financial markets, and institutions that need custom-made advice and financing, for example for major projects such as energy generation or mining.

Standard bank products (such as consumer lending and mortgages) with transparent terms can increasingly be purchased via e-channels. The latter are cost efficient for commoditised credit products and for simple high-frequency bank services such as bill payments, fund transfers, information provision, stock and mutual fund trading, personal planning modules and so on.

Compared with individual investors in corporate bonds, banks have four major comparative advantages in handling credit risks. First, banks have the means and the expertise to monitor and assess the wealth, income, spending behaviour and debt servicing of their customers. Second, they enjoy economies of scale in their credit operations because of the large number of transactions. Third, they are capable of achieving a higher degree of diversification among borrowing customers.

Fourth they can obtain on a continuing basis from their borrowing customers specific information that is not readily available to investors since the borrowers know that their bank, for competitive reasons, will protect proprietary information from public disclosure.

Banks are increasingly at the forefront of using state-of-the-art information technology to protect their market share in the financial services industry against encroachment by new players. Their jump into cyberspace has been spectacular: from dispensing cash and accepting deposits through automatic teller machines from the late 1960s, to the current provision of Internet banking to corporate and individual customers.

Financial firms' considerable investments in IT are aimed at tapping a very large potential market for a wide array of standardisable products or services, such as credit cards, debit cards, stored-value cards, consumer or mortgage loans, fund transfers, foreign exchange, cash and/or asset management, trading in mutual funds and financial instruments, insurance policies, bills payment, corporate research, portfolio evaluation and advice.

Modern banks' activities are based fundamentally on processing information. In this respect their methods of servicing their customers have generally progressed through five stages, beginning in about 1960:

- The automation of the 'back office' and the reduction of paper-based, manually processed operations.
- The provision of self-service banking via ATMs inside or outside the bank premises.
- The provision of banking services via the telephone to customers in offices, shops or at home.
- The provision of Internet banking, further easing customers' access to banking services and allowing new financial service providers to enter the market.
- The delocalisation of the traditional bank-customer relationship with

the arrival of mobile devices that enable customers to interface with their banks and other financial market participants whenever and wherever.

The use of the Internet for transactional purposes has increased considerably for the following reasons: ease of entry by service providers and customers; cost effectiveness (about one tenth of the cost of a transaction in a traditional bank office); and improved transparency in the terms of the products and services offered by banks, including prices.

The Internet has also allowed the rise of independent 'information providers', who search for and aggregate the terms of products and services offered by financial firms. Independent distributors have also sprung up on the Internet, thus widening customers' choice in respect of various products and services, such as mutual funds, deposits, mortgages, consumer credit, life insurance, stockbrokerage, credit cards and so on.

Banks are adding to their traditional function of financial intermediation the novel function of facilitator of e-commerce. In the latter capacity they are currently developing a variety of services, notably:

- Internet portals: these 'supersites' are open to many providers of products or services. They provide potential buyers with an opportunity to view, compare and choose. Offerings need not be limited to financial products or services.
- Certification of identity: each bank certifies the identity of its own account holders, and acts as a channel for its customers to verify the identity of account holders at other banks.
- Assisting small businesses: banks court the custom of small enterprises by offering to set up Web sites for them. These Web sites have interactive transactional capabilities.

Electronic billing: within the framework of their cash management services, banks can offer to companies that send large volumes of bills to their customers an electronic billing and remittance-processing service through the interbank payment system.

Facilitating e-commerce: banks have an interest in offering technology for electronic business-to-business commerce in order to automate the flow of transactions relating to procurement, the distribution of goods and related services. Besides generating fee income from that activity, they expect a positive fallout for other activities, such as cash management.

Electronic money: with the availability of computers equipped with smart card readers, banks are able to provide electronic money that can be stored on these cards for use on the Internet. In addition, electronic cheques are being designed for use by businesses or individuals.

The ongoing cybernetic revolution implies heavy investment by financial firms to strengthen their relationship with existing customers, create new opportunities and fend off competition from other financial and non-financial firms, including technology companies. Yet, potentially profitable IT developments are difficult to identify with certainty, and there is a danger of committing resources to an IT channel that turns out to be economically unviable. In this case the firms concerned could loose substantially in non-amortisable investments and reduced market share or turnover.

SECURITY CONCERNS

E-commerce is particularly vulnerable to technological problems (for example the breakdown of individual computers or networks), and imposters or other parties seeking to harm users or providers. Attacks could include:

- Stealing important information, such as credit card numbers and other personal data.
- Damaging or destroying computer files and contaminating computer systems by planting viruses.
- Illicit operations, such as unauthorised transfers of funds.
- Denying service by maliciously congesting targeted Web sites.

Unless computer security and law enforcement are improved, e-brokerage business-which was estimated to account for about 16 per cent of all stock trade in the US in 2000-and other e-commerce could be hurt. Various users of the Web, including the operators of interbank transfer systems, could be equally hurt by cyber-terrorism. This calls for identification of the Internet's weak links, and for continuous upgrading of security systems in areas such as encryption, digital signatures, finger-print scanning and coding, traffic filters to ascertain legitimate users, and the rerouting of traffic from logged computer servers to others. For the unfettered growth of Internet operations, official security certification at the international level and the prosecution of offenders are essential.

Besides raiders illegally cracking into ostensibly heavily protected computer systems, individual Internet users can be vulnerable to those seeking to embezzle unsuspecting and credulous persons through the use of such claims as 'Get rich quick', 'Free stock' and 'Exceptional high returns', as well as pyramidal schemes and other scams.

Internet fraudsters are being pursued at the international level, and national agencies in 28 countries are monitoring suspect Web sites. The US Federal Trade Commission is spearheading the global sweep, with the help of international agencies. A permanent data base is being established to store information on fraud site operators, their physical locations and the victims of their misdeeds. Fraudulent operators on the Internet are thus increasingly being tracked down.

PUBLIC INTERVENTION

MOTIVATION

Protection of the banking system is of particular concern to the public authorities in modern economies in view of the fact that the banking system is at the centre of the payment and settlement system, the mobilisation of savings, the allocation of credit and the creation of money. Indeed banks provide most of an economy's stock of money through the extension of loans to households and companies. The payment and settlement system is a fundamental infrastructure in a modern economy in that every economic transaction necessitates a payment.

Besides the legal tender-that is the banknotes and coins produced by the monetary authorities-bank deposits lodged by individuals and institutions are a major source of payment funds. Since bank deposits are a leading liquid asset for individual and institutional depositors, banks offer payment services linked to these deposits, and hence they have assumed a central role in the payment system.

The failure of banks-in view of their central role in the payment and financial intermediation systems-thus has a stronger adverse effect on the real economy than the failure of other firms. An efficient financial sector is essential to the growth and stability of modern economies at the national, regional or international levels. Public intervention in the financial sector is therefore prompted by the objective of

- Setting the requisite conditions for the safe and efficient operation of the banking/financial system,
- Forestalling payments crises. Such crises produce considerable ill effects, such as recession, disruption of production, social conflict and loss of property or life. This is readily illustrated by the many crises that hit several countries in various parts of the world during the

1990s. The vulnerability of financial intermediaries-and notably banks-derives largely from five inter-related factors:

- Banks prefer to rely on third-party funding (or debt) in lieu of owner's funding (or equity) because of the lower financial cost of debt financing compared with equity; debt charges are furthermore treated as expenses before the assessment of corporate taxation, which is not the case with dividends. Consequently banks tend to minimise the cushion of equity or risk capital.
- Banks depend for a significant portion of their third-party resources on depositors' funds, which have to be repaid at their face value and on demand (or at very short notice).
- Banks transform liquid or short-term resources into illiquid or longer-term assets in the expectation of reaping higher interest margins. Furthermore they tend to keep a small fraction of their callable deposits in liquid assets, since these assets produce only modest or no income.
- Banks are highly interdependent owing to their intertwined business

relations (interbank lending, syndicated loans, joint clearing and settlement mechanisms, counterparty operations, agency relations, joint ventures and so on). The losses of a defaulting bank spread through the payment and settlement system, and are thus bound to affect other banks.

- Depositors are likely to panic if adverse rumours spread, in view of the maturity mismatch between banks' liabilities and assets and in view of the opacity of information on risks that banks disclose to the public. Depositors are therefore prone to rush to withdraw their funds, not only from unsound or unsafe institutions, but also from solvent institutions.

The principal aim of legislation on and regulation of the financial sector is to protect general welfare and improve market efficiency, notably with respect to consumer protection, transparency, systemic risk and moral hazard. First, consumer protection is needed against the possible abuse of market power by dominant financial intermediaries. Intermediaries have sought to increase their size for multiple reasons, notably to achieve greater efficiency and higher returns through economies of scale (since the initial cost of setting up a financial activity is relatively very large and the cost of an additional unit of product or service is very low or nil), and economies of scope (through the synergy created by offering multiple products to satisfy various complementary needs of customers). Regulators have to ensure that the abovemen-tioned economies benefit consumers.

Second, the financial sector is characterised by information asymmetry, indicating that the parties to a transaction do not have the same information. Indeed depositors have incomplete information on their depository bank. Regulators can require the latter to disclose the information needed to enable depositors and other users of financial services to make sound decisions. Small depositors often lack the willingness, time, skills or resources to identify and analyse the risk of financial intermediaries, delegating that function to the public authorities, which are in a better position to obtain the required information and to impose appropriate penalties on intermediaries that transgress the rules.

Third, regulation can eliminate or moderate systemic risk. The latter results from the potential chain effect of the failure of one intermediary in a given country triggering-through the payment system-liquidity and solvency crises for other intermediaries in the same country, as well as in other countries. The rapid transmission of risk can be explained by the fact that banks are closely interconnected. Solvent intermediaries can be faced by a massive, irrational run by panicking depositors subject to herd-like behaviour and can-in the absence of adequate funding-be obliged to effect a 'fire sale' of financial assets. This will set in train a series of price declines and insolvencies unless the regulators and monetary authorities intervene appropriately and in the early stage of the problem. Fourth, safety nets are put in place to prevent or quell runs on banks that might spread rapidly from weak banks to strong ones. They are normally available through three standby arrangements:

- A lender-of-last-resort service for solvent banks;
- Deposit guarantees-and in some situations an explicit (or implicit) bail-out promise-to individual institu-tions (notably big ones); and
- Intra-day credit from the clearing authorities (viz. the central bank) to participating banks, normally against collateral.

Safety nets carry with them the seed of 'moral hazard'. The latter means that financial institutions and their customers expect central banks, deposit insurance institutions, other governmental agencies and multilateral international organisations to intervene to prevent the failure of a financial intermediary in the event of a financial crisis-a situation which fosters mismanagement.

Public Protection and Market Discipline

Financial crises and their costly aftermath have prompted public authorities to improve their regulatory framework and provide safety nets. The results of this are distorted competition and weakened market discipline. In particular safety nets.

- Reduce the incentive of depositors and other creditors to monitor their bank and to charge that bank in accordance with its risk profile;
- Induce depositors to entrust their funds to banks at lower interest rates than would be acceptable in the absence of deposit insurance;
- Reduce bankers' prudence by enticing them to take greater risks (in the expectation of higher returns) in the knowledge that the funds provided by creditors are secured by deposit guarantees; and
- Enable banks to finance customers at interest costs that are not commensurate with the risk posed by these customers, thereby leading to a suboptimal misalloca-tion of economic resources.

The propensity of management to neglect professional rigour can be counteracted by the effective enforcement of prudential regulations (such as rules focusing on adequate liquidity, exposure limits and risk-adjusted capital), and by imposing appropriate penalties on banks and their managers for irresponsible behaviour. Bank management would accordingly be required continuously to enforce the observance of various laws and regulations, including prudential rules.

This could be verified by efficient control and audit systems within the firm, under the supervision of designated public agencies and accredited independent external auditors. Deviant or fraudulent actions by top management should be subject to appropriate punishment. This could start with a reprimand and ultimately lead to the temporary or permanent withdrawal of operating permits, or jail sentences for executives if warranted.

The involvement of public authorities in regulatory and supervisory functions and safety nets does not mean that market participants can assume risks without bearing the consequences of their actions. In protecting the public interest, bank regulators act as agents for two principals: the taxpayer, who is shielded against the eventuality of being called upon to share the cost of a bank failure; and the customer (whether debtor or creditor), who is safeguarded against exploitation and the misuse of his or her financial resources by unscrupulous parties within or without the bank.

Regulators, as the agent for the taxpayer, do not invariably act in the best interests of the latter as they are supposed to do. Indeed they may be tempted to delay addressing the problems of troubled banks under their jurisdiction in order to cover up past mistakes or oversights in the hope of an improvement in the circumstances of the banks. They are comforted by the fact that insured depositors are protected and that an insolvent bank can continue to operate for a long period. The delay in closing an insolvent bank, with operational losses still accruing, will increase the cumulative losses sustained by the bank. This will in turn increase the cost to the taxpayer, who will be called upon to absorb the losses suffered by insured depositors.

A bank's risks can change rapidly and thus render existing information obsolete. For troubled banks it is recommended that thorough on-site examinations be conducted more frequently than is the case for sound banks. This type of inspection would, however, be costly in terms of the labour of qualified persons assigned to that function, as well as burdensome for the banks being examined as their day-to-day operations would probably be disrupted. Low-risk banks should therefore be subject to a less intensive supervisory programme.

Off-site surveillance complements on-site examination by offering an appreciation of the bank's circumstances on an ongoing basis. This can take the form of

- A series of ratios, known as 'supervisory screens', calculated from the financial accounts of a bank-problems can be detected when the ratios diverge from the standard values established on the basis of past experience; or
- Econometric models based on selected ratios that produce a single number that reflects the degree of solidity of a bank. Econometric models are considered to be more useful than supervisory screens in detecting problems with safety and soundness. Judgement remains, nevertheless, an important element in detecting problem situations. In view of
- The delays in reporting mishaps by the management of troubled banks to the regulatory authorities,
- The inadequate or imprecise measures currently available for assessing bank risks, and

- The lags in corrective measures or sanctions by the regulatory authorities, it is advisable to resort to market signals to trigger managerial rigour, and thus contain or moderate moral hazard.

Governmental entities (such as the Federal Deposit Insurance Corporation, FDIC, in the US) cannot readily recognise changes in the risk profiles of deposit-taking banks. Indeed deposit insurance cannot involve actuarial methods similar to those used, for instance, by the life insurance business.

The latter offers a reliable statistical calculation of the risks and premia needed to build a fund capable of absorbing predictable future losses. However bank failures cannot be accurately forecast: they occur irregularly and very occasionally in large numbers. If the governmental deposit insurance-which substitutes the credit standing of a private bank for that of the central government-undercharges for risk, the bank will in effect be benefitting from a concealed subsidy. Bearing in mind the above considerations, it is essential for the soundness and efficiency of the banking system to price as fairly as possible the risk exposure of each bank.

Towards that objective, transparency of information on a bank's operations enables rational market participants with money at stake to produce a collective judgement on the riskiness of the said bank, and the premia they will require for channelling their savings to it. Markets can evaluate the risk of widely traded financial instruments belonging to entities whose operations are sufficiently transparent.

Market discipline will have been exercised when lending charges (including premia on risks) increase and credit availability decreases in parallel with the increase in the borrower's risk profile. If a bank assumes excessive risks, depositors have the possibility of withdrawing their funds if they doubt the bank's solvency.

In the case of default, management and the shareholders should fully bear the brunt of the losses, followed by subordinate creditors. The orderly liquidation of an insolvent bank benefits the economy in the long term as it prompts the management of other banks to exercise prudence.

This principle should apply to all institutions, regardless of the size and scope of their activities. In the absence of an international framework for handling insolvencies, a professional association of operators and regulators from the financial sector has offered recommendations for the speedy handling of the insolvency of global financial institutions. Market signals could be built into the safety nets to ensure that participants in the financial system have a strong incentive to behave prudently.

Such signals are premised on the existence of transparency (that is, the dissemination of reliable, detailed and up-to-date data on risk exposures), on the efficient functioning of a competitive market place, on rational behaviour by market participants on both the supply and the demand side for funds, and on prompt reaction by all parties concerned. Various measures for the promotion of market signals have been proposed, including the following:

- Regulations could require all banks to issue, besides their share capital, subordinated debt for public subscription. Investors are normally sensitive to a bank's 'prudence and performance' record. The lower the prudence, the higher the cost of placing subordinated debt with potential investors. More generally, the disclosure of a bank's risk-based capital (including information on innovative, complex and hybrid capital instruments) will enable market participants to judge the bank's capacity to absorb financial losses.

This information needs to be complemented, for the benefit of investors, with disclosure on various risk exposures.

A governmental deposit insurance safety net should carry a coinsurance element (for example 20 percent), whereby each depositor shares in the risk by accepting an element of self-insurance and bearing a tranche of the eventual loss on her/his deposit. This coinsurance would encourage depositors, especially large ones, to demand greater transparency from their deposit-taking bank so that they could assess their bank's safety and soundness: they would discipline risky institutions by withdrawing their funds or demanding higher interest rates on their deposits. Should a bank deny its depositors the requisite information, it would be shunned or obliged to pay a risk premium for its opacity.

Partial private insurance or reinsurance of a proportion (say 5 per cent) of a bank's deposits could also be used. Risk-assessed premia on deposits charged by the private sector would then act as a supplementary market signal. A rise in such premia should trigger regulatory action, in the same way as would an increase in the spread required by investors on the subordinated debt of a bank, over and above a risk-free rate (for example that of a governmental security).

A governmental deposit insurance entity-besides using market signals to price its protection of bank deposits-would need the authority to inspect banks and the means to make banks comply. These means could include:

- Penal insurance rates.
- The dismissal and replacement of inefficient or miscreant executives.
- Denying deposit insurance to a delinquent bank.
- Ultimately, the closure of a bank.

The Central Role of Equity

The solidity of a bank in the long term is based on three main pillars: earning capacity, prudence and equity. Prudence calls on management to maintain appropriate liquid reserves to meet unexpected withdrawals of funds, and to avoid excessively risky operations. The survival of a firm in periods of difficulty is dependent on the relative size of equity or owners' capital at risk. Owner's capital demonstrates three characteristics: permanency, a residual status in the distribution of income or assets, and initial responsibility for absorbing eventual losses. Capital's functions are primarily fourfold:

- To cover unexpected losses (expected losses can be integrated into the charges levied on individual products and services, or can be absorbed by specifically constituted loss provisions).
- To finance-in an environment of uncertainty-the start-up costs of a bank's activities (including those relating to physical infrastructure or the acquisition of know-how and talents), and the expansion of these activities over time.
- To secure depositors by increasing the owner's stake in the bank; this serves to moderate the interest paid on deposits and third parties' funds,
- To ensure that the level of capital requirement moves in tandem with the overall risk of a bank's activities.

In view of the fact that equity capital generally costs more than borrowed funds, the firm's top management endeavours to constitute adequate equity base capable of maximising the value of their enterprise. By comparison, public regulators of banks, in prescribing minimum capital requirements, are primarily concerned with protecting the public interest-notably that of ensuring a safe and sound banking system capable of serving all concerned parties efficiently. The first attempt by central bankers and regulators to institutionalise their cooperation in the field of prudential standards was the creation of the Basle Committee on Banking Supervision at the end of 1974. The membership of this committee currently comprises senior representatives of the monetary-supervisory authorities of the major financial centres. The committee has no supranational supervisory authority: its task is to recommend best practice standards and guidelines.

The committee was established in the wake of the foreign exchange turbulences in 1974 that culminated in the collapse of Bankhaus I. D. Herstatt, which defaulted on more than $600 million in claims. More than 12 US-based banks that had paid out Deutschmarks to Herstatt were unable to get US dollars in settlement at the opening of the clearing system in New York at 10. 30 am as Herstatt's had been closed before its dollars could be credited to its foreign counterparties, which suffered considerable losses. The ensuing unsettlement in the interbank trading market hurt other banks, which were charged onerous risk premiums of 2 per cent for six weeks. This type of cross-currency settlement risk is a time-zone-induced credit risk in spot forex transactions and has come to be referred to as the 'Herstatt risk'.

Prompted by the objective of ensuring both prudent behaviour and the convergence of regulatory standards among banks, over the years the Basle Committee has formulated a series of guidelines for national bank regulators.

With the approval of the G10 central bank governors, the committee proposed the application of a framework for minimum regulatory capital, beginning in 1988. Banks operating transnationally were asked to cover four categories of bank loan exposure with minimum capital charges, rising in accordance with their estimated riskiness.

These charges were set at 0 per cent (OECD governments), 1. 6 per cent (banks in OECD countries), 4. 0 per cent (residential mortages) and 8. 0 per cent (all other loans) of the face value of the respective claims. Capital was defined as consisting of two tiers: tier 1 or core capital, comprising common shares and retained earnings; and tier 2 capital, comprising mostly medium- to long-term subordinated debt instruments. In 1997 the committee enlarged the minimum capital requirement for banks to cover market risks, notably with respect to banks' trading portfolios. Equity standards were adopted in 1988 after a negotiated compromise among the committee members.

These standards have proved too simplistic, and often arbitrary or inconsistent. For example, in the case of bank credit the rules assign to the best-rated corporations (AAA) the same minimum regulatory capital coefficient as that for lower-rated corporations, that is, 8 per cent of the face value of such loans. Such rules encourage banks to operate perversely by reducing assets whose risks and capital charges are overestimated by the regulators, and increasing assets whose risks and capital charges are underestimated by the regulators. Use of the static, 'one-size-fits-all' approach also fails to address differences in the nature of banks' businesses.

The standardised uniform weights have not been confined to credit risk, but have also been used in the case of market risks. Indeed in 1997 the committee introduced a regulatory capital charge on the trading account of banks, set at a fixed minimum multiplier of three for value-at-risk (VaR), plus an 'add-on' of one to make a total of four VaR, when the banks' internal models and their stress testing prove to be inaccurate. Stress testing estimates the potential loss resulting from the large changes in key risk factors that can occur in periods of extreme difficulty. During 1999-2001 the Basle Committee embarked on a revision aimed at fine-tuning its regulatory capital framework, guided by four objectives:

- Safety and soundness in the financial system.
- Competitive equality among banks.
- A comprehensive approach to addressing risks.
- Generalised coverage for all banks (the 1988 recommendations were intended solely for internationally active banks) in view of the liberalisation of domestic financial markets.

The committee's 2001 proposals also underline three major requirements:

- Expanding capital requirements to cover additional risks (such as operational and interest-rate risks);
- Giving regulators additional power to raise (above the general

minimum of 8 per cent) a bank's capital adequacy if warranted by the risk encountered by that bank; and

- The disclosure of more details to the general public in order to encourage market participants to differentiate among banks by reference to safe and sound banking practices. The committee has also recommended greater reliance on independent credit rating agencies and on banks' own risk-management models and internal ratings (instead of the preassigned standard ratios imposed by the regulators). The latter recommendation is premised on the assumption that management has full and ready knowledge of the risks of its operations on a continuous basis, and that its models are capable of identifying risk variables and of accurately calculating their weights and behaviour. One can argue that the committee's approach poses several challenges, notably the following:
- The validation of internal models by the regulatory authorities requires a coherent approach to assessing these models, not only within a single country but also across several countries that might use different accounting methods.
- It is possible that certain current or prospective credit rating agencies could supply, in response to demand by or pressure from rated entities, better ratings than would be warranted by strictly objective criteria.
- Credit rating agencies are not likely to have full and immediate knowledge of a bank's rapidly changing risk circumstances.
- The proposed weights for risk exposure, though an improvement over those of 1988, are still rough and static estimates and are often the product of negotiated compromises reached at a given point in time by representatives of the bank supervisory authorities.
- Banks may continue to practice 'regulatory arbitrage' by favouring activities whose regulatory capital requirement underestimates their effective risk.
- The committee has yet to address each individual bank's risk diversification by reference to its full range of portfolios, both on and off balance sheet. Such enterprise-wide calculations for a financial institution can produce an overall risk profile, which can be higher or lower depending on the correlations for defaults and/or credit losses within and across different credit risk concentrations.

Researchers are exploring new avenues for assigning capital charges to assets held by financial intermediaries. They include:

- Precommitment of capital (PCA) to the trading portfolio of a bank. The management of the latter would be asked to choose a level of capital to back the said portfolio over a given period of time. Should the cumulative losses exceed the capital cover at any time during that period the regulators would fine the bank ex-post. The PCA approach could well prompt most banks to develop accurate models and to communicate the results truthfully to the regulators. The task of the regulators would be to choose an appropriate structure of penalties to induce bank managements to moderate their risk levels or provide an additional capital cushion. The stiffer the penalty, the greater the prudence of management in terms of risk taking. PCA would have the advantage of reducing regulators' involvement in the setting of capital requirements by putting the onus on individual bank managements.

- Rewarding banks that avoid losses with a reduction in the standard capital charges. Banks could moderate their risk profile by various means, such as acquiring safe assets, resorting to hedging, disposing of assets (sell-downs or securitization) or enhancing internal controls. Introducing contingent liability for bank stockholders upon the default of their institution. 'Double liability' was applied to national banks in the US from 1863 to 1933. Contingent liability could also be imposed on the managers of failed banks.

Expanding the Reach of Regulation

The gradual dismantling of barriers in financial intermediation and markets has led to greater interdependence at the global level, thereby presenting both opportunities and challenges for competition and risk control. National regulators and supervisors are reluctant to surrender their prerogatives. In the absence of a supranational global regulatory and supervisory entity, which is unrealistic in light of the current and prospective state of world affairs, it is imperative that the various parties in the international financial community enhance their cooperation in order to avoid systemic risk and preserve a sound and resilient global financial market.

International regulatory cooperation has increasingly focused on:

- The observation of uniform principles for healthy risk management and harmonised safe capital requirements;
- Common accounting plans that allow for accuracy and transparency in the reporting of the economic circumstances of financial institutions, and for comparability of reporting techniques across time and space;
- The auditing of the consolidated activities of an enterprise; and
- The appointment of an accredited regulatory agency to act as primary supervisor or principal coordinator of all national regulatory agencies concerned with the world-wide supervision of diversified, transnational financial groups.

Governments interested in boosting their economies have deliberately exonerated from regulation all or selected activities of financial firms. These exonerations vary considerably among jurisdictions. Moreover, regulatory and informational gaps exist even in advanced market economies that are deemed to be well regulated. This is the case, for example, in the US, where the Securities and Exchange Commission does not have the authority to monitor and regulate unregistered affiliates of broker/dealers and futures commission merchants. These companies have large positions in OTC derivatives and are major contributors to hedge funds.

Information gaps exist when risks are not identified and assessed industrywide for the benefit of regulators and operators. Such gaps can well be the source of financial troubles. Indeed this has been the case with the US regulatory system, which does not have a mechanism for pooling information on the risks assumed by financial firms in relation to a specific customer. Industry-wide aggregation of the risks per customer might have alerted the regulators to the excessive leverage of the LTCM, which in 1998 managed to distribute its liabilities among 14 large financial firms. The exposure to the LTCM assumed by each financial firm was not among its largest, and this is the reason why US regulators did not recognise the potential threat posed by the LTCM.

Several European countries have well-established agencies for centralising risk assessment. Their functions are to aggregate the exposures assumed by financial providers vis-à-vis individual customers, be they business enterprises or consumers, and to share the aggregated information with the financial firms concerned. In order to protect their indepen-dence and neutrality, these agencies are not affiliated to any particular private financial firm and usually operate under the aegis of the central bank. The supervisory authorities and the financial firms are therefore able to obtain aggregated information on the size of exposure of an individual customer. With such information, each firm is then able to ascertain the comprehensive exposure its customer has assumed vis-à-vis the financial services industry, and is in a position continuously to monitor its own exposure and judiciously manage its relationship with that customer.

Aggregated information on customers' exposure, which is increasingly available on-line to financial firms, can be of great help in averting the excessive concentration of risks on individual customers within the financial services industry, and in taking timely corrective action. Moreover, under the aegis of the European Central Bank, transnational cooperation among several European risk assessment agencies is expanding the reach of the agencies concerned.

Within the financial sector, the hedge-fund branch is generally under no obligation to disclose risks in its portfolios. The majority of these funds are highly leveraged investment pools (also known as highly leveraged institutions, HLI). Their participants are a few financial institutions or wealthy individuals-no more than 100. They are often organised as limited partnerships and so far have no disclosure requirements. The general partners risk their own money and are responsible for day-to-day management. The limited partners provide their funds for investment by the general partners and do not become involved in management. The latter follow aggressive investment strategies, and take long and short positions with full use of market derivatives.

Recent failings in sophisticated financial firms' models and risk management make vigilance by the supervisory authorities all the more necessary if crises are to be averted or forestalled. In late September 1998 the US Federal Reserve regulators, fearing that a systemic risk might result from the near-collapse of the LTCM, urged that additional financing be provided to this fund by its creditor-investor financial firms. The abrupt and disorderly unwinding of large positions and the liquidation of collaterals held by counterparties would have further strained the financial markets and compounded the difficulties of all participants in the globally interconnected markets.

To limit the ability of financial firms to evade prudential regulation and to close the gap between international supervisory practices, cooperation among

the regulators and supervisors of different countries is necessary. For financial firms operating internationally, it appears reasonable to have as main supervisor the agency from the country where the firm has its central headquarters. It is legitimate for a country to bar the entry of a financial firm if its home country does not have an adequate regulatory-supervisory framework. The Basel Committe called on lender banks to seek both quantitative and qualitative disclosure from borrowing HLIs on their investment risks.

Some transparency is needed if market participants are to anticipate excessively risky situations and avoid aggressive financial strategies that could lead to the collapse of large HLIs, disrupting national and international financial systems. The US authorities favour such a policy for HLIs with capital in excess of $1 billion (less than 20 out of about 2500 funds in the US). The possible failure of any of these large HLIs is deemed to be a source of systemic risk.

It was proposed that they report to the US Federal Reserve their total assets, leverage ratios and market risks, for release in due course to the public. Such legislative disclosure is also espoused by the Financial Stability Forum (FSF), which was created in 1999 by the G7 to forestall crises similar to the Asian and Russian ones of 1997-98. The disclosure requirements could generate market discipline on the part of hedge funds and their counterparties, eventually leading to safer conduct. Should this fail, further legislative action may be needed. The impact of national legislation, even in a major financial centre such as the US, will be limited unless it is emulated by other financial centres. Otherwise fund managers could move offshore in order to maintain secrecy about investment strategies that they consider 'proprietary'. If a large player discloses its strategy, it could be taken advantage of by counterparties or other players, especially when it needs to liquidate its positions.

The Basel Committee on Banking Supervision and its sister bodies the Committee on the Global Financial Systems and the Committee on Payment and Settlement Systems, which operate within the BIS, focus on sound, safe and efficient practices for banks, financial markets and payments systems, respectively. The regulatory aims are shared by other global rule-setting bodies, such as the International Organisation of Securities Commissions (IOSCO) and the International Association of Insurance Supervisors (IAIS). All are concerned with contributing to global financial prudence, and therefore stability.

STATE SUPPORT AND MEGA-INSTITUTIONS

It is reckoned that a few governments of developed market economies that profess to espouse a policy of free and competitive markets in fact follow contrary approaches, offering favourable treatment to certain categories of financial institutions. Recently the debate in Europe has centred on Germany, where the 12 state-owned Landesbanken have been capitalised by regional governments at favourable conditions not available to their competitors and continue to benefit from explicit or implicit state guarantees. This has given these banks higher credit ratings and the possibility of raising funds more cheaply, thereby undercutting their privately owned rivals and allowing them to expand their activities. Such privileges create an uneven playing field at the expense of competitors in national and international markets.

As a result of this governmental support some of the Landesbanken have become very sizeable, including the Westdeutsche Landesbank. The latter is backed by the regional government of North-Rhine Westphalia through unlimited state guarantees and subsidies in the form of property transfer. The European Commission has estimated that the government subsidy amounts to 1. 6 billion Deutschmarks and is asking for its return to the authorities, along with 0. 6 billion Deutschmarks of accrued interest. Governmental support has enabled the Westdeutsche Landesbank to outgrow its regional bank status and become a major commercial bank with offices in 37 countries. It has taken risky exposures, notably in investment banking and lending to emerging markets, such as those in Asia.

Governments in other major market economies have equally failed to maintain a level playing field in their financial markets. In the US, two of the biggest government sponsored financial institutions, the Federal National Mortgage Association and the Federal Home Loan Mortgage Association, were set up by the federal government in 1938 and 1970 respectively and were later transformed into privately owned, profit-making enterprises. Both enjoy certain privileges not available to other private lenders, large or small. In particular they are exempt from state and local corporate income tax, banks can invest in the securities of the two institutions without limitation (that is, the risk concentration rules have been waived), their capital requirements are about one third of those applying to large banks, they benefit from the patronage of the US president who appoints five members of their boards, and the US Treasury provides them with an emergency credit line of $8. 5 billion.

Their quasi-public status enables them to obtain lower-cost funding in financial markets, estimated in 1996 at $6 billion a year on their $1 trillion debt. It is thought that one third of the subsidy is not passed to mortgages but handsomely benefits shareholders, top executives and employees.

The implicit government guarantee is a source of moral hazard, and the borrowing costs of these two institutions do not reflect their risk profile. Without such a guarantee it is likely that they would refrain from extending lower-quality loans: in 2000 some of their borrowers paid a meagre down payment of 3 per cent and allocated 50 per cent of their income to servicing their mortgages (at a time when the standard percentage was a maximum of 36 per cent for housing and other credit expenses). Loans with low down payments are, by statutory requirement, subject to private mortgage insurance. The two institutions were nevertheless held responsible for stifling competition from other private lenders, and for aggravating the credit bubble through their aggressive expansion, thereby putting the US taxpayer at risk if post-bubble difficulties had called for rescue by the government. It is pertinent to note that large national banks finance mortgages with consumer deposits insured by the government-owned FDIC.

Unlike Fannie Mae and Freddie Mac, these banks are not constrained by federal charters to finance domestic housing solely; banks can diversify their activities by offering financial products and services in various markets and countries.

The ongoing consolidation of the financial industry in various parts of the world is producing several large and complex financial firms that engage in a variety of activities. They seek to satisfy the needs and serve the convenience of their customers by offering a broad range of products and services, so-called 'one-stop shopping'. Yet these institutions pose challenges to public policy with respect to (1) their dominant position in selected products and markets and the antitrust implications of this, and (2) governments' reluctance to close institutions whose soundness and safety are in doubt lest their action provokes a systemic risk. The existence of 'too big to fail' (TBTF) institutions has often resulted in public authorities giving implicit guarantees to non-insured depositors and other creditors of these institutions. This policy is bound to deflect from market discipline in the management of mega-institutions.

Large financial institutions have, furthermore, risk exposures in multiple products and sectors, and in extensive geographical areas. Characterised by increasing complexity and diversity, these institutions are accordingly not amenable to standardised rules of risk control. Each needs to construct specifically designed risk models to assess its risks and capital requirements. In view of their potential impact on national or international systemic risks, their operations have to be scrutinised on a continuous basis by a team of highly qualified inspectors. Financial conglomerates now have a greater opportunity to develop in the US market, thanks to the Gramm-Leach-Bliley Act of 1999. The Act effectively dismantled the functional barriers previously imposed on financial providers by the Glass-Steagall Act of 1933. The latter had segregated the ownership and operation of investment banks (securities firms or merchant banks) on the one hand, and deposit-taking institutions (notably commercial banks) on the other. Furthermore the replacement of the Pepper-McFadden Act of 1927 by the Riegle-Neal Interstate Banking and Branching Efficiency Act of 1997 has eliminated geographical barriers to bank extension within the US.

Financial regulatory agencies in certain countries continue to focus on risks and sound practices in their assigned areas in the financial sector: banks, mutual funds, securities and derivatives markets, and insurance. In the US they include the Federal Deposit Insurance Corporation, the Federal Reserve System, the Office of the Comptroller of the Currency, the Office of Thrift Supervision, the Securities and Exchange Commission, the state banking authorities, and insurance regulatory agencies. US bank regulators have joined in the Shared National Credit Programme to assess the risk posed by large syndicated loans to participating banks. The programme does not evaluate other risks. US regulators have not yet properly addressed risks interrelationships across the various segments of the financial sector.

Integrated financial regulation and supervision recognises that the formal separation between financial intermediaries and their products and services is becoming increasingly blurred, especially in view of the growth of financial conglomerates and the increasing substitutability of financial products and services. A single, comprehensive regulatory agency can identify and assess industrywide risks more easily than a fragmented system of multiple agencies, each focusing on different categories of financial services companies. Moreover the centralisation of regulatory functions in one institution yields economies of size and efficiency, and facilitates the recruitment and retention of qualified personnel.

From the standpoint of enterprises, large firms with diverse activities are better off under a single regulatory agency as they avoid having to deal with a multiplicity of agencies. Small firms, however, fear being faced by an overbearing and bureaucratic mammoth to which they have to submit regardless.

The regulation of financial conglomerates poses important challenges with respect not only to setting appropriate prudential rules, but also to avoiding possible conflicts of interest between the different units of conglomerates and their customers, who are entitled to fair and impartial treatment. Greater transparency and timely disclosure of information enables experienced financial customers and analysts to evaluate the terms of the products and services offered, and to assess the risks and results of firms, including their constituent units. Market participants are then able to value shares, subordinated debts and other financial instruments more realistically, thereby prompting management to focus continuously on sustaining productivity and earnings. However at the moment market participants are not fully informed, and some investors may set more store on short-term than on longer-term performance.

Beyond the supervision of risks, public authorities have to concern themselves with the protection of customers of financial conglomerates in two principal areas: consumer privacy and oligopolistic power. With regard to the former, consumers may be concerned about financial firms' legal right to pass on or sell their personal data without prior consent to affiliated or associated companies. The latter include unaffiliated enterprises that perform services for or function on behalf of a financial firm, and joint mechanisms between two or more financial firms for the marketing of financial products and services. The information disclosed can cover, inter alia, the customer's assets, liabilities, sources of income, spending patterns, insurance coverage, retirement plans and even health matters.

The dominance by a small number of financial firms in selected products or markets has been strengthening. The effect of such a concentration could well be to drive up the margins, commissions or premiums that financial conglomerates impose on their services. Moreover such oligopolist control could eventually lead to a reduction in the choices offered to consumers, and increase the opacity of the information available to market participants.

The foregoing calls for constant vigilance on the part of the regulatory authorities which is not always the case. In the UK, for example, the authorities have reportedly tolerated the bending of free market rules. In particular, regulators have allowed the big four UK banks-which control the payment system and about 70 per cent of the personal market-to inhibit competition. These banks' practices included

- Locking in customers by means of high barriers against defection;
- Interbank agreements aimed at discouraging potential entrants;
- Imposing excessive charges that are unrelated to the costs, for example when customers use other banks' cash dispensing machines;
- Charging excessive fees to retailers that accept credit and debit cards; and
- Charging excessive fees for bundled products and services. These

practices have produced excessive profits compared with those made by other enterprises. Furthermore the chairman of the banking review, Don Cruickshank, deemed that the 'over-cosy relationship' between the UK big banks, the government and the regulators was unwarranted for systemic reasons, such as possible bank runs.

FINANCIAL STABILISATION

Sources of Instability

Greed, irrational exuberance and negligence are generally deemed to be at the root of financial crises. According to this interpretation, herd-like euphoria causes decision makers to underestimate risk and/or overestimate returns. A sudden shift in market expectations and loss of confidence-triggered by a particular adverse event-can lead to the opposite process of overestimation ending in a paroxysm of gloom, investor panic and financial contagion.

Crises can also be provoked or exacerbated by unsound or incoherent macroeconomic policies. Alternatively they can be averted, moderated or mastered by judicious policies. To illustrate, a crisis in an open economy can be provoked by an excessive fiscal deficit. The latter will generate a vicious circle of rising domestic demand and prices, followed by the further swelling of public indebtedness.

To stabilise domestic demand, the government may inappropriately resort to monetary measures such as raising interest rates. This will in turn attract foreign hot money, or cause domestic firms to engage in less expensive foreign borrowing: capital inflows will then create additional upward pressure on domestic prices, and lead to an overvalued exchange rate. Deterioration of the country's current account and an increase in its foreign debt will follow. To maintain the exchange rate and the flow of foreign capital, interest rates are raised further, forcing more and more domestic borrowers into liquidity and solvency problems and eventually leading to a cascade of collapses in various sectors and a recession in the domestic economy. This will be accompanied by capital flight and the collapse of the exchange rate. The end result is likely to be a banking crisis.

The globalisation phenomenon, while increasing diversification opportunities, has led to a higher degree of uncertainty, deriving inter alia from the enormous financial resources that can be used for cross-country speculation, potentially leading to destabilisation. The rising interdependence between financial firms and markets has also contributed to an increase in the transmission of risks across institutions and markets. All crises have particular elements of their own.

Fundamental to the Asian financial crisis, which hit Thailand, South Korea, Indonesia and Malaysia in 1997-98, was the conjunction of certain international events with domestic policy and structural distortions, including, notably, the following interrelated factors:

- Banks and corporations in these four countries had resorted to excessive short-term borrowing in US dollars for their local-currency, long-term loans. In the absence of hedging, these banks became vulnerable to the depreciation of national currencies, and to liquidity crises because of their inability to roll over their foreign short-term debts. (The current Basle Capital Adequacy rules appear to have induced banks to favour short-term interbank loans to emerging economies, instead of more appropriate longer-term maturity loans.)
- Given the limited absorptive capacity the Asian national economies faced in the mid 1990s, with a massive influx of foreign capital in search of more attractive opportunities (compared with the yields then obtaining in capital exporting countries) the prices of domestic shares and real assets in the capital-importing countries were allowed to rise considerably, thereby presaging a bust after the boom.

Domestic banks imprudently channelled their lending to certain business sectors of dubious productivity and profitability, including sectors suffering from excess capacity. Furthermore loan reimbursements were not rigorously enforced by bank management, thanks to rampant self-dealing, nepotism, cronyism and corruption. Private projects of high risk or poor profitability benefited from subsidies, cheap credit, authorised monopolistic practices (for example under the aegis of conglomerates) and explicit or implicit government guarantees. State-owned companies (including banks) were extensively used as sources of political patronage.

With rising domestic prices and national currencies effectively pegged to an appreciating dollar, the four economies suffered a reduction in export cost-competitiveness, which in turn reduced their capacity to earn sufficient foreign exchange to meet their foreign-currency-denominated financial obligations on time. Their export earnings suffered further from the stagnation of the Japanese economy, and from competing exports by China, partly boosted by the 50 per cent devaluation of the Chinese currency in January 1994.

Regulatory frameworks and enforcement of the prudential rules governing domestic financial intermediaries proved inadequate. Indeed, regulators condoned and covered up flagrant violations of laws or standards by influential or politically linked executives who had falsified accounts to conceal abuses and losses. In an environment of corruption and bribery, law enforcement officials thus allowed domestic banks to operate with negative capital ratios and flout various other rules.

Early diagnosis of a financial crisis would enable those responsible for its management to produce an appropriate remedy. Some authors have called on the IMF to base its diagnosis on a purely logical, mathematically formalised and econometrically tested model. Such a model would include the interconnections between the factors responsible for the crisis, and the instruments capable of restoring both the soundness of the financial system and economic growth. One should nevertheless be cautious about relying solely on mathematical models based on past experiences to predict future crises and/or prevent their outbreak. Some judgmental discretion may well be needed to reach an innovative or creative approach to interpreting novel situations.

The current supervisory standards in developing and emerging economies need to be improved, guided by proper prudential principles. Financial supervision should be carried out by competent independent examiners whose authority and judgement rests to a significant degree on the integrity of the financial sector. Both external examiners and risk managers of financial firms will need to be provided with appropriate financial and occupational incentives (such as attractive pay and adequate job security) if they are to carry out their functions efficiently. Moreover bankruptcy procedures should be diligently enforced on insolvent institutions.

The developed, richer economies of North America, Europe and Japan have an important role to play in global financial stability. They are the world's major creditor and capital exporting countries, financing inter alia the heavily indebted developing economies. If foreign currency debts and related economic data are fully disclosed without delay by creditor and debtor countries, market forces will be able to alert investors/creditors in time, as well as the supervisory agencies, thereby enabling them to reach sounder decisions.

This will help to forestall crises or at least moderate their impact. The opacity or scarcity of up-to-date reliable information on changing economic conditions in individual countries (and notably emerging economies) have prevented financial markets from functioning efficiently and providing optimal solutions before crises strike. Creditor countries therefore need to improve the supervision of their financial intermediaries' exposure to emerging or developing economies. Facilitating access by the products of poor, heavily indebted developing countries to the markets of developed economies (by waiving duty and quota restrictions) should enhance the ability of these debtor countries to honour their financial commitments and attenuate the intensity of debt crises. In this respect, a proposal was made by the World Bank and the IMF for government ministers to meet within the Development Committee in April 2000 under the joint auspices of the two institutions. The US trade representative would not, however, countenance this approach.

TOWARDS GLOBAL STABILITY

Intergovernmental institutions such as the International Monetary Fund

(IMF), the World Bank and the Bank for International Settlements (BIS) play an important role in promoting global financial stability. The leading governmental members of these institutions represent the world's major financial markets. Crises have prodded these governments to cooperate more closely in respect of

- The exchange, pooling and dissemination of information pertinent to the efficient functioning of world financial markets,
- Greater coordination between national and interna-tional regulatory bodies, and
- The implementation of international best standards and practices.

The foremost multilateral institution in terms of monetary financial cooperation is the IMF. Established in 1945, it works towards various goals: collaboration on international monetary problems, balanced expansion of international trade, exchange stability and the elimination of foreign exchange restrictions. It also provides temporary support to correct maladjustments in members' balance of payments.

Synergetically with the IMF's objectives, the Financial Stability Forum (FSF), established by the G7 in 1999, functions as a coordinator for various institutions with the aim of reducing the risk of global financial instability. It focuses on financial intermediaries, financial markets and payment infrastructures. The FSF does not have an operational mandate and seeks a concerted approach by international organisations and standard-setting entities (for example the BIS, the IMF, the World Bank and the OECD), along with national regulatory agencies, finance ministries and the central banks of the G7 and non-G7 countries with major financial centres.

In view of its status as the global intergovernmental monetary institution (183 countries), the IMF has been entrusted with the major responsibility of promoting global financial stability. Its main role is to help member countries to shore up their balance of payments by providing stand-by facilities, subject to certain rules. Notable among the latter are first, a ceiling of borrowing based on the relative economic weight of the member country) and second, strict enforcement (monitored by the IMF) of an agreed-upon economic programme. These policies aim to promote macroeconomic stability over the long term within the framework of an open market economy.

Governments that experience financial distress often call on the IMF after the fact instead of asking for assistance at the inception of the problem, when the help provided can be more effective and can moderate some of the high economic and social costs of adjustment. In administering its limited resources the IMF has not invariably abided by its own rules.

Moreover it has been directly influenced by its major funders, notably the US, which is the largest contributor to the IMF's resources (17. 35 per cent of the total subscription). One example concerns the 1994-95 financial debacle in Mexico, which led to the exchange rate of the peso plummeting by some 50 per cent on 21 December 1994. At the urging of the US government, the IMF agreed to a stand-by arrangement for Mexico of up to $17. 8 billion immediately after President Clinton announced that the US would provide financial assistance of $20 billion. The total assistance package was raised to $47. 8 billion when Canada and the BIS offered additional aid, beefed-up by a supplementary funding commitment of $2. 8 billion by the World Bank. Several of the member countries complained that the IMF executive Board had not been adequately consulted on the Mexican rescue operation.

Moreover the IMF's financing amounted to 688 per cent of Mexico's subscription quota. The statutory cumulative limit for financial support is about 300 per cent of the member's quota, and is subject to detailed negotiation and agreement between the IMF and the debtor country. The latter normally makes a commitment to reform its macroeconomic and financial policies (with a timetable for targets) in order to ameliorate or eliminate its external payments problem. The US government was concerned-it is pertinent to note-about the negative externalities of the Mexican financial crisis, notably:

- The threat posed to US trade, employment and immigration interests.
- The threat of contagion posed to other countries.
- Solidarity vis-à-vis a fellow member of the North American Free Trade Agreement.
- Concern that Mexico's move towards a market-oriented economy and political democratisation (to be emulated by other emerging economies) could be thwarted.

Critics within the US administration, the US Congress and other creditor countries (the G10) contested the above and further invoked the moral hazard factor as a possible contributor to Mexico's financial crisis. That factor already existed because of the financial assistance provided by the IMF and various creditor nations during Mexico's foreign debt crisis of August 1982. This financial rescue operation could have encouraged Mexico and other emerging capital importing countries to follow risky macroeconomic and financial policies, and unduly encouraged foreign investors or creditor banks to relax their monitoring of risks. Public funds were thus used during the financial rescues of Mexico, South Korea and Russia to repay short-term debt to private parties, despite the fact that these parties had enjoyed high interest rates when they chose to finance these countries.

Foreign banks and investors might, on the basis of past bailouts by the IMF and creditor nations, anticipate similar treatment and therefore take more risks. The IMF's promise to provide financial support to financially distressed member countries therefore entails a moral hazard factor. National deposit insurance mechanisms in creditor counties, which explicitly or implicitly provide banks and their depositors with government guarantees, add to the moral hazard factor. However, no guarantees are cost-free, and several investors and lenders (domestic and foreign) have sustained large losses during past financial crises regardless of the IMF's and creditor nation's support to member governments. To reduce moral hazard and enhance market discipline, lenders and investors should be made to share the cost of crises they have been involved in causing, thus providing them with an incentive to engage in prudent behaviour. Official and private entities have raised several important questions about the optimal future role of the IMF, including the following:

- Should the IMF act more like a central regulatory authority by extending its surveillance function over member countries to cover
- Macroeconomic reforms and stabilisation, and
- Banking and financial market regulation and supervision?
- Should it assist member countries in their endeavour to anticipate, avoid or resolve financial crises, thereby acting as a quasi international lender of last resort for countries hit by creditor panic and currency flight?
- Could the IMF act as an international deposit insurance entity for member countries that borrow on the international financial markets, by levying differentiated premia in accordance with its rating of the creditworthiness of the members concerned? Is it realistic to assume that the IMF has sufficient knowledge and political backing to carry out that function, which would include management of the financial reserves accumulated from such premia?
- Should the IMF be confined to the function of a mediator between creditors (sovereign and private entities) and debtor countries in times of financial distress, and help both parties by facilitating speedy negotiations and workable solutions to settle claims, thereby replacing the ad hoc meetings between public sector creditors (known as the Paris Club) or private sector creditors (the London Club) and the defaulting debtor countries?

Should the IMF continue to address poverty alleviation (mostly through the Poverty Reduction and Growth Facility, and the Heavily Indebted Poor Countries debt relief) or should this be left to its sister organisation, the World Bank, and similar institutions?

Should the IMF maintain its longer-term lending programme (which extends up to 10 years) in order to finance structural reforms in member countries, or should it instead focus on temporary, short-term lending to countries that encounter payment and liquidity problems?

A few critics have questioned the IMF's failure-despite its oversight and conditionality prerogatives-to detect irregularities in member countries, leading to a failure to enforce policy changes and to the misuse of the IMF's resources. They also question the ability of the IMF to forewarn governments about looming crises. IMF officials acknow-ledged in 1999 that they had failed to obtain timely information on some countries that had faced financial distress, although, they had managed to alert certain countries of an impending foreign exchange crisis, to no avail as it turned out. In the case of Thailand, the IMF's warning was reportedly not made public in order to avoid precipitating the very crisis it was aiming to prevent. Moreover crises can deepen or become protracted if appropriate solutions are not adopted in time, or if governments renege on their commitments under the IMF support programmes.

Several entities (official and non-official) have called on the IMF to require greater transparency from member countries so that problems can be identified before they turn into crises. Some holders of high office in government or finance have put in doubt the effectiveness of the IMF's oversight and rescue measures: they consider that its advice is more relevant to past crises than to unfolding ones. For doctrinal reasons or reasons of national interest, very few have called for the outright abolition of the IMF. Most critics suggest that the IMF needs to be more focused and should function primarily as lender of last resort in order to contribute effectively to global financial stability. The emphasis on short-term support to member countries is espoused by the current managing director of the IMF, Horst Köhler, and the US Treasury. Both believe that long-term lending should be primarily the concern of the World Bank. Last-resort lending, as a safety net, carries with it a moral hazard risk.

The members in question are eligible for sufficient last-resort lending, subject to policy conditionality on macroeconomic matters and prudent regulation of their financial sector, with rigorous enforcement of rules and standards.

Lending is made at a penalty rate to limit the demand by countries actually or potentially facing a liquidity crisis, or those susceptible to systemic risk, and on condition that these countries are in a position fully to honour their obligations; for poor countries with no prospect of repaying a loan, aid is more appropriate.

The private sector should carry out its own risk analysis, monitoring and self-regulation; thus capital exporters (creditors and investors), along with capital importers, should have to bear the brunt of the consequences of their risky behaviour by sustaining losses or ultimately being forced into bankruptcy.

The application of reliable accounting, monitoring and regulatory standards, namely those set up by the Basle Committee on Banking Supervision, the IMF Special Data Dissemination Standard, and IOSCO. By enhancing the quality of the available information and assuring the transparency of key data, regulators and markets can more efficiently monitor financial players in the global market.

An embryonic, very modest international lender of last resort facility was started up in April 1999 when the IMF launched its Contingent Credit Lines

(CCL) facility for a two-year trial period. The CCL provides member countries with short term-financing (up to two years) to protect them against contagion risks.

IMF support of this sort is intended to send a message to the international financial community about its confidence in a member's economic policies. The criteria for approval for such support are stringent, and include the prerequisite that 'the member must be implementing policies that make it unlikely it will need to use the resources [sic] and it must not already be facing balance of payments difficulties as a result of contagion'. The CCL support is capped at 500 per cent of the member's quota in the IMF and is subject to a surcharge of 300 basis points in the first year, plus 50 basis points per six-month extension.

Before the IMF can play a genuine lender of last resort role in the world economy the leading creditor countries (the US, the EU and Japan) have to reach a consensus on the IMF's strategy and structure. In particular they have to agree on whether the IMF can substantially increase its members' quota subscriptions and its official borrowing from capital-exporting countries, notably the major industrial countries (the G10). The IMF has yet to tap private sources in the world financial markets directly.

As a universal, multilateral organisation the IMF is likely to have a greater degree of objectivity or neutrality in evaluating data and recommending appropriate policies and reforms than national institutions (although the abovemen-tioned creditor countries will continue to wield considerable influence).

It is more realistic in a world of sovereign states and great diversity to approach global financial cooperation in a gradualistic manner than to attempt a rapid overhaul of the existing web of institutional relations.

Sequencing Liberalisation

Developing countries can expect higher growth in the long run through the gradual liberalisation of their capital accounts, subject to their having sound macroeconomic policies and a solid and well-regulated financial sector. International capital flows are prompted by diverse aims and motives, ranging from productive investment to short-term speculative gains and money laundering.

Unfettered and erratic short-term capital movements can destabilise an economy, especially when the flows are massive in relation to the absorptive capacity of the domestic economy. Some countries, for example South Korea, liberalised short-term financial flows in the mid 1990s while retaining restrictions on long-term capital movements. Such sequencing is deemed inappropriate.

Indeed debt, unlike equity, carries with it the risk of default if debtors fail to pay interest or reimburse capital on time. Moreover debt with a short maturity entails a higher degree of volatility. It is accordingly more rational for governments of developing economies to give priority to the liberalisation of direct investment, followed by equity portfolio investment. Furthermore long-term debt-in contrast to short-term debt-has to be judiciously structured to avoid the bunching of reimbursements.

Charges aimed at discouraging hot capital inflows (that is, short term and speculative) could take the form of fiscal levies or non-interest-earning deposit requirements. These charges would be waived for foreign funds employed over longer periods, thereby providing an incentive for additional productive investment. Capital controls (through fiscal charges or other restrictions) on international financial transactions are prompted by a variety of aims, including:

- Marshalling national savings for domestic use by restricting the outward flow of capital in search of safety or higher returns abroad.
- Enhancing macroeconomic (monetary, exchange rate, growth and so on) stability by moderating the size of foreign pools of capital that can precipitately leave the country.
- Changing the composition of capital inflows, for example by favouring those with longer maturity.
- Reducing the impact of capital inflows on currency appreciation (with its adverse effect on exports) or on monetary expansion (with its inflationary pressures).
- Protecting domestic financial firms until they attain maturity (for example through economies of scale and scope).
- Favouring certain domestic economic activities and/or protecting nationally owned enterprises from foreign acquisition.

Capital controls carry administrative costs, generate corruption, create distortions and institute rigidities in the domestic economy, which then looses the benefits of free trading in assets. These benefits include risk-sharing, diversification, growth, technology transfer and enhanced competitiveness.

Prior to the liberalisation of capital movements, developing countries in an interdependent world economy therefore need to introduce appropriate structural reforms (for example reforms aimed at strengthening the financial sector) and macroeconomic policies that are capable of mobilising domestic savings for productive investment in a market-oriented economy.

As summarised by one well-documented source, 'External financial liberalisation should not be considered an isolated or primary goal, achievement of which automatically raises the sophistication and resilience of the domestic financial system. Rather, it should be part of a concurrent, integrated and comprehensive policy approach to macroeconomic and structural reform with individual elements of this policy package reinforcing each other. '

Even if they have carried out appropriate structural reforms, small and medium-sized economies will continue to fear the adverse effects of massive (measured in proportion to gross domestic product) and speculative cross-border capital flows. They therefore need international organisations to provide some assurance of support in times of trouble if they are fully to liberalise short-term capital movements. The moral hazard such assurance would induce in the behaviour of various economic actors, notably financial firms, has to be weighed against the benefit of preventing the propagation of systemic risk.

9

Measuring Managerial Performance

It should not be necessary to belabor the point that the kinds of men who are chosen to manage an organization, and the kinds of systems that are chosen for measuring and rewarding them, have a profound and lasting impact on the motivational climate of the organization as a whole. Therefore, to the extent that the executive in charge of career management acts as a sort of gatekeeper, regulating the flow of employees into management and of managers into the higher executive ranks, he is in a sense controlling the destiny of the company.

In most companies, the selection of managers is at best a fallible art. In a few companies, it is beginning to be converted into a more systematic and, in some respects, more scientific process. The best of these efforts have been made by American Telephone and Telegraph Company and by Standard Oil Company (New Jersey). Both are, of course, very large companies, and for this reason it would be easy to dismiss research results emanating from them as meaningful only to other corporate giants. But that would be a fallacy in this case, so perhaps it is best to begin by puncturing it.

Large companies do not necessarily need better managers than small companies need, but they do need more of them. The sheer scale on which they must search for and evaluate managerial talent requires that the process be systematized as much as possible. This means that the elements of effective managerial performance have to be identified and that efficient ways of measuring them have to be devised.

In other words, the larger companies, in order to get adequate control of the management selection process, have been compelled to take the lead in researching problems of universal importance to *all* organizations. It was more than just necessity, however, that motivated the move by these big companies into research on management selection. Research is costly, and companies of this size can obviously afford to finance the necessary research effort more easily than a smaller firm could.

There is also a statistical advantage that works in favour of large organizations that attempt this kind of research: their ability to try out various selection systems on more people, so that the sensitivity (or lack of it) of each system can be measured. These measurements on relatively large groups make statistical analysis worthwhile, and without statistical analysis it is impossible to say whether a selection system really works or merely tickles a selector's fancy. Lastly, research of this kind reflects a rather high order of sophistication.

Again, large companies are not necessarily more sophisticated than small ones, and indeed many large companies have not yet ventured into research and develop-ment for their management selection procedures at all. The fact that this research has been done is one more testimony, if any more is needed, to the wisdom and high managerial competence of the companies that have done it. In 1956 the Bell System began a long-term "Management Progress Study" that is destined to continue for some time. More than 400 young men were assessed in depth quite early in their careers. The purpose of these assessments was to determine whether measurements made in the beginning phases of a man's career could be predictive of his subsequent accomplishments and whether further assessments at various later stages of his career could add to an understanding of the reasons why he had developed as he did.

The assessments themselves had several unique features. First, they were unusually comprehensive: They took about three and one-half days from start to finish for each individual. Second, a variety of methods were used, including some unconventional situational tests in which groups of men were observed as they attempted to deal with simulated real-life problems. Consequently, the assessment staff could combine the predictive power of techniques as varied as orthodox interviews and paper-and-pencil tests, on the one hand, and the various situational tests on the other hand.

The results of this potpourri of assessments were considered by a board of judges who had observed the men throughout the various exercises and had developed overall evaluations of each man's strengths and weaknesses on the basis of the combined data available on him from all these sources. In effect, each man who went through the assessment centre was probed and measured by just about every kind of useful psychological technique that could be utilized.

The judges' evaluations, along with the data on which they were based, were filed off company premises and maintained in strict confidentiality, so they could not affect any subsequent selection decisions regarding the men who had been assessed. This insured that the assessments would not become "self-fulfilling prophecies" by influencing the decisions they were ultimately designed to predict. However, as the careers of these men unfolded, the research team followed their progress and correlated it with the original assessments.

Of all the many techniques used, the *situational tests* are of most interest, not only because they are less well known than paper-andpencil tests, but also because the AT&T data clearly indicate that they were the most effective predictors of all. That is, judgments made about the potentialities of the men on the basis of their performance in the situational tests usually came closer to predicting their actual rates of progress than did judgments that were based on the other techniques. However, the best overall predictions were based not on situational tests alone, but on combinations of situational and other tests.

The essence of a situational test is that men are presented, singly or in groups, with a more or less real problem to solve, and they are observed as they try to organize themselves to grapple with it. They receive relatively little guidance or instruction on how to proceed, and therefore they tend to become preoccupied with the problem itself and to be much less conscious than they ordinarily would be of the fact that they are being observed. Specially trained teams of line managers act as observers, rating the men's performance but not aiding them or questioning them as the exercises progress.

Situational tests are admittedly only an approximation of real managerial behaviour, but they are a much closer approximation than most tests, interviews, and other off-the-job procedures can provide. A more important advantage is that, by providing for multiple observers and a standard set of problems to be solved, situational tests offer much better conditions for observing and measuring a man's performance than most on-the-job contexts provide. In that sense, situational tests can be compared to a physical examination: A man's heart may not perform "typically" in his doctor's office, but it is better to evaluate it in the room where the electrocardiograph is situated than to restrict the doctor to feeling the man's pulse while he is on the job.

There are many variations in the way situational tests are presented, but they all have essentially the same inner logic. They all simulate reality, provide relatively little guidance on how to proceed, and leave it up to the individual or group to devise their own strategies for handling the problem as best they can.

There are three main variations to this basic strategy: the *leaderless group discussion*, the business game, and the in-basket exercise. The *leaderless group discussion* (sometimes referred to as the "LGD") consists of presenting a small group of candidates with a problem to discuss. The problem itself is almost always a general one about which all the candidates are likely to be equally knowledgeable or equally ignorant, as the case may be. Other than the fact that they are usually given a time limit and told that the judges will observe but not participate in their discussions, no guidance is given. No chairman is appointed and no rules of procedure are laid down.

The group must, in other words, find a way to organize itself; and in the process of attempting to do this the men have to compete and cooperate simultaneously. Leadership, if it is to emerge at all, must be achieved by consent rather than by assertion. The participants' social skills, verbal skills, and capacity to function in the face of frustration are all put to a direct test. Some variations of the LGD involve mock elections, evaluations of competing business plans, and so on. In every LGD the essential point is that the group must find its own way to begin functioning as a group before it can really deal with the problem it has been given to solve. Because the men are reacting to one another rather than reacting to trying to influence an interviewer, the judges are exposed to a much wider range of their behaviour styles than could be the case in an ordinary interview.

In *business games*, a group of men is given enough background information about a real or mythical business firm to take over its management in a mock decision-making exercise. Usually the group is confronted with some major problem affecting the fortunes of the firm, such as financial overextension or the need to enter a new market. In most cases the men are not assigned specific roles and therefore have to organize themselves into some semblance of a management team; however, in some variations the men are randomly assigned to different functional roles (for example, "treasurer," "plant manager") in order to be sure that several conflicting points of view are championed.

Despite the obvious artificiality and pretense, a well constructed business game quickly captures the imagination of mature participants, and they work at it with considerable vigour and determination. As in the leaderless group discussion, both problemsolving and negotiating skills are called into play, and the judges have an opportunity to observe a wider range of each individual's managerial repertory than would ordinarily be possible. Business games are often used for instruction as well as for assessment, and they have the added merit of lending themselves to critiques from which the men can learn something of value to themselves.

The *in-basket exercise* is usually administered to individuals, although there is no limit to the number of men who can take it simultaneously. Because it too is a simulation of reality and requires the individual to call upon both administrative and social skills to solve the problems with which he is presented, it is properly classified as a situational test. Unlike most LGD's and business games, however, the in-basket exercise lends itself to some degree of standardization.

This, in turn, makes possible an objective scoring system through which the performance of any individual can be directly compared to that of many others who have taken the same exercise before him.

The exercise takes its name from the ubiquitous desk-top box in which managers usually receive their mail. Typically, the individual being assessed receives a background briefing on the fictitious company for which he is supposedly working during the exercise, and a situation is posed in which he must make a large number of decisions during a brief period without being able to consult other people or obtain additional information. This is usually done by asking him to pretend, for the purpose of the exercise, that he has been appointed rather suddenly to take over a key job, that his predecessor and his new staff are unavailable, and that he has come to the new office on a Saturday morning to familiarize himself with the job by going through the papers in his in-basket.

These are a wide assortment of more or less typical letters and memoranda, some more urgent than others. Working within a relatively tight time limit, he must somehow dispose of everything in the in-basket by writing replies, assigning documents to subordinates for handling, or setting them aside for later action. A special questionnaire has been devised through which he can record and explain the various actions he took, and this in turn can be processed by computers to yield a set of overall scores.

The in-basket exercise can be made so realistic that participants and observers alike become enthusiastic about its potentialities for tapping real-life habits and characteristics. This apparent realness is both the main advantage and the main disadvantage of the in-basket technique. On the one hand, close approximation of a real managerial job makes the exercise attractive and acceptable to managers, who regard it as a fairer test of their skills than a more abstract exercise would be. On the other hand, there is as yet very little hard evidence that the results of the in-basket test predict anything at all about a manager's *future* performance or that such predictions can be made more reliably with this than with other, less expensive techniques. However, the ready acceptance of the in-basket exercise makes it difficult to conduct the kinds of studies that would be necessary to put it to this kind of crucial test, simply because it seems hardly necessary. There is enough fragmentary evidence available about the technique's usefulness to raise very high hopes for it. But there have been other instances of promising techniques catching on too quickly to be thoroughly tested, becoming fads, and eventually falling into disrepute. These should encourage a more restrained and orderly approach to the in-basket exercise — and, indeed, to the assessment centre concept as a whole.

The Management Progress Study has aroused enough interest that the basic concepts of assessment are now being applied to management selection decisions in a number of companies. The approach is usually cautious and research-oriented. That is, there is enough confidence in the techniques to encourage their use in addition to — not as a substitute for — the admittedly sketchy data normally available about most managerial candidates. At the same time, by passing large numbers of managers and managerial candidates through the assessment procedures, data can be gathered for eventual comparison with each man's progress in sufficient quantity to permit a more definitive test of the various techniques.

The Bell System itself has been the largest factor in this movement. Because of the interest aroused by the Management Progress Study in the parent company, the Michigan Bell Telephone Company organized an assessment centre in 1958 for the purpose of evaluating the potentialities of employees who had been recommended by their supervisors as candidates for first-line managerial positions. This was quickly followed by similar programs in the other companies in the system. By now, there are more than 40 centers within the AT&T complex which have assessed more than 10,000 men and women for supervisory positions.

Although the techniques used in these assessment centers are essentially the same as those used in the original Management Progress Study, the data are treated entirely differently. The MPS data will remain strictly off-limits to line management so that the men in the study will be neither helped nor hampered in their careers by the assessment results. The Management Progress Study remains, in other words, a scientific venture whose full implications will not be known for some time. The results of the various Bell System assessment centers, on the other hand, are provided to line management and undoubtedly have an important influence on promotion decisions.

Similar assessment centre programs are now operating in The Standard Oil Company (Ohio), Lever Brothers Company, and International Business Machines Corporation, among others. Incidentally, the use of assessment procedures for management selection has an even longer history in Europe than in the United States. The German Army is usually credited with having originated them prior to World War II. The British War Office Selection Boards ("Wosbies," as the troops called them) used them to select officer candidates during the war, and this has led to the very widespread use of these techniques by the British Civil Service since the war. Assessment centre techniques were also used by the U. S. Office of Strategic Services during World War II. Although the OSS procedures aroused considerable interest among American psychologists, they were not used industrially on a large scale until the AT&T Management Progress Study began more than ten years after the war had ended.

The reason for this long hiatus in the development of assessment techniques in the United States was their high cost relative to that of more orthodox methods for evaluating human potentialities. Paper-and-pencil tests are relatively cheap, interviews are not a great deal more expensive, and professionally administered tests are not much more expensive than interviews. It was not clear from the OSS data that the use of assessment centre techniques would add enough precision to the performance predictions that could be made with orthodox techniques to justify the added cost. The AT&T Management Progress Study is the first attempt to answer this question on a sufficiently large scale, and with sufficiently tight controls, to permit a definitive conclusion to be drawn from its results.

Although the Management Progress Study is not yet complete, enough interim measurements have been made of the careers of the men who were assessed to permit some tentative evaluations of assessment itself. So far the available data indicate that the decision of the Bell System companies to establish their own managerial assessment centers without waiting for the conclusion of the Management Progress Study was probably justified. About 79 percent of the men in the original sample who have progressed to middle management had been correctly assessed as having that potentiality by the centers. Further, about 94 percent of the men who have not yet been able to progress beyond the first level of management had been assessed by the centers as probably being limited to that relatively slow rate of advancement.

The assessment centers have, in other words, come remarkably close to predicting how most of the young men in the MPS sample would fare in the Bell System companies five to eight years *after* they were assessed. Whether that rate of accuracy will change when the study has run its full ten-year course remains to be seen; for the moment it appears that the predictions made by the assessment centre staff were very accurate indeed. A conclusive answer to the basic question of the cost-effectiveness of assessment techniques as against that of less expensive techniques cannot be given until the study is completed. However, the current opinion of the AT&T psychologists directing the Management Progress Study is that the extra costs of assessment are fully justified by the accuracy they are apparently able to add to the difficult and crucial art of managerial selection.

The EIMP project (Early Identification of Management Potential) of Jersey Standard was actually begun prior to the AT**T Management Progress Study. However, there is a logic in presenting it after the MPS: AT&T assessed young employees at the beginning of their careers in hopes of gauging managerial potential; the EIMP project focused on managers at all levels who were already well launched on their careers. The two studies are similar in that somewhat more than 400 men were assessed in each and in that the resulting measurements were not permitted to affect the subsequent careers of those who had participated. They also have an essentially similar purpose: to determine whether long-range executive and managerial success can be attributed, at least in part, to characteristics that could be reliably measured years in advance.

The main differences between EIMP and MPS are in the maturity of the men who were assessed and in the techniques used. The Jersey Standard study included men from the entire spectrum of management, ranging from the chairman of the board and the president of the parent company to the lowest supervisory level in some affiliated companies in the New York area. Unlike the AT&T research, the Jersey Standard study included no situational tests or combined judgments.

It was based entirely on paper-and-pencil tests, some of them standardized and some developed especially for this project. The only exception was a personal interview. A projective test was eliminated from the study at a fairly early stage when it was demonstrated that it could not discriminate between managers who had been advancing fairly rapidly and those whose careers had developed more slowly.

All other tests chosen for use in this study proved to have some predictive power. The standardized tests included a modified version of the Miller Analogies Test (a high-level verbal reasoning test, used chiefly to screen candidates for admission to graduate and professional schools); a nonverbal reasoning test; and the Guilford-Zimmerman Temperament Survey (a well-known test designed to measure a number of personality characteristics, some of which were presumed to be important in determining managerial success). The experimental tests which were devised especially for this study included an "individual background survey," which was essentially a biographical questionnaire dealing with the circumstances and history of an individual's youth and early manhood; a "management judgment test," which presented various real managerial problems and alternative solutions; and a "self-performance report," in which the individual was asked to evaluate his own managerial performance.

The data provided by these devices were evaluated in two ways. First, the Jersey Standard research team worked out an index of "overall managerial success to date. " This was calculated by combining position level, rate of salary progress during the previous five years (compared to the average progression for managers at comparable levels), and rankings of managerial effectiveness (prepared by current and former superiors of the men being ranked).

Because the first two elements in the index — position level and salary progress — could be influenced by the age of the individual, a statistical correction was applied which had the effect of eliminating the influence of age on these measures. The three elements were then combined to yield a rating which reflected several relevant aspects of managerial success, instead of only one. This index made it possible to compare the relative success of each of the participating managers up to the time of the study, independently of the advantages which age alone gave to the more senior men. A second and more stringent way of evaluating the test data had to await the passage of time; that is, determining whether the test results were predictive of subsequent managerial success.

The results of the first (or current) analysis of the EIMP data were exceptionally promising and more than justified the burdens of continuing the study over a period of years to determine whether the second analysis would be as successful. The results were expressed in "expectancy charts," one of which is reproduced in the accompanying exhibit. An expectancy chart shows what can be expected to happen, on the basis of experience, if certain information is available which has a known relationship to subsequent events. The chart summarizes the past relationships between "certain available information," on the one hand, and "subsequent events," on the other hand. Expectancy tables can therefore be used for prediction only on the assumption that an individual will turn out more or less the same as the "average" individual having more or less similar characteristics has turned out in the *past*. Whether there is wisdom or the lack of it in making such an assumption depends largely on whether the relationship between available information and subsequent events is stable or transitory.

This is precisely why a second analysis, showing whether a relationship detected at one point in time still exists after a considerable period has elapsed, is necessary whenever a relationship is detected in the first analysis. It is worth noting that it is difficult enough to devise measures of human attributes that are related to *current* performance; when such a measure is devised successfully there is an understandable — but dangerous — tendency to assume that a stable predictor of *future* performance has finally been found. Psychologists have learned the hard way to treat their few successes with current data cautiously. Too often they do turn out to be peculiar to a particular set of individuals or measurements.

An important reason for this instability is that psychologists, in an attempt to rid their predictors of irrelevancies and to make them as precise as possible, deliberately weight the various test scores in such a way as to produce the maximum correlation with current performance. The logic in this is not unlike the logic in focusing a camera: The lens is moved forward or backward until the image of the subject is etched on the focal plane as sharply as the lens itself will allow. Whether the lens must be refocused to take an equally sharp picture on another occasion depends on whether the subject has moved.

Weighting test scores is both necessary and dangerous. It is necessary in that the predictors must be "focused" to operate efficiently; but it is dangerous in that their precision may be illusory and largely due to the particular way in which "current" data were gathered. Weighted current test scores must therefore be treated with caution until a second (future) analysis of their ability to predict behaviour can be made.

The data in our exhibit are based on weighted scores, deliberately introduced by the Jersey Standard researchers to maximize (or, if you will, to focus) the relationship of the test scores obtained by the managers in their sample to their current managerial success at the time they were tested.

The exhibit shows the odds, as it were, that could have been quoted on the likelihood that a manager would be found in the top 33.3 percent of the Jersey Standard "overall success" rankings, judging only by his weighted test scores. If the scores had been entirely unrelated to the success measurement, the managers would have been distributed about equally across both the test and the success measurements. For example, the managers whose test scores were in the top 20 percent would have had about a 33.3 percent chance of placing in the top third — or anywhere else — in the success criterion; and the same would be true of any other 20 percent of the test score groups. Instead there is a regular, sharply defined tendency for the probability of being in the top success group to *increase as* the scores themselves increased. A manager whose test scores were in the top 20 percent was about *19 times more likely* to be in the top success group than one whose scores were in the lowest 20 percent. There can be little doubt that the Jersey Standard research team had focused very sharply indeed on psychological differences between managers that were related to their comparative success levels at the time they were tested.

However, the proof of a psychologist's pudding is never in the eating but in whether it causes heartburn or happiness for years afterward. The EIMP project is still continuing, and the research team continues to follow up the careers of the managers who were tested as much as ten years previously. Although the results of this continuing follow-up have not yet been published, it appears that the system of weighted test scores worked out in the original EIMP study have withstood the test of time.

Whatever it was that the tests measured was stable characteristics that not only differentiated the more successful from the less successful at the time of the original study, but also have continued to influence the varying degrees of success ever since. If anything, the years have tended to heighten the differences detected by the tests. This means that the relationships between weighted test scores and later managerial success will probably be more sharply etched than the ones shown in the exhibit.

What was it, then, that the EIMP tests measured? Actually, a number of factors were involved. The most powerful single predictor in the test battery turned out to be the individual background survey, which was basically a means of recording data about the individual's early life and family background. It appears that biographical instruments of this type are really a sort of indirect personality test, in the sense that adult personality differences can often be traced to trends that had their beginning much earlier in life. However, a biographical survey is more objective than a typical personality test, since most of its questions deal with verifiable matters of record rather than with matters of opinion. This relative objectivity leads, in turn, to a more stable score (and therefore to more accurate prediction) than most personality tests can be expected to achieve.

Basically, the biographical instrument in the EIMP project was measuring the rates at which the managers in the study had become emotionally independent and mature during their youth and early manhood and their ability to set themselves on a well-defined, productive course at an early age. The men who moved farthest and fastest in the Jersey Standard hierarchy had been masters of their own fate from a relatively early age—bad luck and difficult times notwithstanding. They were, in other words, no strangers to success; and for the most part they achieved success by pursuing it, having made such pursuit a habit for most of their lives. Similar findings have occurred in many other contexts, and their implications are rather profound. To suggest that most careers are, in effect, determined before they begin would be going beyond the facts.

On the other hand, there is little reason to doubt that a head start in early life can be turned into a potent advantage by an adult. It is also clear that people who arrive at a full command of their potentialities more slowly, or less completely, than others carry a handicap with them into their adult years at least as far as success in management is concerned. Neither the advantage nor the handicap is absolute: Both can be overcome. Yet it would appear that neither can be overcome easily.

For all practical purposes, the vast majority of humans enter adulthood without a distinct advantage or disadvantage carrying over from their youth. Consequently, what they achieve as adults is a matter of effort, ability, and luck not necessarily in that order. Mental ability was the second most effective predictor in the EIMP battery. This is hardly surprising, since the higher a man rises in executive ranks, the more time he must spend in learning. Executive learning is not the same as children's learning, which is often a matter of memorizing details; nor is it the same as craftsmen's learning, which consists in becoming profoundly familiar with all aspects of a particular, usually rather narrow, set of problems.

Rather, executive learning consists of the quick determination of what is essential in a mass of information which the executive is usually unable to comprehend in any depth. It also consists of determining how those essentials relate to other essentials gleaned from other technologies which he is equally handicapped in understanding. In effect, an executive is in the business of navigating through what are, for him, uncharted waters.

Since he cannot know all these waters well, he had better know his navigation well. This is really just another way of saying that he had better be possessed of a fairly high order of intelligence. It makes sense, then, that the more mentally agile managers in the EIMP study had an advantage with respect to rising to higher executive levels. There is also a sense in which the relationship of mental ability test scores to executive success flies in the face of managerial folklore; and indeed it is necessary to qualify any statement of that relationship rather carefully. Only a few executives are geniuses, and very few geniuses are executives. What is required of an executive is the ability to select, from among other men's insights, those which can be put to practical use — but not necessarily the ability to generate those insights. Consequently, while a highly intelligent man is better equipped for executive responsibility than a man of more ordinary intellect, a brilliant man does not necessarily have an advantage over a highly intelligent man in this respect.

Neither the AT&T nor the Jersey Standard research project has as yet been completed. Indeed, both are continuing programs rather than projects with a deadline. Yet it is already possible to draw some preliminary conclusions from them. Some of the characteristics that enable a man to handle an executive job effectively can be measured when he is still relatively young; these measurements can be made with a combination of situational, biographical, and mental ability tests; and, while he is still young, the individual with the best chance of rising to the top as a mature man is already brighter, more self-possessed, and more able to lead than his peers. The major implication of these results for management is that management development can be focused on men with the greatest probability of benefitting from it. Therefore, it is not necessary to rely on good fortune alone to bring enough well-rounded managers to the forefront when they are needed, because management development is itself a manageable process.

The discovery that the potentiality for high-level managerial work is identifiable at relatively early career stages can help to solve one of management's oldest problems. That is, what is the best way to allocate the necessarily scarce opportunities for optimal career development through rapid promotion and deliberate exposure to varied functional experience? Not even a large company can afford to offer such opportunities to its younger managers indiscriminately.

Early identification techniques offer a rational solution to the problem. At the same time, they could create new problems, chief among which is over reliance on the techniques themselves. No matter how much they are refined, and no matter what new techniques are added to the assessment arsenal, all attempts at early identification will be vulnerable to both the "a" and the "d" types of selection errors.

Another potential problem which could be created by the use of early identification techniques is the development of a "crown prince" atmosphere in the organizations that use them. That is, when some young men are thought to be destined for top-level positions while others are seemingly out of the running almost from the start of the race, the effects on morale and indirectly on productivity are almost certain to be harmful. The solution to both the over reliance problem and the crown-prince problem is to use early identification techniques with restraint and common sense.

This means that although the men who appear to have the greatest potentialities might at first be promoted more rapidly than the others, for all subsequent promotions they would have to compete on equal terms with all other managers at the same levels. Preference should be limited, in other words, to giving the selected men an opportunity to begin developing their managerial skills at a faster rate than their peers. Whether this preferential treatment is continued in further rapid promotions should depend entirely on whether it is justified by superior performance. In other words, if any man is to be given an advantage over his peers it must be clearly due to his accomplishments and not to his sponsors. Of course, the main implication of the studies completed thus far is that properly chosen men *will* tend to justify preferential treatment by performing more capably at every level than managers who have arrived there more slowly than they did.

There is a danger that a rapidly developing manager could be rushed ahead too fast. In that case, not only his career but management's confidence in the early identification system could be damaged unnecessarily. It is worth stressing that the one thing early identification techniques can be expected to do is to show which men are more likely than the rest to develop the capabilities for high-level management. Actual promotions to high-level jobs should be restricted, as they usually are now, to men who have *already developed* these capacities, regardless of whether their long-range potentialities were evident when they were younger.

Meantime, it can be stated with some assurance that further advances in the art of identifying people with high-level potentialities are likely to wait upon developments in other areas. There is no shortage of ways to assess men's potentialities; what is needed now is a much clearer notion of exactly which of their potentialities ought to be assessed. Surprisingly, we still know relatively little about the specific kinds of behaviour that managerial assessment techniques should be designed to predict. There is, of course, a great deal of folklore about what constitutes effective management and what constitutes ineffective management; and much of this has the ring of wisdom to it. But it also has the ring of imprecision and inconclusiveness. In the scientific sense of precise measurement and unambiguous definitions, we really do not know just what kinds of behaviour potentials to look for in prospective managers. This is not because any impenetrable mysteries surround the nature of managerial excellence. It is simply, and embarrassingly, because the necessary techniques for analyzing it have not been applied. This oversight, in turn, is due to a general failure to recognize the inadequacies of most current definitions.

The *prediction of future performance,* which is the essence of selection, and the *evaluation of current performance,* which is the essence of appraisal. We usually consider the way a man handles his job in both contexts, but too often without a clear distinction between the two. As a result, attempts to forecast what a man *could* do get weighted down with a great deal of irrelevant detail, while attempts to improve his current performance and to maintain his motivation are blunted by other irrelevancies. We will consider the application of performance appraisal to both future and current performance but separately. It is logical to continue our discussion on predicting managerial performance by considering the predictive aspects of performance appraisal first.

There are four good reasons why we need to define effective managerial performance more precisely, before we can expect to make much more progress with performance prediction. First of all, the principal ingredient of most management selection programs is and will undoubtedly continue to be nomination. Managers are asked to nominate candidates for other managerial positions from among their subordinates, on the basis of qualities that are presumably revealed in their job performance. The entire ethic of the merit system, promotion from within, and rising through the ranks is tied to the nomination process; it will therefore endure if only because it must endure. Few claims are made for its efficacy as a selection method. But this is precisely why nomination needs to be improved.

The manager who is asked to name employees who have managerial potential usually gets little useful guidance on what to look for and what to ignore or discount. He is hardly to be blamed if he falls back upon a combination of current job performance — which often has dubious relevance to a higher job — and whatever favourite notions he happens to entertain about the qualities that make for good managers.

The typical request to nominate management candidates is in fact quite unfair to the manager who receives it and to everyone else involved. It is founded on the absurd premise that managers, *because* they are managers, somehow know how to identify potential managers. They very often don't. The fact that in some companies there are certain visible similarities among the men who are chosen for management posts only proves that their managers share certain preconceptions. It does not necessarily mean that the qualities of an *effective* manager have been successfully identified. If only to improve the nomination process, and thereby to provide a richer input to more precise methods of assessment, the *behavioral* qualities of effective management should be carefully pinned down.

Second, most attempts to measure the effectiveness of selection systems have run into a sort of semantic sound barrier — an upper limit beyond which measurement itself becomes balky — owing to the elusive nature of the things that selection systems are supposed to predict. For example, it is easy enough to *talk* about "success" or "effectiveness," or to find some other glib way of expressing something we want the selection system to help us to get; but it is not so easy to measure it.

Sooner or later we have to face the practical problem of what to use for a yardstick. When we do that it turns out that "success" and other words like it express very dim concepts indeed. They are not adequately represented by any of the easily obtainable measurements of what people have actually done. The Jersey Standard study, for example, used salary changes as one of its several criteria of managerial success. But the research team used it more because of its convenience and objectivity than because they believed salary to be invariably a close relative of success. On this point, most managers would agree: "It ain't necessarily so. "

Because success is such a loose concept, it is hardly surprising that managers who are asked to rate people according to their success are in fact rating many different things. There is *no* generally acceptable yardstick, and therefore they use whatever yardstick is at hand. The result is a hash. But when you try to correlate something that is reasonably well defined with something that is not, the correlation you obtain can be no more accurate than consistency of the illdefined something lets it be. This is inherent in the nature of correlation, and correlation is by far the most convincing way we have of testing the usefulness of a selection system. One result of this dilemma is that psychologists have wondered for years whether their prediction techniques might not be considerably more accurate than they could prove to their own or anyone else's satisfaction.

This is, in fact, the main barrier to further advances in the state of the art of performance prediction. It is not that the search for newer, more sophisticated predictors needs to be pressed much further at this time. The problem is rather that we are not really sure which of our available predictors are worth the investment of time, money, and talent to develop them further. We won't know until much better performance criteria are developed to replace the ones we have today — better in the sense of being reasonably precise and independent of anyone's personal judgment. This can come only from a reasonably objective definition of the kind of performance that should be expected of managers.

A third reason for attempting to arrive at such a definition has to do with morale. The higher one goes in management, the more ambiguous the requirements of the job become, with the result that performance is not really measured so much as it is reviewed — in the same sense that a critic reviews a play. It is not uncommon for an executive to learn long after he has made a decision that his superiors considered it unwise, because he is in effect playing a game in which the rules are spelled out *ex post facto*. To some extent this is unavoidable, since the full consequences of high-level decisions are difficult to anticipate.

But this uncertainty exacts a price from both the executive and the company he works for. It can hardly fail to make the executive uncomfortable. At times it may also make him defensive and unwilling to think or act independently. When men in high positions choose to play it safe when their business judgment indicates a need for action, it is easy to dismiss the problem as a simple defect in their characters — a selection error. But that would be to fall for the hero fallacy. There is something to be said, therefore, for removing at least some of the ambiguity that surrounds most higher-level jobs; and the way to do that is to define both the unpardonable sins and the unimpeachable virtues as precisely as possible.

The fourth reason for spelling out what we mean by effective managerial performance follows directly from the third. If the rules of the management game are stated unambiguously, it becomes incumbent not only upon the managers, but on *their* managers as well, to abide by those rules. The very act of stating the limits of acceptable and unacceptable behaviour imposes a sort of discipline on top management to stay within them. With their own judges more predictable, managers are less likely to be defensive. As a result, the business of the organization can proceed in a more straight forward manner, with more emphasis upon results and less upon safety, popularity, and second-guessing the men at the top. None of these reasons is new, and one may legitimately ask why they have not long ago impelled a large-scale effort to arrive at an improved definition of managerial effectiveness. The answer is that they have, and that so far none of these efforts has been very successful. The keenest analysis of what's wrong with current systems of managerial performance evaluation has been made by Marvin D. Dunnette of the University of Minnesota. The analysis that follows draws heavily upon his work.

To begin with, many companies still have a predilection for rating their managers in terms of a list of adjectives that are somebody's idea of what a manager ought to be like. These usually sound like a sort of grown-up version of the Boy Scout Oath: Instead of being brave, clean, and reverent, the manager is typically expected to be decisive, articulate, and aggressive — or some other combination of qualities that one can hardly quarrel with. Aside from the unlikelihood that any mortal manager will ever be found who can look good if measured honestly against such sterling criteria, there are serious weaknesses in the adjective approach.

For one thing, the words mean different things to different people and so lead inevitably to a hash. Further, the adjectives are usually rather obviously loaded in a positive or negative direction, so that merely checking them becomes a sweeping judgment of the individual rather than a sharply etched portrait of one aspect of a man. This leads managers to avoid "indictments" by giving nearly everyone a strongly positive rating. While this is understandable, it makes the ratings nearly useless.

Finally, the adjective approach often fails to meet the test of relevance. That is, the qualities described are not always crucial to assessing the value of a man's services, and the adjectives nearly always omit qualities that are more important than those they include.

Another approach is to avoid trying to assess separate components of performance and to concentrate instead on global or overall judgments of what a man has contributed to his organization. One of the merits of the global approach is that it is easier to get judges to agree on generalized ratings than on ratings of separate parts of a man's performance. But balanced against this advantage are several weighty disadvantages.

Assessments that attempt to rate everything about a man at once are so inherently vague that it is impossible to say for certain what goes into them. In effect there is no quality control, and under the circumstances it is fairly likely that irrelevant factors can sway the rating in one direction or another.

Global ratings also tend to underestimate what a man could do at his best and overestimate what he could do at his worst, without indicating which circumstances would enable him to do his best and which would handicap him. One of the more popular trends in performance rating has been to evaluate the results that men achieve, rather than rating the men themselves by their qualities or traits. This represents a laudable attempt to minimize the subjective side of performance rating, and it takes on added respectability from its apparent closeness to Peter Drucker's famous concept of management by objectives. Yet measuring by results and managing by objectives are not quite the same thing. To begin with, there is the inescapable and not-so-easilysolved problem of exactly which results to measure. In many jobs and especially in managerial jobs results are compounded of circumstances, luck, and many people's efforts; and the contribution of any particular person (including a manager) to those results could be anything from minuscule to decisive.

The man whose performance is measured by results may be credited with other people's successes or stigmatized for their failures, unless it can be shown that the results were his and his alone. But that happens only rarely in managerial jobs. Another problem is that the particular results selected for measurement may represent only a part of the job, and not necessarily a large or vital part. Lastly, it is difficult to apply standards to results, so one is often left with the dilemma that measurement by results was intended to avoid: Shall subjective judgment be used to decide which results are "better" than others? While setting objectives is a good way to focus a man's activities and to motivate him in a short-term sense, it is not necessarily an effective way to measure either his contribution or his potentialities.

Perhaps the most important observation to be made about performance rating systems is that they are seldom used with the punctuality or thoroughness that is prescribed for them. Performance rating scales are not, in other words, considered very important by the people for whom they were designed; and this in turn is usually due to the *way* in which they were designed.

They are typically composed of loosely defined or even undefined terms which represent the opinion of someone seldom the manager himself as to what should be rated in a manager's performance. These forms are resisted by managers because they seem, and very often are, irrelevant and unnecessary. The importance of performance rating itself is seldom quarreled with; rather, it is the forms themselves, with their sweeping generalities and their lack of clear-cut standards, that receive the brunt of the criticism.

To be effective, a system of performance evaluation would need to have at least three characteristics: First, the ratings would have to be based on specific, verifiable *events*, not on traits that allegedly encompass a man's personality and not on results in the broad and essentially unaccountable sense. Second, these events would have to be demonstrably significant. It is not enough that anybody's opinion or even so-called common sense indicates that the events are significant; hard evidence should show that they are crucial to effective performance. Third, the scale used for rating each of these events should be firmly anchored in specific, easily recognizable behaviour description, not in ambiguous terms like "average" which mean different things to different people. Attempts to build systems of this kind are currently being made in a number of companies.

Our insistence on basing ratings on events rather than on judgments springs from the need for a stable yardstick. We can usually assume that whenever a yardstick has to be interpreted, even competent interpreters will disagree on the measurements they obtain from it. Thus we are never sure whether such a yardstick has been read accurately or inaccurately, even when we use consensus or some other way of reducing its stretchability. Admittedly, not all the ambiguity is eliminated when we switch from judging traits to asking whether an event has occurred. After all, one can always quibble with the definition of the event. Still, a carefully defined question that seeks a yes-or-no answer is much more likely to lead to agreement between observers than any other kind of question.

There is, of course, a danger in relying on specific events instead of on generalized traits. The events chosen for the rating system may be either irrelevant or insufficient; that is, they may cast no light at all on what kind of performance to expect in the future, or they may reveal only a fraction of what the man has done. Fortunately, both of these dangers can be greatly reduced when the rating system is designed by means of the "critical incident" technique.

This is a method originated by John C. Flanagan of the University of Pittsburgh. It requires the recollection, by persons who were in a position to witness and judge them, of many specific events in which a job was handled exceptionally well or exceptionally poorly. What results from collating and analyzing hundreds of such events is, in effect, the pooled wisdom and experience of the executives who made the judgments. This information can usually be reduced to a manageable number of make-or-break factors. These are, for all practical purposes, the anatomy of the job — its unimpeachable virtues and its unpardonable sins — expressed in terms of specific things that were done rather than in adjectives, adverbs, or other qualifiers. The pertinence of the factors can be guaranteed by selecting only those kinds of incidents that show up repeatedly in many separate recountings; their completeness is assured by thoroughly mining the memories of enough managers.

So much for predicting future performance on the basis of current performance. There remains the thorny problem of current performance itself — whether its measurement contributes to its improvement and, if so, in what way. During the past dozen years or so, this issue has probably generated more heat and less light than anything else in personnel administration. It will probably continue to do so, chiefly because the supporters of performance appraisal claim too much for it, while its opponents, by demanding too much, inevitably acquire a long and impressive list of disappointments with which to damn it.

The rationale underlying performance appraisal is quite simple, and this is indeed the main thing wrong with it. The premise is that if men are told in what ways their performance is deficient, they will naturally want to correct it. This is at best a gross oversimplification of human nature. It would be more accurate to say that most men would want to correct the deficiencies in their performance if they *agreed* that they were deficient and if there appeared to be enough *advantage* in correcting them to justify the effort. But these conditions are extremely difficult sometimes, perhaps, impossible to satisfy. This is the main reason why performance appraisal, when it is practiced at all, so easily leads to resentment and estrange-ment between supervisor and subordinate, on the one hand, or to a mere ritualistic pretense on the other.

Despite the difficulties in making so "straightforward" a programme work, attempts to set matters aright continue. These are of two sorts: administrative and psychological. The administrative attempts consist of various control systems through which personnel departments try, usually with indifferent success, to persuade or coerce managers to confront their subordinates with a frank evaluation of their work. The reason given most often for the relative ineffectiveness of such systems is that top management ignores them and that the rest of management infers that performance appraisal is really only a pious hoax.

The psychological attempts are aimed toward the heart of the matter. They try to remove the underlying resistance to performance appraisal by teaching managers to handle it more adroitly or by restructuring appraisal so that performance is measured against objective standards which the subordinate has helped to select. There can be no serious argument with the value of training and restructuring; but they are not, in themselves, sufficient to make performance appraisal the potent tool for betterment it was intended to be.

Whether an effective system of performance appraisal would actually improve performance is likely to remain an academic question-at least until a way is found, not only to make such a system effective, but to keep it that way. Some experiments suggest that systems based on joint goal setting by supervisors and subordinates can, at least during the life of the experiment, produce increases in productivity. But the real test of any experimental system is what happens when the experimenters, with their vested interest in the system, leave it to be operated by managers whose interest in it depends on how well it has been sold to them. Even effective systems will, in the long run, probably have to rely on the policing abilities of the personnel administrator to see to it that they are used consistently.

There is, however, a subtler advantage to performance appraisal which justifies its use, entirely apart from whether such appraisals improve performance. One of the most common complaints that employees of all kinds, including managers, are likely to express is that they don't know what kind of future they can anticipate for themselves in their companies — or, to use an overused phrase, they don't know where they stand. Traced to its roots, this is usually a way of expressing the discomfort of not controlling one's own destiny.

Assignments, promotions, salary increases events that help to determine the quality of life in an organization too often seem to be decided remotely, in ways that the individual can influence only indirectly if at all. The usual assurances about the merit system are not sufficient to set these anxieties aside, although they can help if they are demonstrably supported by fact. But what is really at stake in each case is a man's future. If he is young enough, he will face the problem of whether to commit himself to his present organization or seek a better future elsewhere.

If he already feels committed, he must make the best of a situation from which he cannot escape. Either way, having one's future largely in the hands of someone else even a benevolent someone else is a rather insecure state of affairs. It is also endemic in organizations of all kinds and, in a sense, the price one pays for being part of an organization in the first place. In the long run, whether this insecurity is assuaged or aggravated can have a significant effect on the quality of a man's motivation.

Performance appraisal is not a complete answer to this problem, but it does give the individual some measure of control over his future in two ways. First, there is at least an implied commitment on the part of the organization to stand behind whatever appraisal the supervisor gives. However vague and inexact it may be, the appraisal is a sort of tacit guarantee, at least for the near term, of the kind of treatment the individual can expect to receive from the organization.

Second, having to reveal the appraisal to the employee imposes a severe discipline upon the supervisor, so much so that many balk at it. Some overreact to the discipline by becoming excessively lenient, letting the employee believe that his work is better than it really is. But under such a system, supervisors are constrained from making the kinds of negative judgments that are too harsh or simply unjustifiable. And it is this constrained, distilled appraisal that becomes a sort of implied contract, at least in the employee's mind, between his organization and himself. In limited and subtle ways, then, a performance appraisal system can let people know where they stand. Is that enough of an advantage to justify the system? It may not seem so, since employees who are appraised and told about it are not necessarily happy, and their work is not necessarily more efficient. But their complaints, if there are any, are likely to centre on less corrosive anxieties, and that is a considerably greater advantage than it may at first appear.

Management too often expects that the elimination of a problem will lead to its obverse; that is, if the cause of unhappiness is removed, people will automatically swing to the other extreme and become happy. It is not difficult to understand why this does not happen. Morale is something like a spring: It can be depressed by a negative pressure or elevated by a positive lift. Releasing either of these influences does not send the spring hurtling in the opposite direction; it merely returns it to a neutral position.

This is the normal condition of morale: neutral, indifferent, motionless. That is all you can expect from relieving a negative pressure upon morale. To move from there to the kind of zest and commitment associated with high morale would require further efforts in other words, a positive lift. Performance appraisal, when sensitively used, relieves one of the more damaging pressures upon morale and permits it to rise, as it were, from a compressed state to a neutral condition. A potential danger is thus removed and the possibility of introducing a lifting force is at least opened. That is not at all a bad bargain.

10

Roles and Responsibilities

AN OVERVIEW

The two college professors could see the look of pain as Liz, a young accountant, looked up from her desk in response to the question that she had been asked during the interview. "It's hard to explain," she said slowly. "I know all the guys around the office will tell you that men and women are treated equally around here. Plus, they probably have data to back it up. But, yes, I have to work harder to get ahead here because I'm a woman. I can't prove it; I just know it in my 'knower.' " Remarks similar to these were heard on several occasions during the course of a research project on women in public accounting. The women who made these remarks were highly successful people on the fast track in large international accounting firms. Moreover, a few of their male colleagues concurred.

Women have been rapidly entering the profession during the last decade and a half. The expansion of opportunities into what was one of the last male bastions to fall has progressed to the point where over 50 per cent of new hires are female in many firms. Brenda T. Acken, who chaired the recent AICPA special committee to examine upward mobility of women in accounting, asserts that within twenty years women are expected to constitute 50 per cent of the profession. The presence of women in the profession has created new ethical dilemmas: issues of equality, issues of upward mobility, issues of propriety, and issues of morality.

ISSUES OF EQUALITY

Irrespective of one's beliefs about women's issues or equality of the sexes, one point is clear: by virtue of the fact that a person is in the profession, she is a member of the professional community. Therefore, the treatment that person receives and the role that person plays must be evaluated within the context of community and the inherent meaning of community membership.

As an example consider that the former code of ethics of the AICPA called "professional courtesy" an "obligation" and that it admonished its members "to deal with fellow practitioners in a manner which will not detract from their reputation and well-being.' From a deontological perspective we may view these as duties owed by members of the community to one another. From a utilitarian point of view we may postulate the consequences that unethical treatment might have upon other members of the community and ultimately upon the profession as a whole.

DUTY

The current movements by accountants who are not in the realm of public accounting to actively seek professional status and recognition. Many believe these accountants have achieved this sought-after status. Therefore it follows that one who is an accountant should conduct herself as a professional.

The question we address here is whether duties owed by or duties owed to professionals change by virtue of the fact that the professional is female. In the absence of some logical reason to the contrary, the answer to this question would have to be no. In the United States and increasingly in other cultures, equality of women in the workplace is at least given lip service. One would presume that"the workplace" would include the professional workplace.

Therefore professional duties are owed to and by all members of the professional community. Yet it is not enough to give assent to this notion; we professionals must act upon it. Professional people should have the opportunity to advance in the profession based upon their professional qualifications and contributions to the firm and to the profession. Professional people should respect one another as persons-as peers in the community.

These are lofty goals, but surely they do not change because of the gender of the community member. As Kant stated, each rational person should be treated as an end and not as a means to an end. By virtue of their admission to the profession women have the right to expect treatment as professionals and have assumed the duty to treat other professionals in a like manner.

Let's say for example that a client has invited Fred to a lunch where some important strategic planning discussions will take place. The client asks Fred to bring"a couple of more" professionals with him. Fred believes that this meeting will have an important career impact upon the people he brings because it will afford them the opportunity to participate in high-level discussions and they will get hands-on experience of the kinds of activity it takes to build a client base.

In Fred's opinion his two most talented and dedicated subordinates are Beth and Bob. He therefore decides that they should attend. Later Fred finds out that the client has scheduled the lunch at a private club in the city with a"men only" policy. So Fred invites John to come to the meeting in the place of Beth.

In this case, Fred has violated a professional duty towards Beth. Beth, through no fault of her own, is being denied an opportunity that she deserves.

This violates a fundamental duty of justice. Fred should have asked the client to schedule the meeting for another place, explaining that Beth was the most qualified person for the engagement.

CONSEQUENCES

Utilitarian ethics support the notion of equality of the sexes in the profession. We need not go to metaphysical utilitarian goals to demonstrate this. The most bare knuckles kind of consequential thinking reveals it. Simply stated, the accounting profession needs women. There is intense and increasing demand for trained and intelligent people in the accountant profession. Women meet a great deal of this demand.

If bright and motivated women are treated unfairly or even if they believe this to be the case, they will take their talents elsewhere. The consequences to the profession would be a severe shortage of qualified people. Therefore treating women as professional peers is not only good ethics; it is also good business.

One final detrimental consequence can accrue to the accounting profession if women in the accounting community are treated unfairly. This is the erosion of the public's perception of the accounting community as a profession. The most important factors in maintaining the benefits of professionalism is that society must recognize the professional status of the group wishing to attain or to maintain professional status. As long as society favours basic fairness and justice towards women in the workplace-and we believe that it does-any profession that treats its female members unfairly or unjustly will do so at its peril.

IS SUES OF UPWARD MOBILITY

Admission to partnership is affected by many considerations, notably technical, management, client relationship and practice development abilities. There is no question about women's technical ability, but traditional beliefs and attitudes regarding other abilities raise questions. For example, are women at a competitive disadvantage in comparison to men in obtaining new audit clients and maintaining existing ones? Is there a women's "network?" Moreover, some partners may believe that men are generally more dedicated than women to a professional career.

One important measure of whether or not women are receiving fair treatment in the profession is evidence of their being promoted and compensated for their professional services.

The AICPA in recognition of this fact recently appointed a special committee to examine two issues:

- That although many women have risen to senior levels in accounting firms, relatively few have been admitted to partnership and

- That many accountants believe admission to partnership is more difficult for women than for men. The report of the Special Committee on Upward Mobility of Women was published in March 1988.

The mere fact that the issues identified by the AICPA are true does not present an ethical problem per se. In order to discern the ethical concerns involved in the upward mobility of women, the reasons for barriers to partnership must be discovered. Three possible reasons are: first, that the cycle is not complete; second, that women leave the profession before being promoted to partner; and third, that because of gender bias women face barriers to partnership.

By stating that the cycle is not complete, we refer to an often expressed belief that women simply have not been in the profession long enough to be promoted to the partner level. Because women began to enter the profession in significant numbers about fifteen years ago and it takes about twelve to fifteen years to be promoted to partner, this argument currently has validity. However, as time passes it will no longer hold water. This reason does not present ethical problems by itself. The other two reasons will not be cured simply by the passage of time. In these two we find issues and dilemmas of interest from an ethical standpoint. We shall therefore focus attention upon the validity of these issues.

The AICPA special committee believes that the factors that affect upward mobility of women are not unique to the accounting profession, but rather are universal obstacles confronting women in the general workplace. However, Cottell and Michael found that while women in the profession encounter many of the same problems faced by their peers in other business situations, public accounting presents several unique aspects.

WHY WOMEN LEAVE

The factors that cause women to leave the profession are entangled with the very same factors that cause barriers to upward mobility for those who do stay in the profession. They can be classified into two broad areas: the balance of personal and professional responsibilities, and real or perceived biases that impede the upward mobility of women in accounting. The balance of personal and professional responsibilities issue is a particularly thorny one in public accounting. In this profession, working hours are not predictable. Clients see CPAs as continuous service providers who should be available when they are needed. This places tremendous burdens upon female professionals, because in most families the woman is the primary manager, according to the AICPA Special Committee. Moreover, family is generally of greater concern to women than to men.

This problem is magnified by a subtle attitude in the business community. Marriage tends to be viewed as an asset for the male executive but a hindrance for the female executive. A wife is a helper who will allow the man to focus more attention towards his business life. For the woman marriage implies that she will have additional responsibilities that will divert her attention from her career responsibilities.

The issue has led some companies and some accounting firms to experiment with what is coming to be known as "the Mommy track." Proponents of this management style suggest that women have the option of a slower career path to partner than the traditional one. The idea is to permit a smaller client load, to allow for flexibility in hours, or to devise other means to help professional women cope with the balance of personal and professional responsibilities.

Women who desire to be on the Mommy track would self-select. In return for the reduced load of clients or hours, they would know that the time to be promoted to partner would be longer. Presumably the option of this alternate track would also be available to men.

The Mommy track issue is controversial and some of the controversy contains ethical overtones. Critics state that the Mommy track will relegate women in the workplace to second-class citizen status.

Moreover, such a policy flies in the face of the American ideal to promote whoever is best qualified and has earned the promotion with hard work. In short, the Mommy track raises the issue of justice for both the person on this career path and for those who are not on the alternate track but are competing for the scarce partner positions. Nevertheless, women interviewed by Cottell and Michael tended to favour at least having the option of an alternate career path. One professional women was actually on a half-time basis with her firm and was quite pleased with the arrangement. Women also leave public accounting because of real or perceived barriers to their upward mobility.

In other words, some women leave the profession because they believe—rightly or wrongly—that opportunities for advancement are better for women in careers outside public accounting. Here the issue becomes entangled with the idea that women are not promoted because of their gender. We are unable to discern the difference between women not being promoted to partner because of gender and their leaving because they "see the handwriting on the wall." This is particularly true in large public accounting firms that have an "up or out" policy under which one either is promoted or is politely asked to leave the firm.

GENDER-BASED BARRIERS

The AICPA special committee and the research of Cottell and Michael revealed several biases women in accounting face. Some are quite subtle. Blatant and obvious discrimination is no longer evident for the most part. More deeply held attitudes and beliefs of both men and women are where we find the ethical issues in today's professional environment.

One gender-specific barrier cited by the AICPA special committee is that women are less aware than men of success criteria in accounting such as visibility within the organization, the benefits of a mentor, and the importance of presenting a successful self-image. Specifically, the committee claims that female professionals think good performance is enough for career advancement. Women also believe that hard work will enable them to overcome any barriers that they might encounter, according to the committee.

Interestingly, the women interviewed by Cottell and Michael did not confirm the findings of the AICPA special committee. Most of these women were aware of success criteria at their firms and did not feel that good performance alone would enable them to get ahead. They realised that they had to do more than work hard to reach their career goals but felt they were unable to engage in some of the forms of office politics necessary for success. Of course, this was a source of frustration to them.

The AICPA special committee stated that women need to learn the importance of working as a team. Some social scientists believe that women have deficiencies in this area because they lack opportunity to participate in team sports. On the other hand, some feminists state that women are by nature better team members because they tend to be conciliators. The jury is still out on this issue.

The AICPA special committee also stated that women receive less advice from their superiors about how to succeed in an organization than their male counterparts. This appears at all three levels of supporting relationships. The committee believes women need increased mentoring opportunities in accounting.

Women face cultural attitudes that can affect their ability to advance in their careers. Many people view women as wives, mothers, and daughters rather than business colleagues. These attitudes are detrimental to women if held by colleagues but devastating if held by clients, since advancement to partner depends primarily upon the ability to build and hold a client base.

As seemingly harmless a matter as the game of golf can cause grief to women in public accounting. Many CPAs use golf to enhance relationships with their clients. However, this is an avenue almost closed to women in the profession. One woman interviewed by Cottell and Michael explained that many men do not like women on the golf course. They feel women slow down the game and lessen the competition. On the other hand, if the woman is an accomplished golfer, they resent being beaten by a woman! This particular woman, who was good at the game, found herself holding back so that she did not commit the sin of winning.

Another cultural attitude concerns personal deportment. Outward expressions of anger and blatant displays of aggressiveness are not only tolerated in men but even admired by some people. For women, on the other hand, such behaviour is viewed as either feminine weakness or unfeminine behaviour. This issue was recently aired in the court suit between Price Waterhouse and Ann Hopkins, a manager who, despite bringing in considerable business to her firm and billing more hours than any other candidate, had failed to make partner. Written evaluations from firm partners branded her " 'macho,' foulmouthed and harsh to co-workers." One partner suggested that she learn "to walk, talk and dress 'more femininely... wear makeup, have her hair styled and wear jewelry.' " In this instance the court upheld lower court rulings that Hopkins had been discriminated against.

A basic issue needs to be resolved with respect to cultural attitudes about women. Should women change? Should they exhibit the kinds of behaviour that have been the keys to success for men in the business and professional community? Many have suggested this course of action and have even suggested that the change begin at the childrearing stage, where boys and girls should be treated more alike.

The other argument states that women are after all basically different from men. Recent research has added evidence to this view. Feminists have begun to adopt this view and state that society and its attitudes need the changing. The business and professional community should recognize, value, and reward those unique attributes that women bring to the workplace by virtue of their femininity. From a community perspective the profession would be expanded and enhanced were it able to embrace this attitude. However, it remains to be seen whether the rigors of the current competitive environment would allow such a change to take root.

Women in accounting encounter stress in the same way as their male counterparts. The AICPA special committee believes that the problem of stress is greater for women than for men. Women feel a greater burden under the balance of personal and professional responsibilities. Women face cultural discrimination. Women perceive that they must perform better than men in order to get ahead. All these things aggravate the stressful environment in public accounting. Thus while everyone in public accounting must face long hours and the stress that goes along with them, women are less tolerant of them. Hence they leave the profession.

The AICPA special committee found that some organizations do not recognize the problems encountered by women. On the other hand, most of the people interviewed by Cottell and Michael—many of whom were at the highest levels of their firms—were not only aware of, but were actively seeking, solutions to the problems faced by women in the profession.

Some of the ongoing policy changes discovered in this research included cafeteria-style benefit packages, in-house day care programmes, flexible hours, and attempts at formal "mentoring" systems. Several of the partners and managers interviewed stated that the primary gender-specific problems female accountants faced were due to clients upon whom the profession and the professional must ultimately depend.

It follows that if women are treated as equal to men in the professional community then they will have equal opportunity for advancement. For the profession to remain a healthy, ethical community, it must forthrightly face the issue of upward mobility for women in real terms. Happily, our profession is continuing to make progress in this area. The AICPA's special committee report contains guidance—both for professional women and for employers of professional women—that has a great deal of merit.

ISSUES OF PROPRIETY

Propriety refers to standards that are "socially acceptable" in conduct or speech. Of course the first question that might be asked is "acceptable to whom?" In our context we speak of acceptable to the community of professionals.

OFFICE ROMANCE

Lisa A. Mainiero has recently published the results of research on dating, sexual relations, and marriage in the workplace. She is surprisingly supportive of such relationships. "Attractions at work are a natural part of the conviviality of daily office life.

They should not be spurned or dismissed as inconsequential. One of the consequences of the new sexual revolution is that men and women will meet, marry, and fall in love on the job. It is unrealistic to think otherwise."

Are ethical issues raised by the occurrence of office romance? While dating and marriage relationships seem strictly personal, they can have ethical implications in two areas addressed earlier in the book.

The first issue is independence. Is it within the standards of the profession for a professional to date the employee of a client? We encounter the same ethical issues here as in any client CPA relationship—independence in fact and independence in appearance.

With respect to independence in fact we must admit that dating relationships may be emotionally charged. In many cases judgment may be clouded. This includes professional judgment. With respect to independence in appearance the issue is particularly murky, since here we speak of independence in the eye of the beholder.

Dating relationships or affairs have the potential to be problematic for the professional. Should such relationships lead to marriage, the questions about independence become even more pronounced. As more and more women come into the business community and as they rise to higher levels in both accounting and client firms, the questions of independence can become more serious. The profession does not have clear guidelines in this area. More thoughtful discussion and consideration are necessary.

The second issue is very much akin to the nepotism issue. Both public accounting firms and other organizations are much more tolerant of office romance than they used to be. Public accounting firms are less tolerant than many other organizations should these relationships lead to marriage, according to Mainiero. She reports that two Big Six firms, Arthur Andersen and Price Waterhouse, strictly prohibit partners from marrying other employees.

SEXUAL STATIC

Sexual static is found when actions in the business community taken for purely business reasons are sometimes misinterpreted by the opposite sex. For example, a male CPA might invite a female colleague to dinner in order to discuss an upcoming audit engagement and she might wrongly interpret this as an unwelcome initiation of romance and thus decline the invitation. Accountants of both sexes are likely to encounter this in any organization. Yet for the female professional in public accounting, the problem can be particularly perplexing with respect to clients.

The building and maintenance of a client base seems to create most of the problem. A common means of maintaining client relationships for the male CPA is to ask a client to dinner and perhaps some socializing afterward. Suppose the CPA is instead an attractive woman in her thirties who asks the client, a married man in his fifties, out to such an evening. Her motives are purely business in nature, but how does the client interpret it? Also, how does that client's wife interpret it? Many women in public accounting believe that this sort of dynamic creates a competitive disadvantage for them.

Cultural attitudes and sexual static can also cause other problems for women in accounting. Accounting, both public and private, is a career that requires the accountant to be gone from the family overnight. Some people believe it is not appropriate for a woman to be away from her family overnight. If the one who holds this belief is a client (for the CPA) or someone high in the organization (for any accountant), a real problem is created for the professional woman.

Sexual static may also cause problems among colleagues. For example, one female accountant we know is a college professor. She relates that no one even takes notice if two men from the otherwise all-male department go to lunch together.

Yet if she goes to lunch with a male colleague, remarks are often heard. These remarks might be made in jest, but they are not funny because they cause pain. Here we have a violation of the duty of non-male ficence caused by sexual static and entrenched cultural attitudes.

ISSUES OF MORALITY

We promised a book not on morality but on practical ethics. Nevertheless, in the realm of men and women in the profession, two ethical issues that arise also have clear moral implications—sexual harassment and certain kinds of office romance. We shall address each briefly.

SEXUAL HARASSMENT

Sexual harassment is an annoying or unwelcome sexual advance or imposition made with the suggestion that inappropriate rewards or penalties will result from compliance or refusal to comply. Most often women are harassed by men who exert some power over them, usually in a job situation. There are occasions where women harass men, and either men or women may be sexually harassed by another person of the same sex. Sexual harassment may also come from coworkers.

Women in traditionally male fields are sometimes systematically harassed by their male peers in an effort to drive them away. People who, because they are the sole support of themselves or their families, need their jobs most desperately may be singled out for sexual harassment because they fear losing their pay. Sexual harassment is not only unethical, it is illegal. By today's standards sexual harassment is so universally condemned that one would not think it worthy of ethical discussion. Yet the phenomenon occurs even among professional people.

We suggest that sexual harassment is particularly abhorrent in the context of a profession. Such conduct strikes at the very heart of the notion of a community of people who respect one another. The unwanted advance need not be overt to constitute unprofessional behaviour.

One woman interviewed by Cottell and Michael related that a partner of a firm had the habit of patting her on the head-something he did not do to her male peers. She asked him not to do it any more, and when it occurred again she left that firm. Here we see a case where the ethical principle of justice was violated. The victim of the harassment left the firm while the perpetrator remained as a member in good standing.

In the final analysis all members of the professional community are victims when sexual harassment occurs. People who are plagued by sexual harassment suffer from tension, frustration, anxiety, and all anger. As a result they either leave the profession or are unable to function properly if they remain. The community is thus deprived of a valued member and the perpetrator who is left unchallenged is free to seek another person to harass.

OFFICE ROMANCE REVISITED

One striking aspect of Mainiero's book is the ethical decision model she repeats throughout the work. That model is hedonistic utilitarianism. Simply stated, Mainiero's advice to her readers is that they should weigh the pleasure they derive from an office romance with the possible consequences-good or bad-that the relationship might have for their career success.

Hedonistic utilitarianism is not an ethical model that thinking people take very seriously any more. The ethics of office romance should involve things other than personal pleasure and career success. The profession is a community, after all, and its ethics should rise to a higher plane. We suggest that either the wider consequences of oflice romance or the rightness or wrongness of such a relationship be taken into account in each individual case. Some office romances are for any number of reasons not within the ethical limits and standards of the accounting profession. For example, an adulterous office romance raises questions of promise keeping and questions of its effects upon families. Exploitative office romance raises questions of non-maleficence and the consequences of promotion for other than reasons of merit, which in turn violates the principle of justice.

Mainiero, who overall seems to favour office romance, gives stern warning against office romance situations where the relationship is between boss and subordinate or mentor and protégée. Two dangers exist in such relationships. First, while the relationship is going on other professionals in the office may resent special treatment they perceive the subordinate is receiving-again the issue of justice is raised. Second, such relationships sometimes turn into sexual harassment cases when the subordinate or protégé desires to end the relationship and the other party desires to continue it.

SOCIAL RESPONSIBILITY ACCOUNTING

THE PURSUIT 0F JUSTICE

Francis de Sales, controller of the Genesee Cable Company, was not pleased with the way the meeting of the management group had gone. At the meeting, the sales manager Teresa Avila had given a brilliant presentation, at the end of which she had recommended that cable service from the Casual Network be offered as part of their regular package in order to boost cable subscriptions. What disturbed Francis was that Casual's fare was widely regarded as soft pornography, a type of television to which Francis was opposed on moral grounds.

At first, John Cross, the president, had seemed to object. John recalled that when Genesee had been competing for the franchise in this community he had stated at a public hearing that Genesee had no intention of offering pornographic material of any type over the cable service. He wondered aloud whether taking on the Casual station wouldn't be breaking a promise to the community.

Yet Teresa had persisted. She noted that a statement made at a public hearing was not legally binding. She also cited her market research, which showed demand for Casual from many people in the community who were not currently subscribers.

What galled Francis most was the fact that Teresa was able to use accounting numbers properly developed in his department to show that by adopting her recommendation Genesee would improve its profits dramatically. At the end of the meeting John seemed to be swayed by the profitability argument, although he did say he wanted to reflect on the recommendation a bit further.

After returning to his office, Francis mused: "Surely there must be more to business than just the bottom line. It seems so irresponsible to break our promise to the community for the sake of making more money. I wonder if accounting, as an information system, might not assign some sort of value to the old-fashioned notion of keeping a promise."

INFORMATION ABOUT RESPONSIBILITY

During the 1970s substantial discussion was available in accounting literature about social responsibility accounting. In recent years this topic has been placed on the back burner. Yet, with increasing attention being given to business ethics, we can expect social responsibility accounting to re-emerge as a "hot" topic.

After all, once society decides that ethical behaviour is a desired trait to be expected of businesses and business personnel, the logical question will follow: Who is and who is not acting ethically or responsibly? This question creates a demand for information, and accounting is one place to which we turn for information about business enterprise.

ETHICS AND ACCOUNTING REPORTS

A leading proponent of social responsibility accounting, defines it as "the process of selecting firm-level social performance variables, measures, and measurement procedures; systematically developing information useful for evaluating the firm's social performance; and communicating such information to concerned social groups, both within and outside the firm." A key accounting role seems apparent here. Accounting, as the language of business, is a primary provider of information. Traditional accounting concerns itself with financial information. In expanding the purview of providing information, we may be going beyond data and interpretation that are clearly financial. Yet ethical process and content may also be "accounted for."

Social responsibility accounting must somehow transform ethical information, which accountants may find "squishy," into financial information, or at least information in financial terms, so that accountants preparing and interpreting the reports are within their professional sphere.

The task here is a formidable one. Accountants must work with identified users of information to ascertain what sort of information is required. Then management must decide whether such information should be reported and, if so, in what form. Once these two barriers are surmounted, the accounting profession will be better able to satisfy the need by coming up with the "how" of reporting.

Much debate has occurred about the desirability of even having social responsibility accounting. Its proponents have suggested several models as starting points for developing this kind of accounting. Our intention is to examine the notion of social responsibility from the point of view of ethics. Two major ethical theories, utilitarianism and deontologism. Utilitarianism can and has been used to create a good case for accountants not to engage in social responsibility accounting. Following that as suggested, present a deontological case in favour of social responsibility accounting.

UTILITARIAN ARGUMENTS

Opponents of social responsibility accounting argue in an analytical rather than descriptive fashion. That is, they approach the entire issue from the standpoint of cost/benefit analysis. Most accountants are quite comfortable with this type of analysis. Cost/benefit analysis is a concept that is deeply rooted in utilitarian ethics. In this analysis the utility defined—that is, the good we maximize—is material wealth expressed in terms of dollars. Simply stated, we sum the cost of an action and compare it with the sum of the economic benefits expressed in financial terms. Under a utilitarian criterion we should undertake a project where the economic benefits exceed the costs.

As an example of this kind of utilitarian reasoning, let's return to the Genesee Cable Company. As part of her research concerning the Casual Network, Teresa asked Francis to provide her a differential cost schedule. This kind of managerial report is a common one in accounting.

The differential cost schedule clearly points to the decision to accept Casual Network programming. The operating income with this option exceeds operating income without it by $162,000. Using the terminology of cost/benefit analysis, we can say that the benefits exceed the costs. This is a straightforward case, since both the benefits and the costs may be clearly identified when the utility that we seek to maximize is monetary wealth measured in dollars.

A careful analysis of the social responsibility accounting issue on this utilitarian ground provides disappointing results for its proponents. From the standpoint of the corporation, the costs of placing any new accounting system into place are substantial. Here the company must consider more than the immediate costs of designing and implementing such an accounting system. Also included should be the possible consequences (costs) of publicly reporting the company's actions in the social responsibility arena.

An honest reporting of these matters could bring consequences that are not in the best interests of the owners or managers of the corporation. These might come in the form of possible calls for increased government action in the affairs of the company, possible action against the company from special interest groups, or lawsuits from parties who believe they have sustained injury from the company's actions. Moreover, these costs of implementing social responsibility accounting are fairly easy to measure using conventional business forecasting methods. We may thus be fairly certain about the magnitude of the costs. Against these costs we should weigh the benefits of social responsibility accounting. Here we run into problems, particularly as far as the accountant is concerned. Accounting tends to deal with information that is specific in nature. Within accounting certain types of information are sanctioned as real and true. Accountants therefore focus their attention upon this type of information to the exclusion of other kinds.

The benefits of reporting social responsibility information fall into a category of information that is not currently sanctioned by accounting. Much of the benefit of ethical behaviour is not obviously financial in nature. Accountants are therefore understandably uncomfortable with attempts to measure this information, let alone report upon it. The benefits of going through this effort are therefore elusive and difficult to express in financial terms. By way of example, let's return to the Genesee Cable Company. Certainly utilitarian arguments may be made to reject Teresa's plan to schedule Casual's programming. In the long run the public, in perceiving that Genesee is a company that keeps its promises and is concerned with community values, will be anxious to have increased business contact with Genesee. In accounting terms we might be tempted to call this goodwill. Yet accountants have recognized the problems associated with measuring goodwill for years.

Today this task is not even attempted unless the goodwill is demonstrated by a purchase transaction on the open market. The economically rational manger would be hard pressed not to offer Casual's programming, especially if he attempted to use cost/benefit analysis in arriving at a decision. The possible benefits of a future good name in the community seem somewhat smaller than the prospect of an increase in profit of $162,000 when we take the cost/benefit point of view. Thus the use of cost/benefit analysis as a criterion for the desirability of social responsibility accounting usually leaves us with heavy, easy-to-measure costs on one hand balanced against vague and seemingly small benefits on the other.

Many accounting writers who have looked at the issue of social responsibility accounting from this utilitarian perspective have been quite pessimistic about its future in accounting. Indeed, the practical application of socially responsible actions themselves finds nearly insurmountable hurdles from a cost/benefit point of view. Yet there are underlying weaknesses in attempts to use cost/benefit analysis or any other utilitarian system in a practical way. These have been identified by Alasdair MacIntyre:

Utilitarian tests must presuppose the application of some prior non-utilitarian principle that sets limits on the range of activities to be considered. Utilitarian tests must presuppose some method of rank ordering the values of good and evil. This method must be non-utilitarian. Different agents will make different assessments of harms and benefits. The question of what is to count as a consequence of a given action must be answered. Boundaries must be placed upon responsibility for consequences.

A time scale must be used in assessing consequences. The question of how far the present should be sacrificed for the future requires a non-utilitarian answer. These weaknesses of the practical application of utilitarianism readily appear in the use of cost/benefit analysis to assess the usefulness of social responsibility accounting. As we have discussed, the weakness of a non-utilitarian principle is encountered in the fact that accounting has traditionally dealt solely with financial information. The ethical benefits in cost/benefit analysis are often difficult to translate into financial terms. Thus, many accountants are uncomfortable entering into this realm.

Cost/benefit analysis presupposes that material wealth is the sole good to be considered. Thus an arbitrary, non-utilitarian method is assumed at the beginning of the utilitarian reasoning process. Yet reasonable people do not really believe that the accumulation of wealth is the only criterion to look at with respect to good and evil.

The final three weaknesses of practical utilitarianism are particularly evident in examining the benefit side of cost/benefit analysis. Hence the frustration with social responsibility accounting among so many accountants. Different agents translate the benefits into financial terms at different amounts. To many accountants this appears to violate the principle of verifiability. Which consequence of an action is the subject of measurement for the accountant also arises. Finally, the entire matter of comparing the present value of probable future benefits with the costs incurred now is a particularly sticky one in cost/benefit analysis.

We see that the deck seems stacked against not only social responsibility accounting but also socially responsible action when we attempt to apply utilitarian arguments. Yet the economic system in which corporations and their managers operate motivates them to take a utilitarian perspective.

Compounding this are forces in the business community that encourage managers to look to short-term rather than long-term results.

A change in the underlying way we view the role of the corporation in society can enable us to more realistically assess not only the need for socially responsible action but also the ways accounting can assist managers and outside readers of accounting reports in the tough choices with respect to these actions. This change is to move towards a deontological perspective.

THE DEONTOLOGICAL VIEW

The use of deontologism for the professions in general and for accounting in particular is not new. Lawyers who defend clients' interests irrespective of the general consequences use deontological reasons to justify this behaviour. Scientists frequently make inquiry into areas where an answer may lead to bad consequences (atomic power, for example). In medicine the doctrine of informed consent, whereby a patient is not subjected to an experiment without his full knowledge and approval, is well entrenched.

Many accountants agree that the Financial Accounting Standards Board should use representative faithfulness (a deontological perspective) over economic consequences (a utilitarian perspective) as a criterion for standard setting. Moreover, the accounting profession in general and certified public accountants in particular have taken great pains to present their field to society as a profession.

Among them are that each is governed by ethical principles that emphasize the virtues of self-subordination, honesty, probity, and devotion to the welfare of those served. CPAs have obligations not only to those served but also to third parties. In fact, the obligations to third parties may supersede the obligation to the party about which the CPA issues a report.

DEONTOLOGICAL FRAMEWORK

Deontological ethics can be applied to situations only if an obligation can be satisfied. The ideas of W. D. Ross, a prominent philosopher of the twentieth century. He provided specific criteria to be used as tests for the existence of an obligation and suggested a set of prima facie duties that represent the main moral convictions of the "plain man."

- Fidelity
- Reparation
- Gratitude
- Justice
- Beneficence
- Self-improvement
- Non-maleficence

We suggest that this list may serve as a starting point for discussion about whether corporations have reporting responsibilities with respect to social responsibility. Two questions must be addressed at the outset. First, do organizations such as corporations have duties that apply to the "plain man?" Second, how shall we know whether a specific duty applies to a particular organization?

Some modern ethicists argue that corporations are moral persons. This is true because people are behind the corporate veil and these people make decisions with moral implications. Society therefore cannot condone as amoral corporate actions that would be considered immoral for the individuals who actually make decisions for the corporation. Portions of the Foreign Corrupt Practices Act that hold corporate officers personally responsible for corporate actions serve as an example of this premise. P. H. Werhane convincingly takes the issue of corporate social responsibility a step farther in Persons, Rights, and Corporations. She argues that corporations have responsibilities apart from the individual responsibilities of persons behind the corporate veil.

She demonstrates that corporations argue for legal rights that must have a moral basis if they are justified. An example of this is the enforcement of contracts, which depends upon the moral duty of fidelity. Moreover, "If corporations have moral rights, then they have the obligations connected with such rights, and they can be held accountable, morally accountable."

If the prima facie duties apply correctly to individuals, including individuals who manage corporations, then they apply to corporations themselves. We may therefore turn to the second question of how to ascertain whether a specific duty applies to a corporation.

S. E. Toulmin has provided a test that may be applied to the prima facie duties: In any particular community, certain principles are current-that is to say, attention is paid to certain types of argument as appealing to accepted criteria of "real goodness," "real rightness," "real obligation," etc. From these the members of the community are expected to regulate their lives and judgements. And such a set of principles of "prima facie obligations" of "categorical imperatives" is what we call the "moral code" of the community.

As citizens, readers of financial reports should be concerned about the actions a company is taking or failing to take in the realm of social responsibility. The socially responsible corporation should therefore report upon how it is meeting or failing to meet its duties to the public. Research among investors and other stakeholders indicates that they are in fact interested in corporate activities that fall within the scope of the prima facie duties. We now explain each of these in terms of the business and accounting community.

Fidelity

Fidelity is the first of two duties that rest upon previous acts. Fidelity is simply the keeping of promises. The promises to be kept may be explicit or implicit.

Many explicit promises are already recognized and reported by corporations. Warranties, for example, are accounted for as contingency liabilities with a corresponding expense. Duties stemming from explicit promises may also raise ethical questions that are not so easily recognized in financial terms.

Let us return to the cable television company case. Management here is faced with a hard choice between its often-stated duty to maximize return for stockholders and the moral duty to keep the corporation's promise. We have demonstrated how the accounting system through the commonly used differential cost schedule uses utilitarian reasoning to report upon future consequences of managerial action. We have shown that such purely utilitarian reasoning, when used alone, would rarely motivate a manager to choose the socially responsible course of action. Yet Francis, and perhaps John, believe that a duty exists here because of the statements made at the public hearing. The duty that they recognize is fidelity.

From the accountant's viewpoint, can a report be developed to assist the decision-making process from a deontological perspective? Moreover, once the choice is made, can it be reported to interested stakeholders in an accounting context?

Reparation

Duties of reparation rest upon a previous wrongful act of the one who has the duty. Examples of duties of reparation in business are quite common and well publicized. The poison gas leak at the Union Carbide plant in Bhopal, India, and Manville's asbestos-related problems provide recent examples. In both cases the victims of actions taken by the company have received monetary compensation.

A clear reporting problem appears to exist in both the Union Carbide and Manville cases; yet, the wrongful act need not be so dramatic for a duty to arise. Suppose our cable television enterprise decides to proceed with the soft pornography offering. Later Francis learns that a father accused of sexually abusing his four-year-old daughter claims that he was motivated to do so after watching a show on Genesee Cable.

Clearly no legal liability exists here under current law. Yet, ethics are usually considered to be on a higher plane than the law. Therefore a duty with corresponding social responsibility accounting implications may arise when no legal liability is present.

Suppose John, Teresa, and Francis are struck with conscience in this matter and therefore are considering paying for the treatment of the little girl. Their consideration might arise from a sense of duty of reparation. Should they later decide to have Genesee make these payments, a social responsibility accounting implication may have been created.

The management of a particular corporation would have the responsibility of deciding the corporation's ethical standards with respect to reparation. The accountant's role would be to report upon the financial implications of meeting those standards. Such reporting might be internal or external. A corporate decision not to accept a reparation duty could also be a reportable event under social responsibility accounting.

Gratitude

Duties of gratitude arise from services done by others for the one who has the duty of gratitude. At first the notion of corporate gratitude may seem questionable, yet official communication from corporations often express gratitude. Annual reports of companies frequently express corporate appreciation for a job well done by employees. Gratitude can be more specific. When Frank Cary retired as the chairman of the board of International Business Machines, the new chairman stated that the company was "indebted" to him "for the wisdom and skill with which he led the company."

The duty of gratitude is not only owed employees. A company might have reason to be grateful to a community, to suppliers, to customers, or to others who interact with it. The duty arises because of the previous actions of the other entities. A question of interest with respect to social responsibility accounting is whether the gratitude expressed by corporations has an associated duty, and whether there is a future cost associated with the duty. If a corporation appreciates efforts by its loyal employees, has a duty been created for the corporation to those employees when economic times are not so good? Does indebtedness of IBM imply that a duty exists? Moreover, if the answers to these questions are yes, what are the costs of fulfilling these duties or not fulfilling them?

On the other hand, a company need not express gratitude for the duty to exist. From the standpoint of ethics an unrecognized duty might exist. Social responsibility accounting may be one vehicle that could assist managers and others in recognizing this duty.

Justice

Duties of justice rest on the fact or possibility of a distribution of pleasure or happiness (or the means thereto) that is not in accordance with the merit of the persons concerned. A duty may arise in such cases to upset or prevent such a distribution. Corporations are frequently confronted with duties that arise from justice. Such duties would create reporting implications under social responsibility accounting.

Suppose that a large corporation is headquartered in a maturing city that contains a ghetto. The youth of the ghetto are unable to attain employment at the corporation because, due to circumstances beyond their control, they are unqualified. In such circumstances enlightened management may believe that it is their duty, and by connection the corporation's, to overturn this state of affairs by providing job training programmes. Such a sense of duty would arise from a concern for justice.

Notice that in this case the sense of duty did not arise from any previous action or promise of the corporation or its management. Duties of justice arise simply because an observed situation is wrong per se. If the corporation recognizes such a duty, a cost may ensue in the future should the corporation create a training programme, for example.

Of interest here is that the corporation does not internalize an externality that it created, an often heard reason for socially responsible action, nor does the corporation take action because it believes that the training programme will benefit it in the long run (a utilitarian argument). Rather the action is undertaken due to a sense of duty.

The duty arises from a concept of justice, perhaps best stated by John Rawls. "Justice is the virtue of practices where there are assumed to be competing interests and conflicting claims and where it is supposed that persons will press their rights on each other.

That persons are mutually self-interested in certain situations and for certain purposes is what gives rise to the questioning of justice in practices couching those circumstances." Rawls argues that every person may be supposed to have a concept of justice. This proposition is true because each person is involved in some relationships with others. In the context of these relationships each person forms a concept of justice for herself as well as for others. Corporate persons would be among those under this societal umbrella.

Beneficence

Like duties of justice, duties of beneficence do not arise because of any culpability on the part of the corporation. Duties of beneficence rest upon the mere fact that there are other beings in the world whose condition can be made better. If the corporation recognizes these beings and is able to improve their condition, then a duty of beneficence arises.

The fact that duties of beneficence are recognized by managers of corporations is demonstrated by the fact that they cause the corporations to make charitable contributions. One is hard pressed to swallow utilitarian reasoning that such contributions may in the long run improve profitability by the creation of goodwill. In fact, the best arguments against such action are utilitarian in nature. Milton Friedman represents perhaps the best-known proponent of this utilitarian point of view.

The Philip Morris Company is well known in some circles as a supporter of the arts. Yet this company does not have a great deal of goodwill in general. Contributions to the ballet are not made in the hope of generating cigarette sales. They are made because people who work for this company believe that society will benefit from having the arts more widely available to the public. In other words, the donations are made because of a sense of duty, the duty of beneficence.

Duties of beneficence on the part of corporations are recognized in the tax laws, in that amounts spent for charity are deductible for tax purposes. They provide an interesting twist in that the duty recognized by the corporation is externalized. Persons who may not recognize the duty become partners in fulfilling the duty in the sense that the government receives less revenue from the corporate source.

Self-Improvement

Duties of self-improvement are the most difficult of Ross's duties of individuals to translate to a corporation. Duties of self-improvement rest on the fact that one can improve her own condition with respect to virtue or intelligence. Interestingly, Ross includes pleasure in the improvement of another's condition but omits it in the improvement of one's own condition. The difficulty with respect to duties of self-improvement lies in defining the corporation when viewing it as something where virtue or knowledge warrant improvement. However, if we accept the notion a priori that a corporation improves itself when it improves its management, duties of self-improvement may be found. An example is the practice of companies paying the cost of sending managers to universities to improve their education. Utilitarians would undoubtedly argue that such action is taken to improve profits through lower costs generated from the better management the corporation expects to receive from better-educated managers. Corporations would undeniably justify this practice on such utilitarian grounds.

However, the imagination must truly be stretched to translate an individual manager's education to the bottom line. A more plausible explanation for such things as classes in human relations might be found in the desire to fulfill a duty for self-improvement. If this is true, does the public bear costs when a corporation does not recognize such a duty? For example, one could argue that by failure to improve managers' knowledge of business ethics, a corporation has caused the public to incur greater risk of unethical conduct by the corporation.

The duty of self-improvement becomes one we may more easily associate with business enterprise if we expand upon Ross's definition a bit. A commonly held and frequently cited belief is that business corporations have the duty to make profits. We may easily accept this notion by stating that the company has the duty to improve itself by improving its financial position. As we do this we agree with Ross that the duty of self-improvement should be subordinated to the other duties.

Non-Maleficence

This is the only duty that is stated in a negative way. Non-maleficence is the duty not to injure others. Duties of non-maleficence are clearly the most compelling; violations of these duties create debate about corporate irresponsibility.

Pollution can serve as an example of how deontological ethics is superior to utilitarian ethics in solving dilemmas. A utilitarian argument for pollution may be made on the basis that those who pollute will generate more profit than those who incur costs to avoid pollution. Yet, reasonable men and women view pollution as undesirable. The utilitarian solution to this dilemma is to argue that the externalities created by the pollution involve more bad than the good created by the profits. The logical conclusion to the utilitarian view is that the responsible corporation should pollute just up to the point where the pollution will not exceed the good generated by the profit and no further. These arguments do not represent the attitudes of plain-thinking people. Indeed, most reasonable people could agree that pollution of the air and water is a prima facie wrong. It is wrong because it is injurious to others irrespective of utility. Because pollution is wrong, members of society, including corporate members, have a duty not to engage in the practice. This is the duty of non-maleficence.

The implications for social responsibility accounting are perhaps most clear under duties of non-maleficence. In the pollution example, those companies that internalize the cost of pollution by purchasing anti-pollution equipment have done their duty and would so report. Those who do not incur these costs will make higher profits, but should be required to report as a social cost the damage the pollution has done or will do.

The duty of non-maleficence could also apply in the Genesee Cable case. As part of his consideration of Teresa's proposal, John might recall an article that asserts that men who watch pornographic material on television develop an attitude towards women that views them as objects to be exploited rather than persons to be respected. John may decide against accepting Teresa's proposal on the grounds that he does not desire Genesee to be a party to fostering such attitudes in the community. In this case he would be acting out of the duty of non-maleficence.

TOWARDS SOCIAL RESPONSIBILITY ACCOUNTING

M. R. Mathews has suggested an excellent classification system through which accounting researchers may look at social accounting. We shall use this framework to suggest how deontological ethics may be incorporated into social accounting.

Under the system, social accounting is divided into two parts, defined by Mathews as social responsibility accounting (SRA) and total impact accounting (TIA) respectively. SRA is voluntary disclosure of information both qualitative and quantitative, made by organizations to inform or influence a range of audiences. The quantitative disclosures may be in financial or non-financial terms. The term Total Impact Accounting (TIA) refers to attempts at measuring, in monetary terms, the total cost of running an organization in its existing form. The total cost of running an organization may be divided between private and public costs.

Social Responsibility Accounting

SRA differs from TIA in that the former is shorter range in nature and does not precisely measure in financial terms for the most part. TIA measures precisely and incorporates social responsibility into the overall accounting system. TIA may be regarded as a more sophisticated or mature form of accounting than SRA. In fact, social costs of the organization would evolve from a SRA system into a TIA system.

The identification of corporate duties would thus be a first step and would fall under SRA. This step would take place at a level akin to the strategic planning function of the organization. A second step, also a part of SRA, would be to identify those actions, or lack thereof, that would have an impact upon or relate to the organization's duties. The final SRA step would be to decide upon an appropriate internal or external reporting medium to inform interested readers about how the organization was fulfilling its self-defined duties.

Total Impact Accounting

The challenge from an accounting standpoint is moving from SRA to TIA. Private costs, as envisioned by TIA, are those costs with which the accounting system of most organizations already deals effectively. The familiar production costs of material, labour, and overhead as well as the periodic expenses of the organization readily come to mind.

Public costs, then, are those that for the most part are borne by society. These public costs are more commonly called externalities. Note that externalities may result in either cost or gain to society. So the plant that pollutes the air in a particular community (a public cost) may also benefit that community through capital formation and the payment of wages (a public gain).

Total impact accounting provides the broad classification into which the deontological basis suggested here will fit. The classifications system could take the form of accounts set up for each of the duties that a company has chosen as applicable to it. So if all the Ross duties were deemed appropriate, the company would set into place seven social responsibility accounts, one for each identified duty. Since doing one's duty has an associated impact upon profit, an account would also be created to summarize those effects over periods of time.

As suggested, call this latter account social capital. A great deal of research needs to be done to perfect TIA. However, we can envision a new statement of social responsibility where public costs and public gains are reported. Public cost would be debited when the corporation, having identified its duty, is either unwilling or unable to fulfill it. Public gain would be credited when the corporation takes necessary steps to do its duty, thereby lowering its profits. The yearly balance of the public costs and gains could be held in an account, social capital, which would be similar to retained earnings.

A "Resolution" of the Genesee Cable Case

In this case the management of the company is faced with the hard choice of offering sexually explicit material after promising not to do so. Offering this programming would increase profits. Forgoing the offering fulfills the duties of fidelity and non-maleficence. It might also preclude the duty of reparation in the future. Under total impact accounting, offering the programming would create a public cost and be so reported. Conversely, forgoing the offering would be reported as a public gain. The amount to be reported would be the amount by which profits increased or were expected to increase as a result of offering the sexually explicit material.

Referring back to the differential cost schedule, we would use $162,000 as the amount to be debited to public cost or credited to public gain. The differential cost schedule serves as an objective document from which the amounts can be verified.

A POSITIVE APPROACH

Much of the current negative reaction to social accounting is due to the utilitarian criticism that corporations have created bad consequences by their past actions. Therefore, they should engage in a sort of public repentance, admit their evil ways, and formally report upon this through accounting. Businesspersons, understandably, do not view such suggestions with much favour. A deontological perspective takes a more positive and more acceptable point of view. Business is asked not to be morally good but to take right actions, thus relieving businesspersons of the concern that their actions will be second-guessed from a moral point of view due to consequences. An aspect of this viewpoint is that the decision not to act is in itself an action. If one can alter circumstances but decides not to do so, then one must take responsibility for the omission just as one must take responsibility for an overt act.

Management Responsibility

The task of formulating and stating the responsibilities deemed appropriate for a particular company rests with the management of the company. That management should believe a company has responsibilities is suggested by social contract theory. Under this theory corporations function within society and require its sanction for their continued existence. A so-called"social contract" is thereby created, which implies that corporations owe society something in return. By formulating responsibilities and discharging them, corporations may be able to fulfill their part of the social contract. That managers do in fact believe they have responsibility towards society has been suggested by several writers. For the most part, managers do not ponder whether or not they should do the right thing. Rather, they seek to know what the right action is.

The penalty for not properly defining the right action is severe. K. Davis has stated that there is an Iron Law of Responsibility:"In the long run, those who do not use power in the manner which society considers responsible will tend to lose it." Businesses that do not establish a track record of responsible decisions are threatened with the prospect of sharing their decision-making discretion with government and with representatives of special interest groups.

The formulation of responsibilities can make the task of properly defining right action an easier one throughout the organization. Moreover, the publication of corporate responsibilities in the form of duties is a proper step in demonstrating responsible action. Taking right action based on these duties can assist the organization in fulfilling it obligation to society and avoiding the penalty of the Iron Law of Responsibility.

The Role of Accounting

The accountant is a key professional involved in assisting management with the task of setting responsibilities and with monitoring progress towards meeting such responsibilities. This may be accomplished by classifying each responsibility perceived by management as a corporate duty under the deontological framework of total impact accounting. Accountants would be responsible for reporting on"how well we are doing," not only in purely profit and loss terms but also in terms of"fulfilling our duty to society."

Further research into total impact accounting may reveal appropriate ways to report upon fulfilling corporate duties. In many cases this would be an internal reporting issue only, so that management can monitor progress towards their responsibility objective and the cost of fulfilling their duties. In other cases management may wish to report to financial statement readers what duties they believe the company has and what private costs have been incurred to reach the public gains.

With respect to external reporting, several writers have noted that managers would naturally have a bias towards reporting the socially responsible actions that they have taken. Correspondingly, they would be reluctant to report upon the organization's ethical failures. Accountants should view this as an opportunity for an increase in their role through the auditing function. The so-called social auditor can monitor total impact accounting much the same as the financial auditor monitors financial statements. The increase in professional responsibility would be both internal and public.

AN EXPANSION OF HORIZON

The argument has been made that adequate measurement tools do not exist to make social accounting feasible. This argument should not be construed as a reason to abandon social accounting but rather as a call for additional research into the area. The body of accounting knowledge is not static but exceedingly dynamic. A statement made by R. T. De George concerning business ethics applies equally well to ethics in accounting:

Business ethics does not consist simply in applying ethical theory or moral norms to cases in business—although it includes this sort of activity.

To stop here is to imply that, although these are new cases, there is nothing new to learn in the field, there is no research required or appropriate, and there is nothing new to be discovered.... If there is a field of business ethics, and if it does not consist simply in applying moral norms or ethical theory to cases in business, it will develop and grow only if there is research to be done and that research is done. The results of such research, as the results of any research, can be taught to students.

Accounting should be developed to provide information to management on the financial implications of acting or failing to act upon ethical issues. If this is accomplished, research into social responsibility accounting can go hand in hand with research in business ethics. A deontological framework provides a starting place for the conduct of such research. By accepting a positive, deontological approach to modern social and ethical issues, accountants will be better able to serve society and thus enhance their claim to ethical professionalism. The task is not an easy one, but the end will not be accomplished unless work is begun.

CASE STUDIES

Responsibility for Reporting

Chris is an internal auditor with the Electro-Solvent Corporation. She had recently returned from a routine inventory visit to one of the company's sites in West Virginia. While relaxing in a motel lounge, she overheard a conversation that startled her and aroused her professional curiosity.Some men from the state environmental protection agency were discussing their activities of the day and disclosed that they involved Electro-Solvent. "It looks as if we have discovered yet another undisclosed toxic waste site here.

That's typical for Electro-Solvent. They have over a dozen questionable sites in the state that we know about. By the time we get through with them they will be out over a half-billion bucks in cleanup costs."When Chris got home she consulted some of the managers about this and discovered that indeed there were several sites that would require cleanup and that the potential was in the hundreds of millions of dollars, more than enough to bankrupt Electro-Solvent.

When Chris asked the controller about reporting this potential liability, she gave her several reasons why the amount was not disclosed on the 10-K or the annual report.

- The company already made footnote disclosure about environmental concerns. Chris noted this disclosure stated that the company did not believe the amounts to be material.
- Since the amount of potential liability was unknown and in the future, the company did not want to unduly worry stakeholders.
- The company intended to sue its insurance company for the amounts in question. Company attorneys believed that they had a reasonable chance to prevail.
- The independent auditors were permitting the disclosure as currently stated.

Responsibility to Stakeholders

Bob Waggener came to work in an extremely expansive mood. As sales manager of the Patch Furniture Company he found himself in an enviable position.

The company had orders for its furniture that far exceeded its capacity. This was in spite of the fact that Patch had recently announced a substantial price increase. All of this was occurring just a few months after most of Patch's competitors had closed their factories and declared insolvency. Patch's very survival at this time was largely due to the efforts of Bob. The company had just come through a period of severe economic hardship for the furniture industry. During this period Bob had cultivated personal relationships with many small, rural furniture stores.

While Patch's competitors were languishing due to a lack of orders from large department stores and retail chains, Patch was barely able to sustain itself with the orders of these small stores. Many of these stores were intensely loyal to Bob and to Patch, even to the point of resisting intense price competition from Patch's desperate competitors.

Bob was looking forward to the meeting this morning that the company president, Sally Duke, had called. When he arrived at the meeting, he found the controller, Barbara West, was also there.

- *Sally*: Bob, I want to congratulate you again for the tremendous job you have done for us over the years. It is obvious that we are now in a position to become extremely profitable now that we have survived that recession.
- *Barbara*: I agree with Sally, Bob, but I now believe the time has come to look forward. Reports coming out of my shop indicate that the time has come to make a change in our marketing strategy.
- *Bob*: How so?
- *Barbara*: We currently have many orders from some large, regional department stores and one national retail chain. Differential cost studies that I have conducted indicate that the most profitable course of action that we can take, given our current capacity, is to accept these large orders and not the orders from the small stores to which you are inclined to sell.
- *Sally*: Bob, I have studied Barbara's reports and believe she is right. We have the responsibility to our stockholders to maximize Patch's profits.
- *Bob*: Sally, if we deny our regular customers their orders they will be forced out of business. These people were the ones who kept us going during bad times. Surely that counts for something. I know these people and don't want to be part of any action that causes them to suffer.

Index

F

G

I

M

N

P

R

S

T

U